Publication No. 13
of the Mathematics Research Center
United States Army
The University of Wisconsin

Asymptotic Solutions of Differential Equations and Their Applications

Rudolph E. Langer

Asymptotic Solutions of Differential Equations and Their Applications

Proceedings of a Symposium Conducted by the Mathematics Research Center, United States Army, at the University of Wisconsin, Madison, May 4–6, 1964

dedicated to PROFESSOR RUDOLPH E. LANGER

Edited by
Calvin H. Wilcox

JOHN WILEY & SONS, INC.
New York · London · Sydney

Printed in the United States of America

PREFACE

Asymptotic solutions of differential equations are an important tool in applied mathematics and theoretical physics, with applications to such diverse fields as boundary layer theory in fluid dynamics, diffraction theory in optics, the theory of thin shells in elasticity, nonlinear oscillations in electrical networks, and quantum mechanics. The theory of asymptotic solutions was initiated by H. Poincaré and G. D. Birkhoff and has been carried forward by Rudolph E. Langer in substantial contributions, both to the rigorous foundations and to the further development of the theory.

This volume contains the Proceedings of a Symposium which was held at the Mathematics Research Center, U. S. Army, on May 4, 5 and 6, 1964 and which was dedicated to Professor Langer at the time of his retirement from his position as first Director of the Center. The purpose of the Symposium was to present a survey of the known theory of asymptotic solutions of differential equations, together with an account of some of the current research on the theory and its applications in mathematical physics.

The Symposium program consisted of ten papers which are published here in full. The papers by W. Wasow and H. L. Turrittin present a survey of the basic theory, together with an account of some of their recent research. Additional new developments of the theory, in several different directions, are presented in the papers by A. Erdélyi, R. W. McKelvey, F. W. J. Olver, and Y. Sibuya. Applications of asymptotic solutions to a number of problems in mathematical physics are presented in the paper by R. A. Clark, N. D. Kazarinoff, R. M. Lewis and C. C. Lin. Professor Langer's influence on research in this field can be seen clearly in the many references to his work which appear in the papers presented here.

The editor would like to thank Millard W. Johnson, Jr., Robert W. McKelvey, J. Barkley Rosser, and Wolfgang Wasow for their participation in planning the program. His special thanks are due to the ten authors whose unhesitating and generous contribution of their time and work made possible the Symposium and these Proceedings.

Calvin H. Wilcox

CONTENTS

Asymptotic Solutions of Differential Equations and Their Applications

WOLFGANG WASOW

Asymptotic Expansions for Ordinary Differential Equations: Trends and Problems

1. Asymptotic Expansions for Linear Systems. The systematic use of matrix notation has made much of the theory of linear analytic differential equations remarkably transparent. Let

$$\frac{dy}{dx} = A(x)y, \qquad x \text{ complex}, \tag{1.1}$$

be a homogeneous system of first order differential equations written in vectorial notation, so that $A(x)$ is an $n \times n$ matrix. If $A(x)$ is holomorphic, i.e., regular analytic at, say, $x = 0$, a classical theorem says that all solutions are holomorphic at $x = 0$. Thus the solutions can be expanded in series of powers of x, and the coefficients can be determined by formal comparison of coefficients.

The natural next question is what happens when $A(x)$ has a singularity at $x = 0$, and the simplest such case is that of a pole. We change the notation and write

$$x^h \frac{dy}{dx} = A(x)y, \qquad h \geq 1, \text{ an integer}, \tag{1.2}$$

for our system, where $A(x)$ is again holomorphic at $x = 0$.

The very special case that (1.2) is a scalar equation can be solved explicitly, and a trivial calculation shows that the solutions are of the form

$$Y(x) = \hat{Y}(x)x^G e^{Q(x)}, \tag{1.3}$$

where

a) G is a, generally complex, constant.

b) $Q(x)$ is a polynomial in x^{-1} of the form

$$Q(x) = \begin{cases} 0, & \text{if } h = 1 \\ \sum_{j=1}^{h-1} Q_j x^{-j}, & \text{if } h > 1 \end{cases} \tag{1.4}$$

c) $$\hat{Y}(x) = \sum_{r=0}^{\infty} Y_r x^r, \quad Y_0 \neq 0, \tag{1.5}$$

is holomorphic at $x = 0$

It is remarkable and satisfying that with suitable mild restrictions and re-interpretations this result remains true for systems as well. Let the following hypothesis be satisfied.

Assumption I: The eigenvalues λ_j of the matrix $A(0)$ are distinct.

Then the system (1.2) possesses fundamental matrix solutions of the form (1.3), where now:

a') G is a constant $n \times n$ matrix

b') $Q(x)$ in (1.4) is a diagonal matrix.

c') $\hat{Y}(x)$ is a matrix function holomorphic at $x = 0$, if $h = 1$. If $h > 1$ then $\hat{Y}(x)$ has, in general, a singularity at $x = 0$. However, this singularity is such that $\hat{Y}(x)$ possesses an asymptotic power series expansion,

$$\hat{Y}(x) \sim \sum_{r=0}^{\infty} Y_r x^r, \qquad x \to 0 \tag{1.6}$$

as x tends to zero in some sector S with vertex at the origin. In fact, to every sufficiently narrow such sector S there exists a fundamental matrix solution for which this statement is true.

The relation (1.) is to be understood in the sense of Poincaré's definition: It means that

$$\lim_{\substack{x \to 0 \\ x \in S}} x^{-m}\Big[Y(x) - \sum_{r=0}^{m} \hat{Y}_r x^r\Big] = 0, \qquad \text{for all } m.$$

The occurrence of asymptotic divergent, instead of convergent, series for $h > 1$ is the most interesting feature of this result. Simple as the statement is, its proof is by no means trivial, and the preceding formulation was achieved only after decades of struggling with special cases. Even the well-known treatise on ordinary differential equations by Ince [1927] shies away from this general theory and gives, instead, considerable space to rather special 19th century investigations that concentrate on exceptional cases in which asymptotic series can be avoided.

There are several known techniques for proving the result stated. We content ourselves with the description of two closely related general schemes, whose variants are also applicable to many other problems in this field. Both schemes have in common that the proof consists of a "formal" and an "analytic" part. Scheme I begins with an inspired guess as to what type of series expansion may be expected to satisfy the differential equation in the "formal" sense: By this we mean that insertion of such an expansion into the differential equation followed by termwise differentiation and algebraic manipulations of the series, as if they were known to be uniformly and absolutely convergent should lead to series in the two members of the equation that can be made termwise equal by a suitable choice of the coefficients in the original expansion. The calculation of these coefficients constitutes the formal part of the argument.

In Scheme II one concentrates, not on the formal solution, but on the formal simplification of the given differential equation, the aim being a formal reduction to some special differential equation, sometimes called "related equation" for which explicit asymptotic solutions are known from other considerations. Again, some successful guessing is essential. The decisive step in this procedure is usually a transformation of the given equation by a linear transformation.

$$y = P(x)\,\tilde{y}\,, \tag{1.7}$$

where $P(x)$ is a matrix function to be suitable determined. Insertion of (1.7) into (1.2) leads to the differential equation

$$x^h \frac{d\tilde{y}}{dx} = [\,P^{-1}(x)\,A(x)\,P(x) \,-\, x^h P^{-1}(x)\frac{dp(x)}{dx}\,]\,\tilde{y}\,. \tag{1.8}$$

One wishes to determine $P(x)$ so that the coefficient matrix in brackets in (1.8) reduces to a matrix function $B(x)$ that is as simple as possible. Thus $P(x)$ and $B(x)$ are related by the equation

$$x^h \frac{dP(x)}{dx} = A(x)P(x) - P(x)B(x) \quad . \tag{1.9}$$

As a differential equation for $P(x)$ this seems to be a harder problem than our original equation (1.2), but this is deceptive for two reasons. First, we need only one of the n^2 independent solutions of (1.9). Furthermore, $B(x)$ plays the rôle of a parameter function. Quite often a skilfull choice of $B(x)$ in some class of particularly simple matrix functions is possible for which (1.9) admits a formal power series solution

$$\sum_{r=0}^{\infty} P_r x^r \quad .$$

For instance, if Assumption I holds, one replaces $B(x)$ by a formal series

$$\sum_{r=0}^{\infty} B_r x^r$$

of diagonal matrices B_r and shows then that the P_r and B_r can indeed be successively determined so as to satisfy (1.9) formally.

In this case, Scheme II consists then in reducing problem (1.2) to a problem

$$x^h \frac{d\tilde{y}}{dx} = B(x)\,\tilde{y} \tag{1.10}$$

of the same type but with a diagonal coefficient matrix $B(x)$. The solution of (1.10) is a trivial matter. Here we have assumed that the second, analytic, part has already been carried out, in which it must be shown that the series

$$\sum_{r=0}^{\infty} P_r x^r$$

and

$$\sum_{r=0}^{\infty} B_r x^r$$

are convergent or asymptotic expansions of functions $B(x)$ and $P(x)$, the former a diagonal matrix, which satisfy (1.9).

The analytic proof, in the asymptotic case, is usually based on a conversion of the differential equation into an equivalent integral equation of Volterra type. We sketch the outlines of this procedure for the Scheme I as applied to our present problem. First a "comparison" equation is constructed whose solutions are known to be asymptotically represented by the formal series obtained in the formal part of the proof. If

$$x^h \frac{d\tilde{y}}{dx} = \tilde{A}(x)\,\tilde{y} \tag{1.11}$$

is such a comparison equation one rewrites the given equation (1.2) in the form

$$x^h \frac{dy}{dx} = \tilde{A}(x)y + [A(x) - \tilde{A}(x)]y$$

and converts this into a Volterra integral equation by the method of variation of parameters, treating the term $[A(x) - \tilde{A}(x)]y$ as if it were a known function. The asymptotic knowledge of the solutions of (1.11) permits an appraisal of the kernel in this integral equation, provided the paths of integration are suitably chosen. This appraisal makes it possible to establish the existence of a solution of the integral equation and to show that this solution is asymptotically equal to a solution of (1.11).

What happens if Assumption I is not satisfied? Leaving aside the relatively simple case $h = 1$, which does not lead to asymptotic series, we can state that even if $A(0)$ has multiple eigenvalues formula (1.3) still describes the asymptotic structure of certain fundamental matrix solutions of the differential equation (1.2), provided we again interpret (1.3) somewhat differently:

a'') G is again a constant $n \times n$ matrix.

b'') Q is again diagonal, but it is now a polynomial in some <u>fractional</u> power $x^{1/p}$ (p a positive integer). No simple rules for the degree of this polynomial or the value of p appear to exist.

c'') $\hat{Y}(x)$ possesses an asymptotic expansion in powers of $x^{1/p}$.

This generalization of the result for distinct eigenvalues is not easy to prove. I have not seen an elegant and transparent treatment. It would be very desireable to have a proof that is as plausible and simple as the theorem.

There are a great many papers dealing with special cases of the theory described. Among the articles devoted to the general theory we mention E. Fabry [1885], W. J. Trijitzinsky [1934], H. L. Turrittin [1955].

<u>2. Connecting Problems.</u> <u>Error Estimates.</u> The theory summarized

in Section 1 gives considerable insight into the nature of the solutions of linear differential equations in the complex plane, but it raises more questions than it answers.

One obvious shortcoming, namely the restriction to singularities of the coefficient matrix that are poles I shall mention only briefly, for no general theory appears to exist for any other type of singularities, except for the fairly obvious fact that it is permissible to replace the assumption that $A(x)$ be holomorphic at $x = 0$ by the weaker hypothesis that it have an asymptotic power series representation, as $x \to 0$ in some sector S.

The result of Section 1 is a local one only. It says nothing about the nature of a fundamental matrix described by formula (1.3) if we leave the neighborhood of the singularity, i.e., $x = 0$ in our formulation. Worse still, the asymptotic series for $\hat{Y}(x)$ represents it in a certain sector S only. If x tends to zero outside of S, this asymptotic representation is, in general, no longer true for the particular fundamental system $Y(x)$ that is so represented in S. It is true that the neighborhood of $x = 0$ can be covered by overlapping sectors in each of which some fundamental matrix exists that has the asymptotic representation described in Section 1, but the linear relations that connect these fundamental matrices are not obtainable from the general theory. These abrupt changes in the asymptotic structure of the solutions of analytic differential equations as certain rays are crossed are referred to as the Stokes phenomenon.

In the physical applications of differential equations it is usually essential to know the behavior of one and the same solution in more than just one such sector, and in regions that are not small neighborhoods of one point. These connection problems are deeper than the theory of Section 1, and there is no hope of achieving results of the same sweeping generality. Special methods of complex variable theory and integral representations for the solutions have to be employed. In this Symposium Professor Turrittin's talk will be devoted to such global questions.

The global theory for differential equations of the type (1.2) has close connections with the local asymptotic theory for differential equations depending in a singular manner on a parameter. This will be explained more fully in the next section, but I can illustrate this connection here by the simplest relevant example:

The behavior of the solutions of

$$\epsilon^2 \frac{d^2u}{dx^2} - xu = 0$$

for small values of the parameter ϵ can be analyzed by reducing this differential equation to the parameterless equation

$$\frac{d^2u}{d\xi^2} - \xi u = 0$$

by means of the simple transformation

$$x = \epsilon^{2/3}\xi \quad .$$

Even if x is restricted to a small disk $|x| \leq x_0$ the variable ξ will range over the domain $|\xi| \leq x_0|\epsilon|^{-2/3}$, i.e., over the whole ξ-plane if ϵ tends to zero.

Although, as we have stated, the linear relations that describe the Stokes phenomenon are not attainable by the methods of Section 1, G. D. Birkhoff [1909] has shown that interesting limited information on these relations can be deduced in this manner. He deals only with the simpler case that Assumption I is satisfied. His method ought to be explored further. It is also applicable to certain problems with a parameter of the form described in the next section. (cf. Wasow [1948]).

From the viewpoint of a numerical analyst an asymptotic series is of little value unless the error involved in truncating the series can be appraised in some constructional and not too wasteful manner. Depressingly little is known in this direction, particularly for series with complex terms. F. W. Olver [1961] has recently done some important work on this problem on which he will report in his talk at this Symposium. For an early contribution see H. Weber [1890].

3. Linear Analytic Differential Equations with a Parameter. Most differential equation problems originating in physical applications involve one or more parameters, and the dependence of the solutions on these parameters is just as important as the behavior with respect to the independent variable. Thus one is led to study vector differential equations of the form

$$\frac{dy}{dx} = A(x, \epsilon)y \tag{3.1}$$

in their dependence on the parameter ϵ. If the coefficient matrix $A(x, \epsilon)$ is holomorphic in both variables in some fixed region of the complex (x, ϵ)-space, say, in $|x| \leq x_0$, $|\epsilon| \leq \epsilon_0$, a classical theorem guarantees the existence of fundamental matrix solutions that are themselves holomorphic in both variables in that region. The convergent series in powers of ϵ for these solutions can be calculated by comparison of coefficients. This is the theoretical basis for many perturbation calculations in mathematical physics.

In analogy with the problem dealt with in Section 1 we next ask for the asymptotic structure of the solutions, as $\epsilon \to 0$, if $A(x, \epsilon)$ has a pole of fixed order h at $\epsilon = 0$. Accordingly, we rewrite our system, in changed notation, as

$$\epsilon^h \frac{dy}{dx} = A(x, \epsilon) y , \qquad h > 0 . \tag{3.2}$$

Again, the scalar case is a helpful guide. It is readily seen that for scalar y there are solutions of (3.2) of the form

$$Y(x, \epsilon) = \hat{Y}(x, \epsilon) e^{Q(x, \epsilon)} , \tag{3.3}$$

where

a) $Q(x, \epsilon)$ is a polynomial in ϵ^{-1} of the form

$$Q(x, \epsilon) = \sum_{j=1}^{h} Q_j(x) \epsilon^{-j} \tag{3.4}$$

with holomorphic coefficients,

b) $\hat{Y}(x, \epsilon)$ has a convergent expansion in powers of ϵ with holomorphic coefficients

$$\hat{Y}(x, \epsilon) = \sum_{r=0}^{\infty} Y_r(x) \epsilon^r . \tag{3.5}$$

Up to a point the extension of this result to systems is quite analogous to the parameterless theory. The analog of Assumption I is

Assumption II. The eigenvalues $\lambda_j(x)$, $j = 1, \dots, n$ of the matrix $A(x, 0)$ are distinct in $|x| \leq x_0$.

Corresponding to every sufficiently narrow section Σ of the ϵ-plane there exists then a fundamental matrix solution of the differential system (3.2) with the representation (3.3), provided we reinterpret the symbols as follows:

a) $Q(x, \epsilon)$ is a diagonal matrix,

b) $\hat{Y}(x, \epsilon)$ is a matrix function that admits an asymptotic expansion

$$\hat{Y}(x, \epsilon) \sim \sum_{r=0}^{\infty} Y_r(x) \epsilon^r, \quad \text{as } \epsilon \to 0 \text{ in } \Sigma . \tag{3.6}$$

The proof of this theorem can be given by arguments resembling the schemes roughly outlined in Section 1. The presence of two complex variables, instead of one, causes some complications, but they are not serious. (See, for instance, G. D. Birkhoff [1908], M. Hukuhara [1937], H. L. Turrittin [1952], Y. Sibuya [1958]). The same cannot be said when Assumption II is dropped. Entirely different and fascinating phenomena may then arise to which we must now turn our attention.

4. Turning Point Problems. For the sake of a simple vocabulary we shall call the point $x = 0$ a turning point for the differential equation (3.2) whenever the eigenvalues of $A(0, 0)$ are not distinct. This name is not descriptive and is usually applied in a somewhat narrower sense, but it serves our purpose.

By means of a skilfull version of what I called "Scheme II" in Section 1, Sibuya [1958] has proved an important theorem the gist of which is that every turning point problem - i. e., the asymptotic description of a differential equation (3.2) near a turning point - can be reduced to a finite set of similar problems each of which has a lead matrix $A(0, 0)$ that is nilpotent. In this reduction the property that the coefficient matrix is holomorphic at $\epsilon = 0$ ha^ to be sacrificed, however: All that can be said of the reduced systems is that their coefficient matrix has in some sector of the ϵ-plane an asymptotic expansion in powers of ϵ with coefficients holomorphic in x. From now on we shall assume that

$$A(x, \epsilon) \sim \sum_{r=0}^{\infty} A_r(x)\epsilon^r, \quad \epsilon \to 0, \quad \epsilon \in \Sigma \tag{4.1}$$

and that $A_0(0)$ is nilpotent.

For certain, rather special, turning point problems Turrittin [1952] has shown the existence of asymptotic expansions of the type (3.3) but involving fractional powers of ϵ. This is quite analogous to what was found to be true in the parameterless case. But when Turrittin's restrictive conditions are not satisfied the analogy with the parameterless case breaks down.

An important and relatively simple turning point problem is connected with the differential equation

$$\epsilon^2 \frac{d^2u}{dx^2} - [x\phi(x) + \epsilon\psi(x, \epsilon)]u = 0, \quad \phi(0) \neq 0 . \tag{4.2}$$

By means of the transformation

$$y_1 = u, \quad y_2 = \epsilon\, du/dx, \; y = \begin{pmatrix} y_1 \\ y_2 \end{pmatrix}$$

it can be written as the system

$$\epsilon \frac{dy}{dx} = \begin{bmatrix} 0 & 1 \\ x\phi(x) + \epsilon\psi(x, \epsilon) & 0 \end{bmatrix} y = A(x, \epsilon)y \; . \tag{4. 3}$$

The leading matrix

$$A(x, 0) = \begin{bmatrix} 0 & 1 \\ x\phi(x) & 0 \end{bmatrix}$$

is nilpotent for $x = 0$, while for $x \neq 0$ its two eigenvalues $\pm\sqrt{x\phi(x)}$ are distinct near $x = 0$.

Away from the turning point the theory of Section 3 applies, but the terms of the asymptotic series so obtained become singular at $x = 0$. Several mathematical physicists have dealt with this problem, which is important in Quantum Theory,and have given convincing but mathematically not quite complete schemes for the asymptotic solution (Wentzel [1926], Kramers [1935], L. Brillouin [1948]). R. E. Langer [1930] developed a new, very fruitful, approach that was mathematically satisfactory. He realized that any attempt at expressing the solution asymptotically in terms of series of elementary functions, such as the representation (3. 3), must fail in regions containing the turning point. A uniformly valid asymptotic expression must contain non-elementary functions that are structurally more closely related to the true solutions. For problem (4. 2) - or, equivalently, (4. 3) - the solutions of Airy's equation

$$\frac{d^2v}{dz^2} - zv = 0$$

turn out to be such functions.

Langer and his pupils have used this basic idea to solve a large number of turning point problems for scalar differential equations of second and higher order. In the earlier papers only the asymptotically leading term was obtained. In 1949 Langer improved his method so as to give full asymptotic series for the solutions. The decisive step is always to relate the solution of the given equation to that of some simpler, structurally similar problem that can be solved explicitly in terms of well known transcendental functions. A partial list of Langer's papers on this subject can be found in the bibliography at the end of this article. See also Cesari [1963] pp. 192-195, for more references to work by Langer and his pupils.

Other mathematicians, among them T. M. Cherry [1949], [1950], Okubo [1961], F. W. J. Olver [1954], [1956], Y. Sibuya [1962], [1963 a], [1963 b], [1963 c] (this is a very incomplete and possibly haphazard selection) have widened the scope of this technique in many directions.

Most of that work deals with scalar equations. In the language of systems this procedure can be described as the reduction of the given problem, by means of what I have called Scheme II, to one solvable by known special functions. The central problem is then the solution, by asymptotic power series with holomorphic coefficients, of the analog of equation (1. 9), i. e.

$$\epsilon^h \frac{dP(x,\epsilon)}{dx} = A(x,\epsilon)P(x,\epsilon) - P(x,\epsilon)B(x,\epsilon) \tag{4.4}$$

for as simple a choice of $B(x,\epsilon)$ as possible.

It turns out that the nature of this problem depends very decisively on the way in which the Jordan canonical form of the matrix $A(x, 0)$ changes at the turning point. A large number of essentially different cases can occur. The value of the exponent h also makes a non-trivial difference. Only a few types of systems have been studied in this manner, most of them such that $A(0.0)$ has either only one Jordan block or is diagonal (see, e. g., Wasow [1963]). In view of these remarks it is not surprising that the simplest equation

$$\epsilon^h \frac{d\tilde{y}}{dx} = B(x,\epsilon)\tilde{y}$$

to which (3. 2) can be reduced by this method is rarely one whose solutions are well studied special functions. Thus, for most systems Langer's procedure effects a simplication, not a solution. Moreover, the analytic part of the technique has not yet been carried out even when the formal reduction is successful, except for certain classes of matrices $B(x,\epsilon)$, for instance, polynomials in x (cf. Sibuya [1962 a]). This is an interesting, wide open field for further study.

A less elegant, but widely applicable technique is what may be called "stretching" and "matching". Its essence is most easily explained by a simple example such as (4. 2). The "stretching" transformation

$$x = t\epsilon^{2/3} \tag{4.5}$$

takes (4. 2) into

$$\frac{d^2u}{dt^2} - [t\phi(t\epsilon^{2/3}) + \epsilon^{1/3}\psi(t\epsilon^{2/3}, \epsilon^{1/3})]u = 0 . \tag{4.6}$$

In this form the differential equation depends regularly on the parameter $\epsilon^{1/3}$ and has therefore a fundamental system of solutions consisting of series in powers of $\epsilon^{1/3}$ whose radius of convergence is positive for any t, but may tend to zero, as $t \to \infty$. Another fundamental system of solutions, involving asymptotic series can be constructed for regions bounded away from the turning point, where the theory of Section 3 applies. If the regions of validity of the two types of expansions can be shown to overlap the linear relation between them can be asymptotically calculated - this is the "matching" - and then any solution may be asymptotically described in domains including the turning point. This basically simple, but technically often tedious, procedure has many useful variants for linear and nonlinear problems other than turning point problems. Its possibilities have not yet been fully explored. For a linear turning point problem treated in this manner see Wasow [1961], [1962].

5. Nonlinear Analytic Equations. Vectorial differential equations of the type

$$x^h \frac{dy}{dx} = f(x, y) \tag{5.1}$$

$$\epsilon^h \frac{dy}{dx} = f(x, y, \epsilon) \tag{5.2}$$

with analytic right hand members are a natural extension of the linear problems (1.2) and (3.2), respectively. The types of still more complicated nonlinear systems for which meaningful questions as to asymptotic expansions of solutions can be asked are, of course, boundless in number. In this survey there is not even room for an adequate description of the work done on equations of type (5.1) and (5.2). We only mention that theories exist for these two equations which approach in generality the corresponding results for the linear case, provided we are dealing with solutions that remain bounded as the singularity is approached in certain directions. The most far-reaching results are due to Iwano [1959], [1962]. The method is again an extension of "Scheme II": Under suitable, not excessively restrictive conditions it is possible to reduce such systems to forms so simple that they can be solved by solving successively a finite sequence of linear equations. Needless to say, these transformations, as well as the solution of the linear equations, involve asymptotic power series.

6. Singular Perturbation Problems: General Remarks. During the last thirty years the interest in asymptotic expansions for differential equations has gained considerable impetus from a type of question of great theoretical and physical interest, the so-called singular perturbation problems. This name describes boundary value problems for differential equations depending on a parameter ϵ in such a manner that the order of the differential equation is lower-but positive- for $\epsilon = 0$ than for $\epsilon \neq 0$.

The passage from inviscid to viscous flows, from geometric to physical optics, from classical to quantum mechanics gives rise to a number of important singular perturbation problems, and there are many others.

When written as first order systems most ordinary differential equations of the singular perturbation type that have been studied are of the form

$$\frac{dx}{dt} = f(x, y, t, \epsilon)$$
$$\epsilon^h \frac{dy}{dt} = g(x, y, t, \epsilon) \quad , \qquad (6.1)$$

where x and y are n and m-dimensional vector functions, respectively. Except for the notation this becomes a special case of equation (5.2) if the first of the two equations (6.1) is multiplied by ϵ^h . However, the general theory for systems of the form (5.2) does not do justice to systems of the special type (6.1). For after multiplying f in (6.1) by ϵ^h we have a problem of the form (5.2) whose first n right hand members vanish identically for $\epsilon = 0$. This is a very special feature that gives rise to interesting special phenomena.

In many applications t represents the time. It is then natural to deal with the real rather than the complex, problem and to drop the requirement that the system be analytic. If all data are infinitely often differentiably one can still hope to attain a full asymptotic expansion for the solutions,inasmuch as any Taylor series, convergent or not, is an asymptotic series for the function it represents. Much of the existing work has been done under milder conditions. Then only finite expansions with a remainder are possible.

Singular perturbation problems arise in such a natural fashion that it is surprising that the first paper on this subject (Tschen, Yü-Why [1935]) was published only 29 years ago! Since then a veritable flood of articles has appeared, the Russians and - to a somewhat lesser extent - the Americans dominating the field.

What makes these problems particularly interesting is the occurrence of discontinuous limit functions, as ϵ tends to zero. Trivial examples of this can be given. The most elementary calculation shows that the scalar differential equation

$$\epsilon u'' + u' = 0 \tag{6.2}$$

under the boundary conditions

$$u = \alpha, \text{ at } t = 0, \qquad u = \beta, \text{ at } t = 1 \tag{6.3}$$

is solved by a function $u(t, \epsilon)$ such that

$$\lim_{\epsilon \to 0+} u(t, \epsilon) \equiv \beta, \qquad \lim_{\epsilon \to 0-} u(t, \epsilon) = \alpha \quad , \tag{6.4}$$

which means that the limit function has a jump discontinuity at the right or left endpoint, respectively, unless $\alpha = \beta$. This behavior is typical: If the solution of a boundary value problem for an equation of type (6.1) converges at all, as $\epsilon \to 0$, (more often than not it diverges, except in problems from physics) it will, in general, approach a limit function with jump discontinuities. For small non-zero values of ϵ the solution is, of course, continuous but it changes very rapidly in a narrow interval about the point where the the discontinuity appears. If these narrow intervals are at the boundary they are fittingly called "boundary layers" after the best known such phenomenon which arises in fluid dynamics.

Observe that the limits in (6.4) are solutions of the "reduced" or "degenerate" equation $u' = 0$ obtained for $\epsilon = 0$. They are the solutions of this first order equation characterized by one of the two boundary conditions (6.3). This loss of boundary conditions in the passage to the limit is typical.

7. Singular Perturbations. Linear Boundary Value Problems. For linear singular perturbation problems with boundary conditions at two points there exist essentially two approaches in the literature. The first is very natural from our present viewpoint, though not trivial to carry out: On the basis of the general theory explained in Section 3 one can calculate asymptotically a fundamental system of solutions. The particular linear combination of these solutions that satisfies the boundary conditions is then determined in the obvious manner by solving a linear algebraic system of equations. This leads, in particular, to general rules as to which boundary conditions characterize the limit function, if it exists. (See Wasow [1944] for the case of a scalar equation of order n and Harris [1962] for the more difficult case of a system.)

The second method, developed by Višik and Lyusternik [1957], is more sophisticated. It disdains the use of fundamental systems, a feature which makes it applicable to partial differential equations as well and - in modified form - to nonlinear equations. The solution is tentatively written as the sum of three formal series. One of them is in powers of ϵ. The other two series are exponentially negligible for small ϵ, except in the boundary layers near the two end points.

The purpose of these two series is to supply the appropriate boundary layer corrections. If the boundaries are at $t = 0$ and $t = 1$, say, these series are also power series when written in terms of the "stretched" variables $\sigma = t/\epsilon$ and $\tau = (1-t)/\epsilon$, respectively. Typically, the coefficients involve exponential factors such as $e^{-\sigma}$ or $e^{-\tau}$, which are the reason why these series are neglibible unless $t = O(\epsilon)$ or $1-t = O(\epsilon)$.

Višik and Lyusternik give an algorithm for the successive calculation of the terms of these three series. Every partial sum satisfies all boundary conditions. The analytic part is quite different from what has been described here before. The remainder term is estimated, not in terms of the maximum modulus norm, but in a certain integral norm suitably adapted to the nature of the problem. This involves techniques familiar in Functional Analysis.

The methods of these authors are flexible and powerful. Their potentialities are probably not yet exhausted.

8. Singular Perturbations: Nonlinear Problems. The standard initial value problem for nonlinear singular perturbation problems of the type (6.1) has been very thoroughly explored by A. B. Vasil'eva [1959], [1963]. The second of these papers contains an extensive bibliography of work on this and related problems by many authors.

Her method can be regarded as a variant of that of Višik and Lyusternik. It results in an asymptotic series expansion composed of two parts, the second of which is the boundary layer correction and is asymptotically negligible outside the boundary layer.

Let

$$x = \alpha, \quad y = \beta, \quad \text{for } t = 0 \ (\alpha, \beta \text{ independent of } \epsilon)$$

be the prescribed initial conditions. The first part of the asymptotic solution consists of series

$$x = \sum_{r=0}^{\infty} x_r(t)\epsilon^r, \qquad y = \sum_{r=0}^{\infty} y_r(t)\epsilon^r \tag{8.1}$$

that satisfy the differential system (6.1) in the formal sense. This approach leads to a recursive sequence of differential equations for the coefficients $x_r(t)$, $y_r(t)$. Here, however, one meets with the peculiar problem that the initial values $x_r(0)$, $y_r(0)$ are not directly available for $r > 0$. One might think that, since for the true solution $x(t, \epsilon)$, $y(t, \epsilon)$ we must have $x(0, \epsilon) = \alpha$, $y(0, \epsilon) = \beta$, those initial values ought to be $x_0(0) = \alpha$, $y_0(0) = \beta$, $x_r(0) = y_r(0) = 0$, $r > 0$. However, this is generally not true, except for the first of these conditions, because in the boundary layer near $t = 0$ the true solution is not represented by series of the form (8.1). Thus a deeper investigation is needed.

To this end, Miss Vasil'eva performs the usual stretching transformation. If $h = 1$ - the only case we will consider - the stretching transformation is $t = \tau\epsilon$. In terms of τ the system (6.1) is no longer a singular perturbation problem. It can be solved by convergent power series in ϵ, which describe the solution in the boundary layer. A careful study of the matching requirement of this expansion with the one of type (8.1) leads her to a very elegant explicit formula for the initial values $x_r(0)$, $y_r(0)$. The series (8.1) obtained in this way are an asymptotic representation for the solution <u>outside</u> the boundary layer.

Going beyond this result, Miss Vasil'eva succeeds in finding an asymptotic expansion for the solution that is uniformly valid inside as well as outside the boundary layer. It is obtained by adding the two series expansions mentioned so far and subtracting from this a third series obtained by re-writing (8.1) as double series in t and ϵ according to t and ϵ combined. Unfortunately it is impossible to give more details in this brief survey.

Nonlinear two-point boundary value problems of the singular perturbation type lead to still greater complications. Even for relative simple problems of the form

$$\begin{aligned} &\epsilon u'' = F(u, u', t, \epsilon) \\ &u = \alpha \text{ at } t = 0, \qquad u = \beta \text{ at } t = 1 \end{aligned} \tag{8.2}$$

only partial results are available. It turns out, for instance, that if F, as a function of u', grows with order of magnitude greater than $O(u'^2)$, as $u' \to \infty$, the problem (8.1) generally does not even possess a solution for small ϵ. The quasilinear case, when F is linear in u' has been treated by Višik and Lyusternik [1958]. They use a variant of their theory in their previously quoted paper [1957]. A sketch of an extension of this method to certain more strongly nonlinear problem is given in a subsequent paper by these authors [1960]. The quasilinear case has also been treated, by an entirely different method,in an earlier paper by Wasow [1956].

<u>9. Singular Perturbations: Periodic Solutions.</u> If the right members

of (6.1) are periodic in t, or independent of t, periodic solutions may exist. For perturbation theory the first question is whether the assumed existence of periodic solutions for the reduced equation

$$\begin{aligned} \frac{dx}{dt} &= f(x, y, t, 0) \\ 0 &= g(x, y, t, 0) \end{aligned} \tag{9.1}$$

implies the existence of nearby periodic solutions for the full problems. If the answer is in the affirmative one then wishes to expand this solution in some convergent or asymptotic series for small ϵ.

This problem can be regarded as a two-point boundary problem with certain special features that require special methods. The principal distinctive fact about this problem is the absence of boundary layers. This is plausible inasmuch as there are no two distinguished boundary points as such in this problem. A consequence of this is that small periodic perturbations exist even in cases where the corresponding fixed initial or boundary value problem may diverge as $\epsilon \to 0$. In other words, the theory can be developed under milder hypotheses.

Among the papers dealing with the existence (and uniqueness) problem only we mention L. Flatto and N. Levinson [1955], because it contains some ideas that were exploited by E. R. Rang [1957], [1963], who proved the most general theorem concerning series expansions for such periodic singular perturbations.

Rang's method is an extension to quite general systems of a procedure of Wasow [1950] which in its turn is based on a formal scheme suggested by I. M. Volk [1948].

The system discussed by Rang is more general than (6.1), being of the form

$$\Omega(\epsilon) \frac{dx}{dt} = F(x, t, \epsilon), \tag{9.2}$$

where

$$\Omega(\epsilon) = \operatorname{diag}(\epsilon^{h_1}, \epsilon^{h_2}, \ldots, \epsilon^{h_n}) \tag{9.3}$$

with

$$0 = h_1 = h_2 = \ldots = h_m,$$

$$0 < h_{m+1} < h_{m+2} < \ldots < h_n .$$

The scheme proposed by Volk consists in solving the differential system by a series of the form

$$x(t, \epsilon) = \sum_{r=0}^{\infty} p_r(t, \epsilon)\epsilon^r \tag{9.4}$$

(This is not a power series in ϵ !), where the $p_r(t, \epsilon)$ are periodic solutions of a recursive set of linear differential equations obtained by formal insertion into (9.2) and comparison of powers of ϵ with the following unusual modification: the factor $\Omega(\epsilon)$ in the left member is treated as if the ϵ in it were a second, independent parameter. Each of the linear differential systems for the $p_r(t, \epsilon)$ is therefore itself a singular perturbation problem. Under suitable hypotheses Rang shows that periodic solutions $p_r(t, \epsilon)$ exist and that the series (9.4) converges.

There exists another, more striking, type of singular perturbation problems with periodic solutions, the so-called relaxation oscillations. The solutions of(9.1) lie on the manifold $0 = g(x, y, t, 0)$ in the (x, y, t)-space. It can be shown that the full system (6.1) may sometimes have periodic solutions that tend to a periodic limit functions with jump discontinuities, as $\epsilon \to 0$. In the (x, y, t)-plane these limit functions are curves composed of arcs lying on different branches of the manifold $g(x, y, t, o) = 0$ together with connecting arcs along which t is constant. The most general investigation of such relaxation oscillations, as far as existence and uniqueness is concerned is due to N. Levinson [1951]. The series expansions for such solutions are very hard to obtain. Much effort has been spent to find series,for small ϵ ,for the period $T(\epsilon)$ in the autonomous case. The required calculations are depressingly involved, even when x and y are one-dimensional. Better methods would be highly desirable. (See J. Haag [1943], [1944] and A. A. Dorodnicyn [1947].)

REFERENCES

1. Birkhoff, G. D., On the asymptotic character of the solutions of certain differential equations containing a parameter. Trans. Amer. Math. Soc. 9 (1908), 219-231.

2. Birkhoff, G. D., Singular points of ordinary linear differential equations. Trans. Amer. Math. Soc. 10 (1909), 436-470.

3. Brillouin, L., A practical method for solving Hill's equation. Quart. Appl. Math. 6 (1948), 167-178.

4. Cesari, L., Asymptotic behavior and stability problems in ordinary differential equations, 2nd ed., (1963), 271 pp. Springer Verlag and Academic Press.

5. Cherry, T. M., Uniform asymptotic expansions. J. London Math. Soc. 24 (1949), 121-130.

6. Cherry, T. M., Uniform asymptotic formulae for functions with transition points. Trans. Amer. Soc. 68 (1950).

7. Dorodnicyn, A. A., Asymptotic solution of the Van der Pol equation. (Russian) Prikl. Mat. Meh. 11 (1947), 313-328.

8. Fabry, E., Sur les intégrales des équations différentielles linéaires a coéfficients rationnels. Thèse, 1885, Paris.

9. Flatto, L., and Levinson, N., Periodic solutions of singularly perturbed systems. J. Rational Mech. Anal. 4(1955), 943-950.

10. Haag, J., Etude asymptotique des Oscillations de rélaxation. Ann. Sci. Ec. Non. Sup. 60 (1943), 35-111.

11. Haag, J., Exemples concrètes d'étude asymptotique d'oscillations de rélaxation. Ann. Sci. Ec. Non. Sup. 60(1944). 73-117.

12. Harris, W. A. Jr., Singular perturbations of two-point boundary problems. J. Math. Mech. 11 (1962), 371-382.

13. Hukuhara, M., Sur les propriétés asymptotiques des solutions d'un système d'équations différentielles linéaires contenant un paramètre. Mem. Fac. Eng., Kyushu Imp. Univ., 8(1937), 249-280.

14. Ince, E. L., Ordinary differential equations, Longmans, Green and Co., London, 1927.

15. Iwano, M., Intégration analytique d'un système d'équations nonlinéaires dans le voisinage d'un point singulier, I, II; Annali Mat. Pura Appl., 44 (1957), 261-292, and 47 (1959), 91-149.

16. Iwano, M., On a system of non-linear ordinary differential equations containing a parameter II. Kodai Math. Sem. Reports 14 (1962), 95-109.

17. Kramers, H. A., Das Eigenwertproblem im eindimensionalen periodischen Kraftfelde. Physik 2(1935), 483-490.

18. Langer, Rudolph E., On the asymptotic solutions of ordinary differential equations with an application to the Bessel functions of large order. Trans. Amer. Math. Soc. 33 (1931), 23-64.

19. Langer, Rudolph E., On the asymptotic solutions of differential equations with an application to the Bessel functions of large complex order. Trans. Amer. Math. Soc. 34 (1932), 447-480.

20. Langer, Rudolph E., The asymptotic solutions of certain linear ordinary differential equations of the second order. Trans. Amer. Math. Soc. 36 (1934 a), 90-106.

21. Langer, Rudolph E., The solutions of the Mathieu equation with complex variable and at least one parameter large. Trans. Amer. Math. Soc. 36 (1934 b), 637-695.

22. Langer, Rudolph E., The asymptotic solutions of ordinary linear differential equations of the second order with special reference to the Stokes phenomenon. Bull. Amer. Math. Soc. 40 (1934 c), 545-582.

23. Langer, Rudolph E., On the asymptotic solutions of ordinary differential equations with reference to the Stokes' phenomenon about a singular point. Trans. Amer. Math. Soc. 37(1935), 397-416.

24. Langer, Rudolph E., The asymptotic solutions of ordinary linear differential equations of the second order, with special reference to a turning point. Trans. Amer. Math. Soc. 67 (1949), 461-490.

25. Langer, Rudolph E., The solutions of the differential equation $v''' + \lambda^2 zv' + 3\mu\lambda^2 v = 0$. Duke Math. Journ. 22 (1955 a), 525-542.

26. Langer, Rudolph E., On the asymptotic forms of ordinary linear differential equations of the third order in a region containing a turning point. Trans. Amer. Math. Soc. 80 (1955 b), 93-123.

27. Langer, Rudolph E., The solutions of a class of ordinary linear differential equations of the third order in a region containing a multiple turning point. Duke Math. J. 23 (1956 a), 93-110.

28. Langer, Rudolph E., On the construction of related differential equations. Trans. Amer. Math. Soc. 81 (1956 b), 394-410.

29. Langer, Rudolph E., On the asymptotic solutions of a class of ordinary differential equations of the fourth order with a special reference to an equation of hydrodynamics. Trans. Amer. Math. Soc. 84 (1957), 144-191.

30. Langer, Rudolph E., The asymptotic solutions of a linear differential equation of the second order with two turning points. Trans. Amer. Math. Soc. 90 (1959 a), 113-142.

31. Langer, Rudolph E., Formal solutions and a related equation for a class of fourth order differential equations of a hydrodynamic type. Trans. Amer. Math. Soc. 92 (1959 b), 371-410.

32. Langer, Rudolph E., Turning points in linear asymptotic theory. Boletino Soc. Mat. Mexicana, 1960.

33. Levinson, N., Perturbations of discontinuous solutions of non-linear systems of differential equations. Acta Math. 82 (1951), 71-106.

34. Okubo, Kenjiro, On certain reduction theorems for systems of differential equations which contain a turning point. Proc. Japan Akad. 37 (1961), 544-549.

35. Olver, F. W. J., The asymptotic solution of linear differential equations of the second order for large values of a parameter (307-327); the asymptotic expansion of Bessel functions of large order (328-368). Phil. Trans. Royal Soc. A 247(1954).

36. Olver, F. W. J., The asymptotic solution of linear differential equations of the second order in a domain containing one transition point. Philos. Trans. Soc. London, Ser. A, 249 (1956), 65-97.

37. Olver, F. W. J., Error bounds for the Liouville-Green (or WKB) approximation. Proc. Cambridge Phil. Soc. 57 (1961), 790-810.

38. Rang, Edward R., Periodic solution of singular perturbation problems. Technical Report #1, Department of Mathematics, University of Minnesota (1957), 72 pp.

39. Rang, Edward R., Periodic solutions of singular perturbation problems. Proceedings of International Symposium on Non-linear Differential Equations (1963), 377-383, Academic Press.

40. Sibuya, Y., Sur réduction analytique d'un système d'équations différentielles ordinaires linéaires contenant un paramètre. J. Fac. Science, Univ. of Tokyo (1) 7(1958), 527-540.

41. Sibuya, Y., Asymptotic solutions of a system of linear ordinary differ ential equations containing a parameter. Funkcialaj Ekvacioj, 4 (1962 a) 83-113.

42. Sibuya, Y., Formal solutions of a linear ordinary differential equation of nth order at a turning point. Funkcial. Ekvac. 4 (1962b), 115-139.

43. Sibuya, Y., Simplification of a linear ordinary differential equation of the nth order at a turning point. Arch. Rat. Mech. Anal. 13 (1963 a), 206-221.

44. Sibuya, Y., Reduction of the order of a linear ordinary differential equation containing a small parameter. Kodai Math. Seminar Reports, v. 15 #1, (1963 b) 1-28.

45. Sibuya, Y., Asymptotic solutions of a linear ordinary differential equation of nth order about a simple turning point. Internat. Sympos. Nonlinear Mechanics, (1963 c), pp. 485-488, Acad. Press, New York.

46. Trjitzinsky, W. J., Analytic theory of linear differential equations, Acta Math. 62 (1934), 167-226.

47. Tschen, Yü-Why, Uber das Verhalten der Lösungen einer Folge von Differentialgleichunen, welche im Limes ausarten, Comp. Math. 2 (1935) 378-401.

48. Turrittin, H. L., Asymptotic expansions of solutions of systems of ordinary differential equations. Contributions to the Theory of Nonlinear Oscillations II; Ann. of Math. Studies, No. 29 (1952), 81-116, Princeton Univ. Press.

49. Turrittin, H. L., Convergent solutions of ordinary linear homogeneous differential equations in the neighborhood of an irregular singular point. Acta Math. 93 (1955), 27-66.

50. Vasil'eva, A. B., On repeated differentiation with respect to the parameter of solutions of systems of ordinary differential equations with a small parameter in the derivative. (Russian). Mat. SB. (N. S.) 48(90) (1959), 311-334.

51. Vasil'eva, A.B., Asymptotic behaviour of solutions of certain problems for ordinary nonlinear differential equations with a small parameter multiplying the highest derivatives (Russian). Uspehi Mat. Nauk 18 (1963), 15-86.

52. Višik, M.I. and Lyusternik, L.A., On the asymptotic behavior of the boundary problems for quasilinear differential equations (Russian). Dokl Akad. Nauk. SSSR 121 (1958) 778-781.

53. Višik, M.I. and Lyusternik, L.A., On initial jumps for non-linear differential equations containing a small parameter (Russian), Dokl. Akad. Nauk SSSR (1960) 1242-1245.

54. Višik, M.I. and Lyusternik, L.A., Regular degeneration and boundary layer for linear differential equations with small parameter (Russian). Uspehi Mat. Nau, (N.S.)12(1957), 3-122. Amer. Math. Soc. Translations Ser. 2, v. 20 (1962), 239-361.

55. Volk, I.M., On periodic solutions of autonomous systems (Russian). Akad. Nauk SSSR Prikl. Mat. Meh. v. 12 (1948), pp. 29-38.

56. Wasow, W., On the asymptotic solution of boundary value problems for ordinary differential equations containing a parameter. J. of Math. and Phys. 32, 173-183 (1944).

57. Wasow, W., The complex asymptotic theory of a fourth order differential equation of hydrodynamics. Ann. of Math. 49 (1948), 852-871.

58. Wasow, W., On the construction of periodic solutions of singular perturbation problems. Contributions to the theory of Nonlinear Oscillations, Annals. of Math. Studies v. 20 (1950), 313-350.

59. Wasow, W., Singular perturbations of boundary value problems for nonlinear differential equations of the second order. Comm. Pure. Appl. Math. 9 (1956) 93-113.

60. Wasow, W., Turning point problems for systems of linear equations. I. the formal theory. Comm. Pure Appl. Math. 14 (1961), 657-673.

61. Wasow, W., Turning point problems for systems of linear differential equations. II. The analytic theory. Comm. Pure Appl. Math. 15 (1962), 173-187.

62. Wasow, W., Simplification of turning point problems for systems of linear differential equations. Trans. Amer. Math. Soc. 106 (1963), 100-114.

63. Weber, H., Zur Theorie der Besselschen Funktionen. Math. Ann. 37(1890), 404-416.

64. Wentzel, G., Eine Verallgemeinerung der Quantenbedingung fur die Zwecke der Wellenmechanik. Z. Physik 38 (1926), 518-529.

HUGH L. TURRITTIN

Solvable Related Equations Pertaining to Turning Point Problems

1. Introduction. As Professor Wasow has already indicated, a great amount of thought and ingenuity has been directed toward simplification of turning-point problems. When one has done his best in this regard, he is still faced with the problem of solving the simplified or related equation that is finally obtained. In some cases, as Wasow pointed out, the large parameter λ can be removed by a transformation of the form

$$z = t\lambda^{p}, \qquad p > 0, \tag{1}$$

where t is the original independent variable and z is the new independent variable. Usually we are interested in the behavior of solutions as $t \to 0$ and $\lambda \to \infty$. It is then clear from (1) that for the resulting equation the behavior of solutions must be known when z is both large and small. In short solutions in the large are needed.

It is to this problem that we direct our attention. Some of the main efforts that have been made to calculate solutions in the large will be traced. For example in 1936 in Henry Scheffé's thesis, see reference [28], written under Professor Langer's direction, it became necessary to solve the equation

$$\frac{d^{n}w}{dz^{n}} - z^{v}w = 0, \tag{2}$$

where $n \geq 2$ and v is a positive integer. The complete solution in the large for this equation was finally obtained in 1950, [19], [35].

More recently Langer found it necessary in treating certain third and fourth order equations to solve in the large an equation of the form

$$\frac{d^{3}w}{dz^{3}} + z\frac{dw}{dz} + cw = 0, \tag{3}$$

where c is a constant, see ref. [22], [23] and [25]. The solution of this problem was facilitated by the use of E. M. Wright's work [37], [42] on the generalized hypergeometric function.

Let us begin the more technical aspects of our subject by considering first the simplification and standardization of differential equations which do not involve a parameter.

2. Matrix differential equations. As Wasow has pointed out, considerable progress has been made in studying the behavior of solutions of equations of the form

$$\frac{dZ}{dx} = x^{r-1}\left(\sum_{k=0}^{\infty} A_k x^{-k}\right) Z , \tag{4}$$

where r, the rank of the system, is a non-negative integer, [20], [31]. The unknown $Z(x)$ and the constant coefficients A_k are n-th order square matrices and the indicated series is presumed to converge for all sufficiently large values of $|x|$.

G. D. Birkhoff in two papers in 1909 and 1913, [1] and [3], attempted to terminate the infinite series in (4) and produce a new reduced equation of the form

$$\frac{dY}{dx} = x^{r-1} \sum_{j=0}^{s} C_j x^{-j} Y \tag{5}$$

by using one of two types of transformations:

Type I. $Z = B(x)Y$,

where the n^2 elements in matrix B are all analytic in some neighborhood of $x = \infty$ and the determinant $B(\infty) \neq 0$.

Type II. $Z = V(x)Y$,

where $V(x)$ can be represented by a convergent series of the form

$$V(x) = x^g \sum_{j=0}^{\infty} V_j x^{-j} ,$$

where the lead matrix $V_0 \neq 0$; g is an integer and the determinant of $V(x)$ is non-vanishing in some neighborhood of infinity, $r_1 \leq |x| < \infty$. The determinant of the lead matrix V_0 may, however, be zero.

G. D. Birkhoff asserted that, if an appropriate transformation of Type I were used, the s in (5) need not exceed r. However in 1953 Gantmacher, [13], produced a counter example showing that Birkhoff had made an error.

In a recent paper in the Transactions [34], Turrittin has attempted to make clear to what extent Birkhoff was right and to what extent he was wrong. For instance there is always some cutoff; i.e., form (5) can always be reached by a suitable transformation of Type I for some sufficiently large finite value of s.

If $r = 0$, and this is the case covered by the counter-example, Birkhoff would have been right if he had made his s one unit larger and, if the more general transformation of Type II were used Birkhoff would have been right when $r = 0$. More generally when $r > 0$ and transformations of Type II are used Birkhoff is still correct provided the characteristic roots of A_0 are all distinct.

When A_0 has multiple roots, the situation is complicated and obscure. It was my hope to present on this occasion further results relating to this problem; but very serious difficulties have appeared and there is only one rather special new fact to be presented:

Theorem. A second order equation

$$\frac{dZ}{dx} = x^{r-1}\left(\sum_{k=0}^{\infty} A_k x^{-k}\right)Z \quad , \tag{6}$$

where the indicated series converges if $|x| > \alpha > 0$, can always be reduced to form (5) with $s = r$ by a transformation of Type II provided the asymptotic solution of (6) does not contain fractional powers of $1/x$.

Proof: As stated, if $r = 0$ or if the roots of A_0 are distinct, the theorem is known to be true. Let us use induction on the rank r. There is no loss in generality in assuming A_0 is in Jordan canonical form. If

$$A_0 = \begin{Vmatrix} \rho & 0 \\ 0 & \rho \end{Vmatrix} ,$$

make a transformation

$$Z = \exp\{\rho x^r/r\} Y \tag{7}$$

which merely annuls the A_0 matrix and makes no other changes and thus, cancelling out an x, produces a new equation of rank $(r-1)$. The series, by the hypothesis for the induction, in this new equation can be truncated to form (5) with r replaced by $(r-1)$ and $s = r - 1$. The ρ's on the main diagonal would then be replaced in matrix A_0 by using the inverse of transformation (7), bringing the equation back to form (5) with $s = r$ and we would have produced the desired result.

In the event that

$$A_0 = \begin{Vmatrix} \rho & 1 \\ 0 & \rho \end{Vmatrix} \quad \text{and} \quad A_1 = \begin{Vmatrix} a_{11} & a_{12} \\ a_{21} & a_{22} \end{Vmatrix}$$

again the ρ in A_0 is annulled by transformation (7) and, if fractional powers do not appear in the asymptotic expansion, as is assumed, we must also at this juncture have $a_{21} = 0$. This being the case a shearing transformation

$$Y = \begin{Vmatrix} x & 0 \\ 0 & 1 \end{Vmatrix} W$$

reduces the rank a unit and our induction is again brought into play and the inverse of (7) is used as before and our theorem is proved.

The most disconcerting thing about this result is that there is a strong indication that the theorem is valid regardless of the order of the equation provided the fractional powers of x do not appear in the asymptotic solutions; but this can be presented only a conjecture since a proof has not been found.

Let us return to equation (4) to determine a formal series solution $Z_\infty(x)$ running in general in fractional powers of x, say in powers of $1/x^{1/p}$. To this end one might begin by reducing (4) by a standard procedure, [33], to an equation of the form

$$(8) \qquad \frac{dY}{dt} = t^{q-1} \left\| \delta_{ij}\{\rho_i(t) I_i + J_i t^{-q}\} + \sum_{\nu=q+1}^{\infty} B_{ij\nu} t^{-\nu} \right\| Y ,$$

where in general t is a fractional power of x; i.e. $t = x^{1/p}$. Also here $i, j = 1, \ldots, m$ and the I_i's are identity matrices of appropriate orders; δ_{ij} is the Kronecker delta; the J_i's are square matrices with zeros on 1's, or a mixture of 0's and 1's running down the first subdiagonal of J_i and all other elements of J_i are zeros. The $\rho_i(t)$ have the form

$$\rho_i(t) = \rho_{i0} + \rho_{i1} t^{-1} + \dots + \rho_{iq} t^{-q} .$$

The integer q will usually exceed r. The ρ_i are distinct and, if the first q coefficients of say ρ_i and ρ_j are alike and $i \neq j$, then the last coefficients ρ_{iq} and ρ_{jq} will not differ by integers. Once form (8) is reached it is not difficult to compute the desired formal series solution $Z_\infty(x)$.

In the older literature there is considerable emphasis on the rank r; but recently in the Duke Journal, [36], it has been shown that in a very simple fashion the rank r of any system of type (4) can be reduced to rank $r = 1$ by increasing the order n of the system. Actually this rank reduction does not seem to be helpful at all in some cases in solving a given equation. In fact the true difficulty of the problem is more properly measured by the size of the q in (8) than the r in (5).

3. The problem in the large. Let us now consider an equation in Birkhoff's reduced form, namely

$$\frac{dY}{dx} = x^{r-1} \left(\sum_{j=0}^{r} A_j x^{-j} \right) Y \tag{9}$$

and let $S_1, \dots, S_h$ represent a sequence of successively adjacent and possibly overlapping appropriately chosen sectors covering completely the neighborhood of $x = \infty$ and suppose the sectors are listed in clockwise order. Also let $Y_i(x)$, $(i = 1, \dots, h)$ be a true fundamental solution of (9) with an asymptotic representation $Y_\infty(x)$ in S_i. In general $Y_i(x)$ and $Y_{i+1}(x)$ are not the same matrices and yet, as is well known, they are linearly related; i.e., there exists a constant matrix C_i such that $Y_{i+1}(x) = Y_i(x) C_i$, $(i = 1, \dots, h)$, where we set $Y_{h+1}(x) \equiv Y_1(x)$.

If one wishes to know the behavior of solutions of (9) in the complete neighborhood of $x = \infty$, in general not only must the $Y_\infty(x)$ and the various $Y_i(x)$'s be known; but one must also find the Stokes matrix multipliers C_i. The determination of these multipliers may be called the sector connection problem.

Although in general equation (9) has an irregular singular point at $x = \infty$, the origin $x = 0$ is a regular singular point and thus a convergent solution $Y_0(x)$ can be found running in powers of x and involving possibly a finite number of powers of $\log x$. Since there are no other singular points, the series solution $Y_0(x)$ converges for all finite values of x.

The matrices $Y_1(x), \dots, Y_h(x)$ are linearly related to $Y_0(x)$; i.e., there is a new Stokes multiplier C_{i0} such that $Y_i(x) = Y_0(x) C_{i0}$,

$(i = 1, \ldots, h)$. The computation of these C_{i0} 's may be called the two-point connection problem.

It is obvious that, if this later problem can be solved, the sector connection problem is automatically solved, for then $C_i = C_{i0}^{-1} C_{i+1,\,0}$. Once the C_i and C_{i0} 's are known, we say the problem is solved in the large.

4. Solution in the large by matching. Since the region of convergence of the series $Y_0(x)$ extends from the origin into the remote portions of each of the sectors S_i, where we have an asymptotic expansion $Y_\infty(x)$ for the solution $Y_i(x)$ in sector S_i, one can pick a point $\hat{x}$ far out in sector S_i and, making the right choice for the multiple valued functions involved in the asymptotic expansions, we get an approximate evaluation for $C_{i0} \cong Y^{-1}(\hat{x})\, Y_\infty(\hat{x})$. This technique of comparing two solutions at a point could be called asymptotic matching. In many problems, to-date, this is the best evaluation we can make for the C_{i0} 's. Actually in carrying out this approximation the asymptotic series is cut short and usually only a few of the elements in the C_{i0} 's can be found with reasonable accuracy by this asymptotic matching. The other elements remain essentially undetermined.

Occasionally accuracy can be improved as Dingle, [6], has shown by using convergence factors; but in the more complicated cases it is not clear that suitable convergent factors can be introduced that will provide satisfactory accuracy for all elements in the Stokes multipliers.

However, the situation is not always so unsatisfactory, for referring to our equation (8), if $q = 1$, or if $m = 2$, or if all the roots ρ_{i0} are distinct, then the divergent asymptotic series $Y_\infty(x)$ can, using Borel summability, be replaced by a convergent generalized factorial series $\widetilde{Y}_\infty(x)$ and we then have a precise evaluation

$$C_{i0} = Y_0^{-1}(\hat{x})\widetilde{Y}_\infty(\hat{x}) \quad ,$$

for the Stokes multipliers and at least in theory our problem in the large has been solved by convergent matching.

It might conceivably turn out that the asymptotic series even converged and then it would not be necessary to attempt to sum and introduce factorial series. In a recent paper Hukuhara and Iwano, [21] have made a study of the possible number of such convergent solutions. Actually such convergence rarely occurs.

In an actual case, if one were to compute the multipliers to some prescribed degree of accuracy, the computations would be very lengthy indeed for we would be dealing with slowly convergent series.

To-date, however, no convergent matching process is known that will supply multipliers in all cases.

Let us look at the simplest recalcitrant case; i.e., in (8) let $n = m = 3$; $q = 2$; $\rho_{10} \neq \rho_{20} = \rho_{30}$ and $\rho_{21} \neq \rho_{31}$ and think of our equation as a vector rather than a matrix equation. One would like to have three independent convergent vector solutions both at the origin and at infinity. The three convergent solutions are available at the origin and they do converge for all finite values of x and curiously enough one of the vector solutions at ∞ can be summed and represented by a convergent factorial series, while no means has been found so far to sum the other two series. One might think the known convergent vector solution at infinity could be used to reduce the order of the equation to $n = 2$ and that then the new equation of order 2 might be more amenable to treatment. Let us see what can be done in this direction.

5. Equations involving factorial series. It is fairly obvious, if the plan just described can be carried out, that the reduced second order equation that one will obtain will no longer be of precisely the type we have been considering, for in the new equation

$$\frac{dZ}{dx} = G(x)Z$$

the coefficient matrix $G(x)$ would no longer be a convergent power series in $1/x$; but instead it would involve a convergent factorial series. Therefore, one is inclined to believe we should have studied equations involving factorial series at the outset. The basic class of functions under consideration is then to be shifted from those that are analytic at ∞ to those that can be represented by convergent factorial series.

Let us recall that, if a matrix $A(z)$ can be represented by a factorial series

$$A(z) = \sum_{k=0}^{\infty} \frac{k!A_k}{z(z+1)\dots(z+k)}$$

convergent in some right-half plane $\text{Re } z > \lambda$; then $A(z)$ can also be represented as a Laplace transform; i.e., there exists a matrix $B(t)$ such that

$$A(z) = \int_0^{\infty} e^{-zt} B(t)\,dt$$

and $B(t)$ is analytic in a region D of the t-plane extending to infinity as shown in the following figure, which is the image of the circle $|v-1| < 1$ under the transformation $v = e^{-t}$.

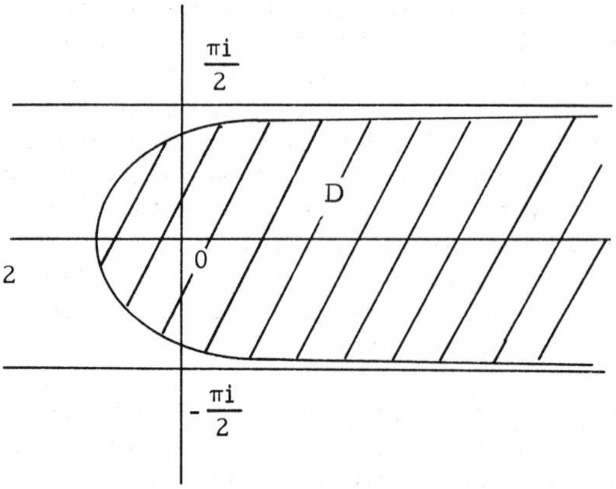

Figure 1

Moreover in D the function $B(t)$ has at most exponential growth as $t \to \infty$. Likewise in the open region D the derivative $B'(t)$ has only exponential growth, a fact that apparently has not been previously emphasized and would be needed in the proof of a theorem about to be stated. To verify this later fact one notes that the Laplace transform of $B'(t)$ is $\{zA(z) - A(0)\}$ and therefore

$$\int_0^\infty e^{-zt} B'(t)\,dt = \sum_{k=1}^{\infty} \frac{k!A_k}{(z+1)(z+2)\ldots(z+k)}$$

and, since this right-hand member converges in a half-plane, it is known [15] this sum can be replaced by an equivalent convergent factorial series. This in turn implies $B'(t)$ has at most exponential growth in D.

Two new theorems relating to the topic at hand are at our disposal.

Theorem I. Let $r = 0$ or 1 and consider the equation

$$\text{(10)}\qquad \frac{dU}{ds} = s^r\Big(\sum_{k=0}^{\infty} \frac{k!A_k}{s(s+1)\ldots(s+k)}\Big)U = \begin{Vmatrix} A_{11}(s) & A_{12}(s) \\ A_{21}(s) & A_{22}(s) \end{Vmatrix} U,$$

where the indicated factorial series converges in some right half-plane and the lead matrix has the form

$$A_0 = \begin{Vmatrix} A_{110} & 0 \\ 0 & A_{220} \end{Vmatrix} .$$

Furthermore suppose that, if $r = 0$, no characteristic root λ_j of A_{110} differs by an integer from a characteristic root μ_i of A_{220}; or, if $r = 1$, that none of the differences $\pm(\mu_i - \lambda_j)$, $i \neq j$, fall in region D; then there exists a transformation

$$U = \begin{Vmatrix} I_1 & Q_{12} \\ Q_{21} & I_2 \end{Vmatrix} V ,$$

where I_1 and I_2 are identity matrices and the series

$$Q_{ij} = \sum_{k=0}^{\infty} \frac{k!Q_{ijk}}{s(s+1)\dots(s+k)}$$

for Q_{12} and Q_{21} are both convergent in some right half-plane, which will convert equation (10) into a new equation of the form

$$\frac{dV}{ds} = \begin{Vmatrix} B_{11} & 0 \\ 0 & B_{22} \end{Vmatrix} V ,$$

where

$$B_{ij} = \sum_{k=0}^{\infty} \frac{k!B_{iik}}{s(s+1)\dots(s+k)} , \qquad (i = 1, 2) ,$$

is convergent in some right half-plane and $B_{ii0} = A_{ii0}$.

This theorem is a modified form of Sibuya's block diagonalization process, [30]. Here the emphasis is on the use of factorial series. The restriction, when $r = 1$, relating to the differences $\pm(\mu_i - \lambda_j)$ is not as severe as it appears, for, if the condition is not satisfied, one can still get block diagonalization by using generalized factorial series of the form

$$\sum_{k=0}^{\infty} \frac{k!A_k}{x(x+\gamma)(x+2\gamma)\ldots(x+k\gamma)} \quad .$$

Theorem II. Consider an equation of the form

$$(11) \qquad \frac{dY}{dx} = \left(\sum_{k=0}^{\infty} \frac{k!A_k}{x(x+1)\ldots(x+k)} \right) Y \quad ,$$

where the matrix factorial series converges in some right-half-plane. Assume, without loss of generality, [33], that the lead matrix has the form

$$A_0 = \| \delta_{ij}(\rho_i I_i + J_i) \| \,, \qquad (i = 1, \ldots, m) \,,$$

where the notation is the same as in equation (8) and, if $i \neq j$, ρ_i does not differ from ρ_j by an integer. Then equation (11) has in some appropriate right half-plane a fundamental convergent factorial series solution of the form

$$Y(x) = \left(Y_0 + \sum_{k=0}^{\infty} \frac{k!Y_{k+1}}{x(x+1)\ldots(x+k)}\right) \| \delta_{ij} t^{\rho_i} \exp\{J_i \log t\} \| \,,$$

where the Y_0, Y_1, ... are appropriate constant matrices.

The proof for both of these theorems is quite similar and follows what is now a standard procedure [5], so the details will only be briefly indicated here and limited to the case $r = 0$. When $r = 0$, one finds that the matrix Q_{12} to be used must be a solution of the equation

$$(12) \qquad \frac{dQ_{12}}{ds} = A_{12} + A_{11}Q_{12} - Q_{12}A_{22} - Q_{12}A_{21}Q_{12}$$

and that $B_{22} = A_{22} + A_{21}Q_{12}$. Matrix Q_{21} and B_{11} satisfy analogous equations. Since the A_{ij} are convergent factorial series, they have a Laplace integral representation

$$A_{ij}(s) = \int_0^{\infty} e^{-st} C_{ij}(t)\,dt \quad .$$

Proceeding momentarily only formally, let

(13) $$Q_{12}(s) = \int_0^\infty e^{-st} R(t)\, dt \; ;$$

then the formal Laplace transform of the singular Volterra integral equation

(14) $$-tR(t) = C_{12}(t) + \int_0^t C_{11}(t-\tau) R(\tau)\, d\tau - \int_0^t R(t-\tau) C_{22}(\tau)\, d\tau$$

$$- \int_0^t R(t-\tau) \left[\int_0^\tau C_{21}(\tau - \nu) R(\nu)\, d\nu \right] d\tau$$

will be precisely equation (12). We shall hear more about such integral equations from Professor Erdélyi later in our program. In (14) the matrices C_{ij} are known to possess convergent series representations of the form

$$C_{ii}(t) = \sum_{k=0}^{\infty} C_{iik} t^k \qquad (i = 1 \text{ or } 2)$$

and

$$C_{ij}(t) = \sum_{k=1}^{\infty} C_{ijk} t^k \qquad (i \neq j, i, \; j = 1, 2) \; .$$

One would show first that the integral equation (14) possesses an analytic solution of the form

(15) $$R(t) = \sum_{k=0}^{\infty} R_k t^k$$

convergent in some circle of convergence about the origin $t = 0$. This would be done by substituting formally the series (15) into the integral equation and computing the coefficients $R_0, R_1, R_2, \ldots$ one after the other. Then, using a dominant integral equation built from dominant factorial series, the note of growth of R_n as $n \to \infty$ can be estimated and the convergence and existence of a solution of the integral equation can then be established.

Next $R(t)$ would be continued analytically into region D and using the fact that the $C_{ij}(t)$ grows at most at an exponential rate in D one can deduce from the integral equation itself that $R(t)$ also has only exponential growth at most in D. We can then use (13) to define the desired matrix $Q_{12}(s)$ and thus finally prove our theorem.

Since block diagonalization can be carried out, we may as well at the outset assume that in equation (10) the roots of the lead matrix A_0 are all alike when $r = 1$ and that A_0 is in the Jordan classical canonical form. If in particular $A_0 = \rho I$, the rank may be reduced to zero and we are back to the case $r = 0$ with a convergent factorial series solution. If A_0 has ones on the first subdiagonal, a shear would be used to remove the 1 's and, if this can be accomplished without introducing fractional powers of s, again a convergent factorial series solution could be obtained.

If the shear introduces fractional powers of s, we are completely blocked, and summation of the divergent asymptotic series appears to be impossible, since a fractional power of x, such as $1/x^{1/2}$, can not be expressed in terms of a convergent factorial series.

If in (10) $r > 1$ and block-diagonalization with factorial series is attempted, we proceed as outlined and an analytic solution $R(t)$ is found. Then when the rate of growth of $R(t)$ is estimated directly from the integral equation, it turns out $R(t)$ now can grow as fast as e^{t^2} or faster and the Laplace transform of $R(t)$ becomes meaningless and the block diagonalization with convergent factorial series is not possible.

One might hope to break out of these difficulties when $r > 1$ by reducing the rank of (10) to $r = 1$ by increasing the order at the outset. When this is done some block diagonalization is possible. However, to return to the recalcitrant case where in (8) the $n = m = 3$; $q = 2$; $\rho_{10} \neq \rho_{20} = \rho_{30}$ and $\rho_{21} \neq \rho_{31}$, what happens, when the order is raised from $n = 3$ to $n = 6$ to reduce the rank from 2 to 1, is that the block diagonalization does indeed yield two separate systems, one of order $n = 2$ and the other or order $n = 4$. The new system of order $n = 2$ can be solved in terms of convergent factorial series; but the system of order $n = 4$ is of rank $r = 1$ and the necessary shearing leads to fractional powers and we are again at a dead-end. Thus in this instance no convergent matching would be possible and there appears to be no hope of getting such a process without some entirely new insight and approach to the problem.

What other methods are available?

6. <u>The Ford technique.</u> In 1936 Walter B. Ford, [10], introduced a new method of computing Stokes multipliers when considering an equation of the form

$$(16) \qquad z^2(a_0 + a_1 z + a_2 z^2)\frac{d^2y}{dz^2} + z(b_0 + b_1 z + b_2 z^2)\frac{dy}{dz}$$

$$+ (c_0 + c_1 z + c_2 z^2) y = 0 \ .$$

If certain special cases are set aside, equation (16) possesses two independent convergent solutions of the form

$$(17) \qquad \begin{cases} y_1(z) = z^{h_1} \sum_{n=0}^{\infty} g_1(n) z^n \\ \\ y_2(z) = z^{h_2} \sum_{n=0}^{\infty} g_2(n) z^n \end{cases} \quad \text{where} \quad \begin{cases} g_1(0) = 1 \\ \\ g_2(0) = 1 \end{cases}$$

and two other convergent solutions of the form

$$(18) \qquad \begin{cases} \bar{y}_1(z) = \left(\frac{1}{z}\right)^{k_1} \sum_{n=0}^{\infty} \frac{\bar{g}_1(n)}{z^n} \\ \\ \bar{y}_2(z) = \left(\frac{1}{z}\right)^{k_2} \sum_{n=0}^{\infty} \frac{\bar{g}_2(n)}{z^n} \end{cases} \quad \text{where} \quad \begin{cases} \bar{g}_1(0) = 1 \\ \\ \bar{g}_2(0) = 1 \end{cases} \quad .$$

To determine the linear relationships between these two sets of solutions Ford's plan was roughly as follows:

The $g_1(n)$, for instance, treated as a function of the complex variable n, satisfies a three term recurrence relation of the form

$$p_2(n) g_1(n + 2) + p_1(n) g_1(n + 1) + p_0(n) g_0(n) = 0 \ ,$$

where the coefficiencts p_0, p_1, p_2 are certain known second degree polynomials in n. This difference equation can be solved and two independent solutions $G_{11}(n)$ and $G_{21}(n)$ can be found and in this case, save for a certain multiplying coefficient, each solution can be expressed as a factorial series convergent in some right half-plane. Furthermore, we know that $g_1(n)$ is some linear combination of G_{11}

and G_{21}, say

$$g_1(n) = c_{11}G_{11}(n) + c_{21}G_{21}(n) \quad .$$

Similarly $g_2(n)$ can be expressed in the form

$$g_2(n) = c_{21}G_{12}(n) + c_{22}G_{22}(n) \quad ,$$

where the $G_{12}(n)$ and $G_{22}(n)$ are also known expressions involving convergent factorial series. The evaluation of the multipliers c_{ij} for the problem at hand, as appears later from Ford's analysis, is essentially equivalent to the evaluation of the Stokes multipliers for the original differential equation (16). Thus the Stokes multiplier problem for the differential equation is transferred into a Stokes multiplier problem for difference equations.

This latter problem can often be solved by using convergent processes. In Ford's problem $g_1(0)$ and $g_1(1)$ are known and so $g_1(n)$ for successively larger and larger values of n can be computed directly from the difference equation itself until one obtains the values of say $g_1(m)$ and $g_1(m+1)$, where m is sufficiently large to fall in the half-plane of convergence of the series representing $G_{11}(n)$ and $G_{21}(n)$. At this juncture one solves the two equations

$$\begin{cases} g_1(m) = c_{11}G_{11}(m) + c_{21}G_{21}(m) \\ g_1(m+1) = c_{11}G_{11}(m+1) + c_{21}G_{21}(m+1) \end{cases}$$

for the desired multipliers c_{11} and c_{21}.

Once this is done, the asymptotic behavior of a function of the form

$$\sum_{n=0}^{\infty} G_{11}(n)\, z^n$$

in the neighborhood of $z = \infty$ must be determined. To do this Ford expressed the first $(n+1)$ terms of the series as a sum of residues. For this purpose he used a contour integral around the path C shown in Figure 2 and wrote

$$\sum_{k=0}^{n} G_{11}(k)\, z^k = \frac{1}{2i}\int_C \frac{G_{11}(w)(-z)^w\, dw}{\sin \pi w} \quad .$$

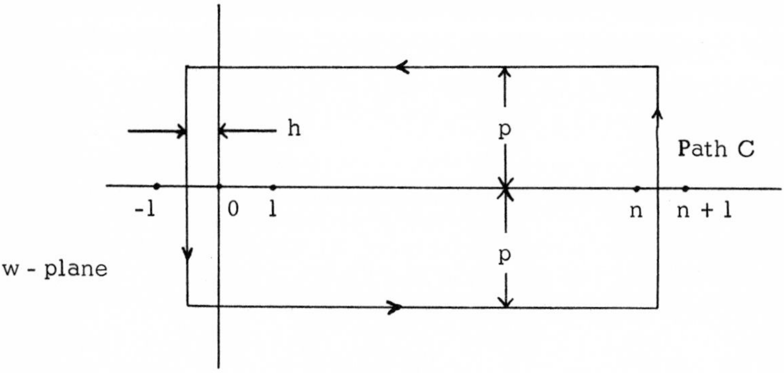

Figure 2

One finds that as $p \to \infty$ the contribution to the integral on the two horizontal paths approach zero. As the right boundary is moved farther from the origin more and more terms of the series

$$\sum_{k=0}^{\infty} G_{11}(k) z^k$$

are summed and by increasing h more and more residues come from the poles of the function $G_{11}(w)$, making up a sum which is essentially the desired asymptotic expansion of

$$\sum_{k=0}^{\infty} G_{11}(k) z^k$$

for large values of z in an appropriate sector.

There are a number of details related to this process that need careful consideration and for the equation chosen by Ford this procedure can be pushed through and the asymptotic expansions can be identified with the series (18). Thus the problem is completely solved in the large by convergent processes.

The strength and weaknesses of the Ford method appear already in Ford's original presentation. In considering equation (16) a number of special cases came up and most of them Ford was able to handle by modifications in his analysis. However, he was not entirely successful in all cases and was blocked completely in two cases:

Case I: Suppose $a_0 = \mu^2$, $\mu \neq 0$, $a_1 = 2\mu$ and $a_2 = 1$ and also suppose the roots h_1 and h_2 corresponding to the indicial equation

$$\mu^2 h^2 + (b_0 - \mu^2) h + c_0 = 0$$

do not differ by an integer. In this event to carry through Ford's method and have convergent processes one must be able to sum the asymptotic solutions of the difference equation satisfied by the g's and express them as a convergent factorial series in a right half-plane. Despite the recent efforts and advances in solving difference equations that have been made particularly by Culmer [4], [5], Harris [14], [16], [18] and Sibuya [17] the solutions in this case can not be summed by any known method. Thus Ford's technique fails in this case. Incidently, this problem could be solved in the large by the convergent matching method first described and so we see the two procedures do not cover the same class of problems.

Case II: Let $a_0 = 1$, $a_2 = a_1 = 0$, and $b_2 \neq 0$ and assume the roots of the indicial equation

$$h^2 + (b_0 - 1) h + c_0 = 0$$

do not differ by integers. Then we obtain a more typical case showing the difficulties involved in carrying out Ford's program. Here there is no difficulty in getting solutions of the difference equation in terms of convergent factorial series, [27]. The difficulties lie elsewhere. One even gets asymptotic expansions for the functions defined in (17) which are valid in the neighborhood of infinity, but the new difficulty lies in the fact that the expansions are valid in sectors that are <u>too narrow</u>. The sectors do not cover completely the neighborhood of infinity, four narrow sectors are left uncovered.

Furthermore, in the sectors where we do have asymptotic expansions, each of the y 's is a sum of two asymptotic expansions and one of these expansions completely dominates the other throughout the sector. This means as far as the asymptotic expansions are concerned, one might as well not even write the subdominant expansions in the sum and this in turn implies one gets some, but not all, of the Stokes multipliers.

In short, if one is to succeed completely by Ford's method, it is crucial to obtain asymptotic representations in maximal sized sectors to cover the entire neighborhood of $z = \infty$. In Ford's second exceptional case, it is not clear just how to do this, nor is it certain that it can be done.

7. Okubo's problem. In a recent paper Okubo [26] has put a great deal of thought on maximalization of sector size in studying the behavior of solutions of a system of equations of the form

$$t\frac{dx}{dt} = (A + tB)x \quad ,$$

where x is an n-component vector and A and B are n by n constant matrices. It is presumed B is diagonal and that the diagonal elements are all distinct. Furthermore, it is assumed that A has no two eigenvalues which have an integral difference. There are other restrictions also on the roots. Okubo has almost solved his problem in the large completely. In the special case $n = 2$ he has indeed succeeded; but, if $n = 3$, in his formulas, as he points out, there is still an additional error term $O(t^h)$ for some appropriate $h > 0$, which for complete success should not be present. He conjectures that this error term need not really appear in the formulas and proves this to be true when $n = 2$.

It should be emphasized however, that when $n = 2$, the situation is far simpler than when $n \geq 3$. For example, an equation of Okubo's type when $n = 2$ can be solved completely in the large without making any restrictions whatsoever on the nature of the roots of either matrix A or B. To see this note first of all that a vector equation of the form

$$(19) \qquad t\frac{dx}{dt} = \left\| \begin{matrix} 0 & t \\ -a_2-b_2t & -a_1-b_1t \end{matrix} \right\| x$$

is equivalent to the single second order equation

$$t\frac{d^2x}{dt^2} + (a_1 + b_1t)\frac{dx}{dt} + (a_2 + b_2t)x = 0$$

and this latter equation has been solved completely and systemmatically in the large, see Higher Transcendental Functions, Bateman Manuscript Project, vol. 1, p. 249.

Consider then, a more general second order matrix equation of the form

$$(20) \qquad t\frac{dX}{dt} = (A + Bt)X \; .$$

Case I: Suppose

$$B = \begin{Vmatrix} \rho & 0 \\ 0 & \rho \end{Vmatrix} ;$$

then one integrates at once and obtains a fundamental solution

$$X = \exp \{ \rho t I + A \log t \} .$$

Case II: If

$$B = \begin{Vmatrix} \rho & 1 \\ 0 & \rho \end{Vmatrix} ,$$

an exponential transformation $X = e^{\rho t} Y$ will annul the ρ in B ; so one may as well assume that

$$B = \begin{Vmatrix} 0 & 1 \\ 0 & 0 \end{Vmatrix} \quad \text{and} \quad A = \begin{Vmatrix} a_{11} & a_{12} \\ a_{21} & a_{22} \end{Vmatrix} .$$

A substitution

$$X = \begin{Vmatrix} 1 & m \\ 0 & 1 \end{Vmatrix} Y$$

will convert (20) into the equation

$$t \frac{dY}{dt} = \left\{ \begin{Vmatrix} 0 & t \\ 0 & 0 \end{Vmatrix} + \begin{Vmatrix} a_{11} - m a_{21} , & a_{12} + m(a_{11} - a_{22}) - a_{21} m^2 \\ a_{21} & , \quad a_{21} m + a_{22} \end{Vmatrix} \right\} Y .$$

One selects m so that

$$a_{12} + m(a_{11} - a_{22}) - a_{21} m^2 = 0$$

and annuls the element $(a_{11} - m a_{21})$ by a transformation

(21) $$Y = t^{a_{11} - m a_{21}} Z ,$$

thus producing an equation of type (19), which can be solved in the large.

This procedure would be blocked only if $a_{12} \neq 0$, $a_{11} = a_{22}$ and $a_{21} = 0$ and in this exceptional case one may integrate and obtain a fundamental solution

$$X = t^{a_{11}} \begin{Vmatrix} 1 & t + a_{12} \log t \\ 0 & 1 \end{Vmatrix} .$$

Case III: In the event that B has distinct roots there is no loss in generality in assuming

$$B = \begin{Vmatrix} 0 & 0 \\ 0 & \rho \end{Vmatrix} .$$

If $a_{12} \neq 0$; let

$$X = \begin{Vmatrix} 1 & 0 \\ m & t \end{Vmatrix} Y ,$$

where m is a root of the equation $a_{12}m^2 + (a_{11} - a_{22})m - a_{21} = 0$ to get a new equation of the form

$$\frac{dY}{dt} = \left\{ \begin{Vmatrix} 0 & a_{12} \\ 0 & \rho \end{Vmatrix} + \frac{1}{t} \begin{Vmatrix} c_{11} & 0 \\ m\rho & c_{22} \end{Vmatrix} \right\} Y .$$

Again c_{11} can be annulled by a transformation to type (21). Next to replace a_{12} by unity let $t = x/a_{12}$ and we are back to an equation of type (19) with a solution in the large.

If at the outset $a_{12} = 0$; but $a_{21} \neq 0$, set

$$X = \begin{Vmatrix} 0 & 1 \\ 1 & 0 \end{Vmatrix} Y$$

and proceed as just indicated. If $a_{12} = 0$ and $a_{21} = 0$, integrate and

$$X = \left\| \begin{matrix} t^{a_{11}} & 0 \\ & \\ 0 & e^{pt} t^{a_{22}} \end{matrix} \right\| .$$

Thus solutions in the large for (20) are always available.

Before considering the situation when $n = 3$, it should be pointed out that the computation of the Stokes multipliers for equation (19), as well as for equations (2) and (3), has been carried out without using a matching process. This evaluation of Stokes multipliers without matching has been done essentially in just two types of problems; either the equations have been simple enough so that the solutions can be represented by contour or line integrals, usually of the Laplace or Fourier type, with the integrands in known closed forms or that the coefficients $g(n)$ of the convergent power series solutions satisfy two term scalar difference equations, which, as is well known, possess explicit solutions in terms of Gamma functions.

The importance of differential equations leading to only two term difference equations was recognized by Scheffé, [29]. He showed that if proper transformations are made, one is always lead to solutions of the generalized hypergeometric equation. This means the thorough and extensive work of E. M. Wright [37], [42] and others on the asymptotic behavior of generalized hypergeometric functions can be brought at once to bear on the problem at hand.

There is strong indication then that in these two special cases; i. e., when Laplace or Fourier integral representations in closed form for solutions are available [12], [8], [9] or two-term scalar difference equations appear, the Stokes multipliers can be determined completely and explicitly in terms of known functions. This situation however, has not been systematically explored and certain troublesome special cases can come up.

The problem of finding solutions in the large of Okubo's equation

$$(22) \qquad t\frac{dx}{dt} = (A + Bt)x ,$$

when the vector x has more than two components, is on the face of it a natural extension of Scheffé's concept of two-term scalar recurrence relations, for the coefficients in the solution satisfy a two term matrix recurrence relation; but since closed form solutions in terms of Gamma functions are no longer available, serious complications appear.

The single n^{th} order equation which is analogous to Okubo's problem takes the form

$$(23)\qquad \frac{d^n y}{dx^n} + \sum_{j=0}^{n-1} \left(\sum_{k=0}^{n-j} c_{jk} x^{-k} \right) \frac{d^j y}{dx^j} = 0 \quad .$$

However, if $n > 3$, it is not at all clear just how one would systematically proceed to convert (23) into a system of type (22) or to convert (22) into (23). In fact at this point one runs into a number of difficult problems relating to equivalence classes of equations. If $n = 2$ there is no difficulty in converting (23) into (22). If $n = 3$ to convert (23) into (22), make a change of variable $y = x^{\mu} w$ and select μ so that the new equation has the form

$$\frac{d^3 w}{dx^3} + \left(\frac{a_1 + b_1 x}{x}\right)\frac{d^2 w}{dx^2} + \left(\frac{a_2 + b_2 x + c_2 x^2}{x^2}\right)\frac{dw}{dx} + \left(\frac{b_3 + c_3 x + d_3 x^2}{x^2}\right) w = 0$$

or in matrix notation

$$(24)\qquad \frac{dW}{dx} = \left\| \begin{matrix} 0 & 1 & 0 \\ 0 & 0 & 1 \\ \dfrac{b_3 + c_3 x + d_3 x^2}{x^2} & \dfrac{a_2 + b_2 x + c_2 x^2}{x^2} & \dfrac{a_1 + b_1 x}{x} \end{matrix} \right\| W.$$

Equation (24) is not in Okubo's form, but it can be converted into Okubo's equation by a transformation of the form

$$W = \left\| \begin{matrix} x & 0 & 0 \\ 0 & x & 0 \\ \xi x & \eta x & 1 \end{matrix} \right\| Z$$

provided η is a root of the equation

$$(b_1 - \eta)(b_1 \eta - \eta^2 + c_2) - d_3 = 0$$

and

$$\xi = b_1\eta - \eta^2 + c_2 .$$

By way of conclusion let me emphasize once again that new ideas and new methods for solving ordinary differential equations in the large are much needed. If new special transcendental functions are to be studied and eventually tabulated, one place to begin would be to carefully analyze all possibilities that come up when faced with an equation of the Okubo type when $n = 3$. If one were to ask what new functions should be tabulated to cover this case; it would be difficult to answer, for before getting to the new functions, one would like to separate out all the special cases that would lend themselves to expression in terms of functions already known and tabulated. For instance one would like to know how to determine all cases that could, after appropriate transformations, be integrated in closed form; which equations could actually be reduced to two separate systems of order 1 and 2 respectfully; what equations could be handled by the Laplace or Fourier integral representation technique, which would lead essentially to two-term recurrence relations, etc. These then are only a few of our problems for the future.

REFERENCES

1. G. D. Birkhoff, Singular points of ordinary differential equations, Trans. Amer. Math. Soc., 10 (1909), 463-470.

2. __________, General theory of linear difference equations, Trans. Amer. Math. Soc., 12(1911), 243-284.

3. __________, Equivalent singular points of ordinary linear differential equations, Math. Ann. 74(1913), 134-139.

4. W. J. A. Culmer, Convergent solutions of ordinary linear homogeneous difference equations in the neighborhood of an irregular singular point, Ph. D. thesis, Univ. of Minn., Aug. 1959.

5. W. J. A. Culmer and W. A. Harris, Jr., Convergent solutions of ordinary linear homogeneous difference equations, Pac. Jour. of Math., 13(1963), 1111-1138.

6. R. B. Dingle, Asymptotic expansions and converging factors, Proc. Royal Soc. of London A 244(1958), 456-491 and 249 (1959), 270-283.

7. A. Erdélyi, W. Magnus, F. Oberhettinger and F. G. Tricomi, Higher transcendental functions, vol. 1, p. 249; Bateman Manuscript Project, Mc-Graw Hill, 1953.

8. A. Erdélyi, Asymptotic representations of Fourier integrals and the method of stationary phase, J. Soc. Indust. Appl. Math., 3(1955), 17-27.

9. __________, Asymptotic expansions of Fourier integrals involving logarithmic singularities, J. Soc. Indust. Appl. Math., 4(1956), 38-49.

10. W. B. Ford, Studies on divergent series and summability, Sci. Series Univ. of Mich., vol II, Macmillan 1916.

11. __________, The asymptotic developments of functions defined by Maclaurin series, Sci. Series, Univ. of Mich., vol. XI, George Banta Publ. Co., 1936.

12. K. O. Friedrichs, Special Topics in Analysis, notes, New York Univ., 1953-54.

13. F. R. Gantmacher, The theory of matrices, vol. 2. Chelsia, New York, 1959.

14. W. A. Harris, Jr., Linear systems of difference equations solvable by factorial series, Tech. Summary Report No. 213, U.S. Army Math. Research Center, University of Wisc., Madison, Wisc., Dec. 1960.

15. W. A. Harris, Jr. and H. L. Turrittin, Reciprocals of Inverse Factorial Series, Funkcialaj Ekvacioj, 6(1964), 37-46.

16. W. A. Harris, Jr., Linear systems of difference equations, Contributions to differential equations, 1 (1963), 489-518.

17. W. A. Harris, Jr. and Y. Sibuya, Note on linear difference equations, Bull. Amer. Math. Soc., 70(1964), 123-127.

18. W. A. Harris, Jr., Equivalent classes of difference equations, Contributions to differential equations, 1(1964), 253-264.

19. J. Heading, The Stokes phenomena and certain n^{th} order differential equations, Proc. Cambridge Phil Soc., 53(1957), 399-411 and 56(1960), 329-341.

20. M. Hukuhara, Sur les points singuliers des équations différentielles linéaires, III., Mem. Fac. Sci., Univ. Kyusyu, A. 2(1942), 127-137.

21. M. Hukuhara and M. Iwano, Étude de la convergence des solutions formelles d'un système différentiel ordinaire linéaire, Funkcialoj Ekvacioj, vol. 2, No. 1, June (1959), 1-18.

22. R. E. Langer, The solution of the differential equation $v''' + \lambda^2 z v' + 3\mu\lambda^2 v = 0$, Duke Math. Jour. 22(1955), 525-542.

23. ___________, On the asymptotic forms of ordinary linear differential equations of the third order in a region containing a turning point, Trans. Amer. Math. Soc., 80(1955), 93-123.

24. ___________, The solutions of a class of ordinary linear differential equations of the third order in a region containing a multiple turning point, Duke Math. J., 23(1956), 93-110.

25. ___________, On the asymptotic solutions of a class of ordinary differential equations of the fourth order with a special reference to an equation of hydrodynamics, Trans. Amer. Math. Soc. 84(1957), 144-191.

26. K. Okubo, A global representation of a fundamental set of solutions and a Stokes phenomenon for a system of linear ordinary differential equations, Jour. Math. Soc. of Japan, 15 (1963), 268-288.

27. T. K. Putta Swamy, The solution of certain ordinary linear differential equations in the large, Master's Thesis, May, 1963, Univ. of Minn.

28. H. Scheffé, Asymptotic solutions of certain linear differential equations in which the coefficients of the parameter may have a zero, Trans. American Math. Soc., 40(1936), 127-154.

29. ___________, Linear differential equations with two-term recurrence formulas, Jour. of Math. & Phys., 21(1942), 240-249.

30. Y. Sibuya, Simplification of a system of linear ordinary differential equations about a singular point, Funkcialoj Ekvacioj, 4(1962), 29-56.

31. W. J. Trjitzinsky, Analytic theory of linear differential equations, Acta Math. 62(1934), 167-227.

32. __________, Laplace integrals and factorial series in the theory of linear differential and linear difference equations, Trans. Amer. Math. Soc., 37(1935), 80-146.

33. H. L. Turrittin, Convergent solutions of linear homogeneous differential equations in the neighborhood of an irregular singular point, Acta Math., 93(1955), 27-66.

34. __________, Reduction of ordinary differential equations to the Birkhoff canonical form, Trans. Amer. Math. Soc., 107 (1963), 485-507.

35. __________, Stokes multipliers for asymptotic solutions of a certain differential equation, Trans. Amer. Math. Soc., 68(1950), 304-329.

36. __________, Reducing the rank of ordinary differential equations, Duke Math. Jour., 30(1963), 271-274.

37. E. M. Wright, The asymptotic expansion of the generalized Bessel function, Proc. London Math. Soc. (2), 38(1934), 257-270.

38. __________, The asymptotic expansion of the generalized hypergeometric function, Jour. London Math. Soc., 10(1935), 286-293.

39. __________, The asymptotic expansion of integral functions defined by Taylor series, Phil. Trans. Royal Soc. London, A 238(1940), 423-451 and A 239(1941), 217-232.

40. __________, The asymptotic expansion of the generalized hypergeometric function, Proc. London Math. Soc. (2), 46(1940), 389-408.

41. __________, The generalized Bessel function of order greater than one, Quarterly J. Math., Oxford Ser., 11(1940), 36-48.

42. __________, The asymptotic expansion of integral functions and of the coefficients in their Taylor series, Trans. Amer. Math. Soc., 64(1948), 409-438.

SUPPLEMENTARY REFERENCES

E. W. Barnes, The asymptotic expansions of functions defined by Taylor's series, Phil. Trans. 206A (1906), 249-297.

__________, The asymptotic expansions of integral functions defined by generalized hypergeometric series, Proc. London Math. Soc., ser. 2, 5(1907), 59-116.

__________, A new development of the theory of hypergeometric functions, Proc. London Math. Soc., ser. 2, 6(1908), 141-177.

A. Erdélyi and C. A. Swanson, Asymptotic forms of Whittaker's confluent hypergeometric functions, Memoir Amer. Math. Soc., No. 25 (1957), 1-49.

J. Horn, Verwendung asymptotischen Darstellungen zur Untersuchung der Integrale einer speciellen linearen Differentialgleichung, I, Math. Annalen, 49(1897), 453-472.

H. K. Hughes, On the asymptotic expansions of entire functions defined by Maclaurin series, Bull. Amer. Math. Soc., 50 (1944), 425-430.

__________, The asymptotic developments of a class of entire functions, Bull. Amer. Math. Soc., 51(1945), 456-461.

J. Malmquist, Sur l'étude analytique des solutions d'un systeme d'équations différentielles dans le voisinage d'un point singular d'indétermination, I & II, Acta Math., 73(1940), 87-129; 74(1941), 1-64.

W. Wasow, A study of the solutions of the differential equation $y^{(4)} + \lambda^2(xy'' + y) = 0$ for large values of λ, Ann. of Math., 52(1950), 350-361.

ROBERT M. LEWIS

Asymptotic Methods for the Solution of Dispursive Hyperbolic Equations

Contents

1. Introduction. In recent years asymptotic methods have been developed for the solution of certain boundary-value problems and initial-value problems for partial differential equations. These problems involve a parameter, and the methods provide one or more terms of the asymptotic expansion, say for large values of the parameter, of the solution of the problem. They are often applicable to problems for which exact solutions are not known, and even for problems which can be solved exactly it frequently happens that only the asymptotic expansion of the solution is sufficiently simple to be useful in practical applications. Furthermore, it is invariably true that the methods which yield the asymptotic expansion directly are very much simpler than the procedure which involves first finding the exact solution, and then its asymptotic expansion.

An important class of asymptotic methods is characterized by the fact that certain curves, often called "rays", play a central role in the theory. The rays are of fundamental importance because all of the functions which make up the various terms of the expansion can be shown to satisfy ordinary differential equations along these curves. Thus, in a sense, the method is one which reduces partial differential equations to ordinary differential equations.

The "ray method" has been extensively developed, primarily by J. B. Keller and his co-workers at New York University, for the reduced wave equation

$$\Delta v + k^2 n^2(X)\, v = 0 \tag{1}$$

and related elliptic equations. When applied to (1) the method yields a "geometrical theory of diffraction" [1] which generalizes the classical theory of geometrical optics. The extensive literature on the asymptotic theory of the reduced wave equation and Maxwell's equations has recently been unified and summarized in [2]. The reduced wave equation is, of course, obtained from the wave equation

$$\Delta u - \frac{1}{c^2(X)}\, u_{tt} = 0 \tag{2}$$

by the substitution $u(t,X) = v(X)\,e^{-i\omega t}$. Then $k = \omega/c_0$ and $n(X) = c_0/c(X)$. (c_0 is a convenient constant. The large parameter is ω or k.) Similarly the "symmetric hyperbolic" system of equations

$$\sum_{\nu=0}^{n} A^{\nu} \frac{\partial u}{\partial x_{\nu}} + Bu = 0, \quad (x_0 = t) \quad , \tag{3}$$

is reduced by the substitution $u(t,X) = v(X)e^{-i\omega t}$ to the system

$$\sum_{\nu=1}^{n} A^{\nu} \frac{\partial v}{\partial x_{\nu}} + (B - i\omega) v = 0 \quad . \tag{4}$$

Here $X = (x_1, \ldots, x_n)$, A^{ν} and B are real $k \times k$ matrices which are functions of X, A^0 is positive definite, and $A^1, \ldots, A^n$ are symmetric. The asymptotic theory of (4) for large ω has been studied in [3].

The original hyperbolic system (3) contains no parameter. However, P. D. Lax [4] has obtained the asymptotic solution of the initial-value problem for (3) with "oscillatory initial data" of the form

$$u(0,X) = e^{i\lambda s(X)} z(X) \quad . \tag{5}$$

In Lax's problem the large parameter λ appears only in the initial data, and specifically in the form (5). The role of the rays is played by the "bicharacteristics" which are space-time curves that generate the characteristic hypersurfaces of (3).

In this paper we shall examine a method which is applicable to the solution of initial value and initial-boundary value problems for symmetric hyperbolic systems of the form

$$\sum_{\nu=0}^{n} A^{\nu} \frac{\partial u}{\partial x_{\nu}} + \lambda B u = f(t, X; \lambda) \tag{6}$$

with initial conditions

$$u(0, X) = u_0(X; \lambda) \quad . \tag{7}$$

The large parameter λ appears in the system of differential equations (6), multiplying the undifferentiated term Bu. It is well-known (See [5], p. 191) that the presence of such terms leads to the phenomenon of dispersion*, and the large parameter in the dispersive term ensures that these phenomena appear in the asymptotic solution. For this reason the asymptotic method when applied to (6) leads to results which are quite different from the solution of Lax's problem. For the dispersive system (6) the bicharacteristics no longer serve as "rays." In fact the rays do not lie on characteristic hypersurfaces,

* For dispersive systems, different frequency components of a wave travel with different velocities; this leads to distortion of wave forms and other interesting physical phenomena.

and they represent trajectories of points which move with an appropriately defined "group velocity." Thus, for example, the asymptotic construction of the Riemann function, which is defined by (6) and (7) with $f = 0$ and $u_0 = \delta(X)$, leads to rays that emanate from the origin in space-time and fill out the interior of the characteristic conoid. The parameter λ also appears in the source term f of (6) and the initial data function u_0 of (7). We will see that the simplest type of expansion is obtained when u_0 is oscillatory, i.e., of the form (5). However it is possible to obtain asymptotic solutions of (6.7) when λ appears in u_0 and f in a variety of different ways. This leads to a variety of different types of asymptotic solution, each of which is characterized geometrically by a typical ray pattern. Some of these will be examined in sections 3 and 4 of this paper.

An interesting example of a dispersive symmetric hyperbolic system of the form (6) is given by

$$(8) \qquad \nabla \times H - \epsilon \frac{\partial E}{\partial t} = J, \quad \nabla \times E + \mu \frac{\partial H}{\partial t} = 0, \quad \frac{\partial J}{\partial t} - \epsilon \phi^2 E = 0 .$$

The first two equations are simply Maxwell's equations for the electric and magnetic fields E, H in M.K.S. units. The third equation is obtained by assuming that the current J is entirely due to the motion of electrons with charge e, mass m and number density $\eta(X)$, and that these electrons satisfy Newton's equation with the force term given by eE. In (8) ϕ is the "plasma frequency" defined by

$$(9) \qquad \epsilon \phi^2 = \frac{\eta e^2}{m} .$$

The system (8) describes the propagation of electromagnetic waves in certain plasmas such as the ionosphere. For the case of harmonic time dependence (8) reduces to the well-known equations of the (isotropic) magneto-ionic theory [7]. Let us introduce the velocity of light $c = (\epsilon\mu)^{-\frac{1}{2}}$, an average plasma frequency ϕ_0, and a characteristic length* $\underline{a}$. We then replace E, H, J, X, t in (8) by E', H', J', X', t' and set

$$(10) \quad \sqrt{\epsilon}\, E' = E, \sqrt{\mu}\, H' = H, \; J' = \sqrt{\epsilon}\, \phi J, \; X' = aX, \; ct' = at, \; \phi(X) = \phi_0 b(X) .$$

---

* For problems with boundaries $\underline{a}$ denotes a typical boundary dimension. For problems with non-constant $\phi(X)$ $\underline{a}$ is an average value of the function $\phi(X)/|\nabla\phi(X)|$. Thus $\phi(X)$ changes by a small fraction of itself over distances small compared to $\underline{a}$.

Then (8) becomes

$$E_t - \nabla \times H + \lambda b(X) J = 0, \quad H_t + \nabla \times E = 0, \quad J_t - \lambda b(X) E = 0 \quad . \tag{11}$$

The (large) parameter λ is given by

$$\lambda = \frac{\phi_0 a}{c} \quad . \tag{12}$$

X and t are dimensionless space and time variables and $b(X)$ is a dimensionless function proportional to the plasma frequency.

It is now an easy matter to verify that (11) is of the form (6) with $f = 0$. In this case u is the column vector with components

$$(E_1, E_2, E_3, H_1, H_2, H_3, J_1, J_2, J_3) \quad , \tag{13}$$

A^0 is the 9×9 identity matrix, and A^1, A^2, A^3 are 9×9 matrices defined by

$$\sum_{\nu=1}^{3} k_\nu A^\nu = \begin{bmatrix} 0 & -(K) & 0 \\ (K) & 0 & 0 \\ 0 & 0 & 0 \end{bmatrix}, \qquad B = \begin{bmatrix} 0 & 0 & bI_3 \\ 0 & 0 & 0 \\ -bI_3 & 0 & 0 \end{bmatrix} . \tag{14}$$

Here I_3 is the 3×3 identity matrix and (K) is the 3×3 matrix

$$(K) = \begin{bmatrix} 0 & -k_3 & k_2 \\ k_3 & 0 & -k_1 \\ -k_2 & k_1 & 0 \end{bmatrix} \tag{15}$$

Since (K) is anti-symmetric we note that A^ν is symmetric and B is antisymmetric. The last condition implies that the system conserves energy and is important for our expansion procedure as we will soon see.

H and J are easily eliminated from (11) to obtain the second order system of equations

$$E_{tt} - \Delta E + \nabla(\nabla \cdot E) + \lambda^2 b^2(X) E = 0 \quad . \tag{16}$$

If b is independent of x_3 and $E = \mu(x_1, x_2) A_3$, where μ is a scalar function and A_3 is a unit vector in the direction of the 3 axis, then $\nabla \cdot E = 0$ and (16) reduces to

(17) $$u_{tt} - c^2(X)\Delta u + \lambda^2 b^2(X)\, u = 0 \ ,$$

with $c = 1$.

Equation (17) is a simple example of a dispersive hyperbolic equation that conserves energy, and it serves admirably as a model for demonstrating our method of asymptotic solution. In Section (2), (3), and (4) we shall develop methods of obtaining asymptotic solutions of initial and initial-boundary value problems for (17) and for the same equation with an inhomogeneous (source) term. In our work we shall deal only with (17) and in sections (3) and (4) we shall, for simplicity, further restrict our considerations to the case of one space dimension. However, we emphasize that the methods are quite general. Research currently in progress has established that they are applicable to symmetric hyperbolic systems of the form (6) (with anti-symmetric B) in any number of dimensions. The main condition necessary for application of the method can best be described in terms of the "dispersion equation"

(18) $$\delta(k_1, \ldots, k_n, \omega) = 0$$

which can be obtained by requiring that a plane wave of the form

(19) $$u = (\text{const.}) \exp\left\{ i\lambda\left(\sum_{\nu=1}^{n} k_\nu x_\nu - \omega t\right)\right\}$$

be a solution of the partial differential equation with constant coefficients. Then the condition is that the solutions

(20) $$\omega = h(k_1, \ldots, k_n)$$

of (18) be real for real $k_1, \ldots, k_n$. (To what extent this requirement can be relaxed is not yet clear.)

For (17)

(21) $$\omega = \pm\sqrt{c^2 k^2 + b^2} \ ; \ k^2 = \sum_\nu k_\nu^2 \ ;$$

and for (6) (with constant coefficients and $f = 0$) the dispersion equation takes the form

(22) $$\det G = 0; \quad G = Q - A^0\,\omega \ ; \ Q = \sum_{\nu=1}^{n} k_\nu A^\nu - iB \ .$$

That this equation has only real solutions ω for real k_ν follows from the fact that A^0 is positive definite and Q is Hermitian, for ω is an eigenvalue of the Hermitian matrix $(A^0)^{-\frac{1}{2}} Q (A^0)^{-\frac{1}{2}}$.

Before proceeding to the detailed discussion of our method we would like to point out that it is also applicable to the very important case of dispersion of electromagnetic waves in dielectrics. This case is not included in (6) because the electric and magnetic field vectors E, H in a dispersive dielectric satisfy the system of differential and integral equations*

$$\nabla \times E + \frac{1}{c}\frac{\partial H}{\partial t} = 0, \quad \nabla \times H - \frac{1}{c}\frac{\partial D}{\partial t} = 0 \ ,$$

$$D(t,X) = E(t,X) + \int_0^\infty f(\tau, X)\, E(t-\tau, X)\, d\tau \ . \tag{23}$$

Here we have, for simplicity, taken the magnetic permeability to be $\mu = 1$. The dielectric permeability ϵ is a function of frequency, and f is given by

$$f(t,X) = \frac{1}{2\pi}\int_{-\infty}^{\infty} e^{-i\omega t}[\epsilon(\omega, X) - 1]\, d\omega \ . \tag{24}$$

Since ϵ is dimensionless it must be a function of ω/ω_0 where ω_0 is a characteristic frequency of the dielectric. We now replace

$$X,\ t,\ \omega,\ \epsilon,\ f \ \text{ by } \ X',\ t',\ \omega',\ \epsilon',\ f'$$

and introduce a characteristic length $\underline{a}$. Then we set

$$X' = aX,\ ct' = at,\ \omega' = \omega_0\omega,\ \epsilon'(\omega', X') = \epsilon(\omega, X),\ af'(t', X') = cf(t, X). \tag{25}$$

With this transformation (23) and (24) become

$$\nabla \times E + \frac{\partial H}{\partial t} = 0, \quad \nabla \times H - \frac{\partial D}{\partial t} = 0, \quad D(t,X) = E(t,X) + \int_0^\infty f(\tau, X)\, E(t-\tau, X)\, d\tau, \tag{26}$$

$$f(t,X) = \frac{\lambda}{2\pi}\int_{-\infty}^{\infty} e^{-i\omega\lambda t}[\epsilon(\omega, X) - 1]\, d\omega \ . \tag{27}$$

---

* See [8], section 58. In order to compare easily with [8] we use Gaussian units here.

Here

$$\lambda = \frac{\omega_0 a}{c} \quad . \tag{28}$$

Although the system of equations (26) is quite different from (6) a very similar asymptotic method is applicable to the solution of (26) for large λ.*

Let us indicate briefly the steps involved in the asymptotic method. For problems which can be solved exactly**, examination of the asymptotic expansion of the solution shows that it consists of a sum of terms, each of which is an asymptotic power series in λ^{-1} involving a "phase function" and an infinite sequence of "amplitude functions". For complex problems, we therefore assume that the solution is also given by a sum of such series. By inserting such a series into the partial differential equation, we find first that the phase function satisfies a first order partial differential equation which can be solved by the "method of characteristics".*** The characteristic curves are of course the rays which we have mentioned. They are space-time curves. The characteristic (ordinary) differential equations will be called "ray equations". Thus, by the method of characteristics the phase function can be obtained by integrating an ordinary differential equation along the rays. We also find that the amplitude functions satisfy ordinary differential equations along the rays and that these "transport equations" can be solved. In order to find the rays, and the phase and amplitude functions, it is necessary to specify initial conditions for all of these ordinary differential equations. In some cases (for example, the case of oscillatory initial data) the required initial conditions follow directly from the data of the problem. In others the initial conditions are obtained from the solution of a "canonical problem". A canonical problem is one with the same local features as the given problem. It is, however, sufficiently simple to be solved exactly. The required initial conditions for the given problem are obtained by examination of the asymptotic expansion of the solution of the canonical problem.

It is by now clear that the asymptotic method involves several unproved assumptions. It is therefore reasonable to ask whether it can be proved that it does indeed yield the asymptotic expansion of the exact solution of the given problem. No complete proof of this fact has been given. Nevertheless there is abundant evidence of the validity of the method. This evidence has, so far, been obtained in two ways:

---

* We hope to complete our research on systems of the form (6) and (26) in the near future.

** For example, problems with constant coefficients and no boundaries.

*** See [5], Chapter II.

1. Problems for (17) in one space dimension can be solved exactly by fourier analysis with respect to t. The resulting ordinary differential equation (with independent variable x) can be solved asymptotically by standard methods for ordinary differential equations (W. K. B. method). Then the asymptotic expansion of the resulting integral representation can be obtained by the "method of stationary phase" and related methods. In every case that has been examined the resulting asymptotic expansion of the exact solution agrees perfectly with the results obtained in this paper by the "ray method". These investigations yield not only confidence in the validity of the ray method but also an appreciation of the great simplicity of that method when compared with the approach just outlined.*

2. In the case of initial value problems for (6) with oscillatory initial data it is possible to estimate** the remainder of the asymptotic series by energy inequalities. This approach is similar to one outlined by Lax for the initial value problem (3, 5), and yields an indirect proof of the asymptotic nature of the expansion in this case.***

The ideas developed in this paper had their origins mainly in the work of J. B. Keller [1, 2] and G. B. Whitham [6]. The latter approached the problem of the propagation of dispersive waves from a physical point of view, with considerable success. Our results in sections (3.4) and (4.1) are easily seen to be equivalent to Whitham's results. In attempting to develop Whitham's approach into a systematic expansion procedure, we first introduced the large parameter λ as in (6), (11), (17) and (26, 27). This enabled us to proceed in a manner very similar to Keller's method for the reduced wave equation. The essential idea of the "canonical problem" also had its origins in Keller's work.

Some features of the expansion we shall employ are similar to those of expansions that have been used for the time-dependent Schroedinger equation. In fact the mechanical terms which we shall use such as "Hamiltonian", "Lagrangian", etc. occur quite naturally when the expansion is applied to the initial value problem for the Schroedinger equation. In this case the appropriate large dimensionless variable is $\lambda = \frac{ap}{h}$ where $\underline{a}$ is a characteristic length $\underline{p}$ is a characteristic momentum and h is Planck's constant. We have

---

* The author is indebted to Mr. N. Bleistein who has carried out these comparative studies and is currently engaged in other critical examinations of the ray method.

** So far we have been able to obtain estimates in the L_2 norm (energy norm). It is not clear whether pointwise estimates can be obtained by these methods.

*** It is worth noting that such indirect proofs are much more difficult, if not impossible in the case of elliptic equations such as (1) and (4).

found it convenient as well as suggestive to continue to use the mechanical terms for all our equations.

Before proceeding to the asymptotic solution of (17) we add one final remark: If we introduce the transformation

$$x' = \lambda x, \quad t' = \lambda t, \quad u'(t', x') = u(t,x) \tag{29}$$

(17) becomes

$$u'_{t't'} - [c'(x')]^2 \Delta_{x'} u' + [b'(x')]^2 u' = 0 . \tag{30}$$

Here

$$c'(x') = c(x) = c(x'/\lambda), \quad b'(x') = b(x) = b(x'/\lambda) . \tag{31}$$

Thus, in finding asymptotic solutions for $\lambda \to \infty$ of problems for (17), the transformation (29) shows that we will also be obtaining asymptotic solutions for large t', x' of corresponding problems for equation (30) in which no parameter appears. It should be pointed out, however, that (31) implies that

$$\frac{\partial c'}{\partial x'_\nu} = 0\left(\frac{1}{\lambda}\right), \quad \frac{\partial b'}{\partial x'_\nu} = 0\left(\frac{1}{\lambda}\right) . \tag{32}$$

Therefore, for the case of variable coefficient functions, the asymptotic solutions, as applied to (30), are valid only for slowly-varying coefficient functions. If boundaries are present in the problem for (17) then (29) shows that the corresponding boundaries for (30) must have large dimensions.

In all of the succeeding sections, vectors are denoted by capital letters. We also employ the summation convention with respect to repeated indices.

2. <u>Asymptotic series solutions of a hyperbolic equation</u>. Let us assume that a solution $u(t,X) = u(t, x_1, \ldots x_\mu)$ of (1.15) has an asymptotic expansion of the form

$$u \sim e^{i\lambda s(t,X)} \sum_m (i\lambda)^{-m} z^{(m)}(t,X) ; \quad z^{(m)} = 0 \text{ for } m = -1, -2, \ldots . \tag{1}$$

By inserting (1) in (1.17) and equating to zero coefficients of $(i\lambda)^{-m}$ we obtain the <u>dispersion equation</u>*

* Here the dispersion equation is a partial differential equation for s whereas in section 1 it was an algebraic equation. No confusion will arise from the double meaning of the term.

(2) $$c^2(X)\, s_{x_\nu} s_{x_\nu} - s_t s_t + b^2(X) = 0 \ ,$$

and the transport equations

(3) $$2\left(s_{x_\nu} z^{(m)}_{x_\nu} - c^{-2} s_t z^{(m)}_t\right) + z^{(m)} \Box s + \Box z^{(m-1)} = 0;\ m=1,2,\ldots \ .$$

Here $\Box s = s_{x_\nu x_\nu} - c^{-2} s_{tt}$.

We choose a constant reference speed c_0 and introduce the following notation, which will be used throughout the paper:

(4) $$x_0 = c_0 t,\ k_\nu = s_{x_\nu},\ k_0 = s_{x_0} = -\frac{\omega}{c_0},\ \omega = -s_t,\ K = (k_1, \ldots, k_\mu) \ ,$$
$$\hat{K} = (k_0, K),\ \hat{X} = (x_0, X),\ k^2 = k_\nu k_\nu,\ \hat{k}^2 = k_0^2 + k^2 \ .$$

Then the dispersion equation takes the form

(5) $$c^2 k^2 - \omega^2 + b^2 = 0 \ ,$$

or, if we solve for ω ,

(6) $$\omega = h(X,K) = \pm h_0(X,K);\ h_0(X,K) = \sqrt{c^2 k^2 + b^2} \ .$$

For each of the two values of the Hamiltonian, h, the dispersion equation can be written in the form

(7) $$h(X,K) - \omega = h(X,K) + c_0 k_0 = 0 \ .$$

We now define the quantities

(8) $$g_\nu = \frac{\partial h}{\partial k_\nu} = \frac{c^2 k_\nu}{\omega},\ g_0 = c_0,\ G = (g_1, \ldots, g_\mu),\ \hat{G} = (g_0, G) \ ,$$
$$\hat{g}^2 = g_0^2 + g^2,\ g^2 = g_\nu g_\nu = c^2(1 - b^2/\omega^2) \ .$$

G is the group velocity vector, and g is the group speed. By analogy with plane wave solutions of (1.17) we see that it is appropriate to refer to ω and K as (angular) frequency and propagation vector, or if we wish to emphasize the mechanical analogy we may refer to K as the momentum vector.

In the following it will be noted that we shall make no essential use of the explicit form (6) of the Hamiltonian function. For this reason it is not surprising that our methods can be applied to a large class of partial differential equations, as we have asserted in the introduction.

2.1. the ray equations. The first order partial differential equation (Hamilton-Jacobi equation) (7) can now be solved by introducing the characteristic equations (Hamilton's equations of motion)

(9)
$$c_0\dot{t} = \dot{x}_0 = c_0 = g_0, \ \dot{x}_\nu = \frac{\partial h}{\partial k_\nu} = g_\nu, \ -\dot{\omega} = c_0\dot{k}_0 = 0, \ \dot{k}_\nu = -\frac{\partial h}{\partial x_\nu}; \ \nu = 1, \ldots, \mu \ .$$

Since $\dot{t} = 1$, we may choose the independent variable in this system of ordinary differential equations to be t. Each solution of (9) defines a curve $X(t)$ in X-space or equivalently a space-time curve $[t, X(t)]$ which we shall call a ray. From (4) and (9) we now have

$$\dot{s} = \frac{ds}{dt} = s_t + s_{x_\nu} \dot{x}_\nu = \ell \tag{10}$$

where ℓ is the Lagrangian,

$$\ell = k_\nu \dot{x}_\nu - h = k_\nu g_\nu - \omega = k_\nu \frac{\partial h}{\partial k_\nu} - h \ . \tag{11}$$

2.2. solution of the dispersion equation. An initial value problem for $s(t, X)$ can now be solved by means of (9) and (11). Let $\Sigma = (\sigma_1, \ldots, \sigma_\mu)$, and let

$$t = t_0(\Sigma) \ , \ x_\nu = x_{\nu 0}(\Sigma) \ ; \quad \nu = 1, \ldots, \mu \tag{12}$$

be the parametric representation of a hypersurface on which s has the prescribed values

$$s[t_0(\Sigma), \ x_{\nu 0}(\Sigma)] = s_0(\Sigma) . \tag{13}$$

Then differentiation of (13) with respect to σ_j yields

$$k_\nu \frac{\partial x_{\nu 0}}{\partial \sigma_j} - \omega \frac{\partial t^0}{\partial \sigma_j} = \frac{\partial s_0}{\partial \sigma_j} \ ; \quad j = 1, \ldots, \mu \ . \tag{14}$$

(14) and (6) provide $\mu+1$ algebraic equations for the determination of $\omega = \omega_0(\Sigma)$ and $k_\nu = k_{\nu 0}(\Sigma)$, $\nu = 1, \ldots, \mu$, at each point Σ of the initial hypersurface (12). Then $t_0(\Sigma)$, $x_{\nu 0}(\Sigma)$, $\omega_0(\Sigma)$, $k_{\nu 0}(\Sigma)$, provide initial values for the solution of (9). If this solution is denoted by $x_\nu = x_\nu(t;\Sigma)$, $k_\nu = k_\nu(t;\Sigma)$, $\omega = \omega(t;\Sigma) = \omega(\Sigma)$; then $x_\nu[t_0(\Sigma);\Sigma] = x_{\nu 0}(\Sigma)$, $k_\nu[t_0(\Sigma);\Sigma] = k_{\nu 0}(\Sigma)$, and $\omega(\Sigma) = \omega_0(\Sigma)$. In terms of this solution (10) may be integrated to yield

$$(15) \qquad s[t, x_\nu(t;\Sigma)] = s_0(\Sigma) + \int_{t_0(\Sigma)}^{t} \ell[x_\nu(t';\Sigma), k_\nu(t';\Sigma)]\,dt' \ .$$

Corresponding to the two values of (6), (15) yields the two solutions of the initial value problem for s.

The initial value problem for s is considerably simplified if the initial hypersurface is the hyperplane $t = t_0$. In this case we may determine $k_{\nu 0}(\Sigma)$ and $\omega_0(\Sigma)$ at once. We set

$$(16) \qquad t_0(\Sigma) = t_0, \; x_{\nu 0}(\Sigma) = \sigma_\nu; \; \nu = 1, \ldots, \mu \; ;$$

in (12). Then (14) and (6) yield

$$(17) \qquad k_{j0}(\Sigma) = \frac{\partial s_0}{\partial \sigma_j}; \; \omega_0(\Sigma) = h\left(\sigma_\nu, \frac{\partial s_0}{\partial \sigma_\nu}\right) = \pm\sqrt{c^2(\Sigma)\frac{\partial s_0}{\partial \sigma_\nu}\frac{\partial s_0}{\partial \sigma_\nu} + b^2(\Sigma)} \, .$$

It is interesting to note that (11) implies that s is constant on rays if and only if $k_\nu \frac{\partial h}{\partial k_\nu} = h$. But this is equivalent to the condition that h be homogeneous of degree one in K. In this case the original partial differential equation contains no lower order terms and is non-dispersive. For non-dispersive equations it is easily seen that the dispersion equation (as a differential equation for s) is the "characteristic equation", the level surfaces of its solution $s(t,X)$ are characteristic hyper-surfaces of the original equation, and the rays lie on the characteristic surfaces. None of these statements are true for dispersive equations such as (1.17).

2.3. <u>solution of the transport equations</u>. We turn our attention now to the transport equations (3) which may be written in the form

(18)
$$\dot{z}^{(m)} + \left(\frac{c^2}{2\omega}\Box s\right) z^{(m)} = z_t^{(m)} + g_\nu z_{x_\nu}^{(m)} + \left(\frac{c^2}{2\omega}\Box s\right) z^{(m)} = -\frac{c^2}{2\omega}\Box z^{(m-1)}; \; m = 0, 1, 2, \ldots \, .$$

If we set $z^{(0)} = z$, the zero order equation is

$$\dot{z} + \left(\frac{c^2}{2\omega}\Box s\right) z = z_t + g_\nu z_{x_\nu} + \left(\frac{c^2}{2\omega}\Box s\right) z = 0. \tag{19}$$

These are ordinary differential equations along each ray. To solve the homogeneous equation (19) we first note that

(20)
$$\Box s = s_{x_\nu x_\nu} - c^{-2} s_{tt} = c^{-2}\omega_t + \frac{\partial k_\nu}{\partial x_\nu} = \frac{\partial}{\partial x_0}\left(\frac{\omega}{c^2} c_0\right) + \frac{\partial}{\partial x_\nu}\left(\frac{\omega}{c^2} g_\nu\right) = \hat{\nabla}\cdot\left(\frac{\omega}{c^2}\hat{G}\right)$$

where

$$\hat{\nabla} = \left(\frac{\partial}{\partial x_0}, \nabla\right), \quad \hat{G} = (g_0, G), \quad g_0 = c_0 \quad . \tag{21}$$

Then (19) can be written in the form

$$\frac{2\omega}{c^2}\hat{G}\cdot\hat{\nabla}z + z\hat{\nabla}\cdot\left(\frac{\omega}{c^2}G\right) = 0 \quad , \tag{22}$$

or

$$\hat{\nabla}\cdot\left(\frac{z^2\omega}{c^2}\hat{G}\right) = 0 \quad . \tag{23}$$

For an arbitrary domain D in Σ-space we now apply Gauss' theorem to the "ray-tube" in $\hat{X}$-space determined by: Σ in D , $t_1 \le t \le t_2$:

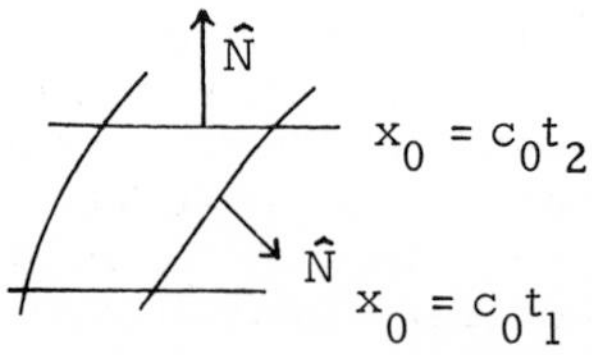

Since $\hat{G} = (c_0, G)$ is everywhere parallel to the rays $\hat{X} = (x_0, X) = [c_0 t, X(t,\Sigma)]$, (23) yields

$$0 = \int \hat{\nabla}\cdot\left(\frac{z^2\omega}{c^2}\hat{G}\right)dx_0\cdots dx_\mu = \int \frac{z^2\omega}{c^2}\hat{G}\cdot\hat{N}dS = \left\{\int_{t=t_2} - \int_{t=t_1}\right\}\frac{\omega z^2 c_0}{c^2}dx_1\cdots dx_\mu$$

(24)

$$= \left\{\int_{\substack{t=t_2\\(\Sigma \text{ in } D)}} \quad \int_{\substack{t=t_1\\(\Sigma \text{ in } D)}}\right\}\frac{\omega z^2}{c^2}c_0|j|d\sigma_1\cdots d\sigma_\mu \ .$$

Here j is the Jacobian,

$$j(t,\Sigma) = \frac{\partial(x_1,\ldots,x_\mu)}{\partial(\sigma_1,\ldots,\sigma_\mu)} = \det\left[\frac{\partial x_\nu(t;\Sigma)}{\partial\sigma_i}\right] . \tag{25}$$

Since D was arbitrary and ω is constant on a ray (24) implies that $\frac{z^2 j}{c^2}$ is constant on a ray (provided j does not vanish). Thus the solution of (19) is given by

$$z(t) = z(t_0)\frac{c(t)}{c(t_0)}\left[\frac{j(t_0)}{j(t)}\right]^{1/2} . \tag{26}$$

Here $z(t) = z[t,X(t,\Sigma)]$, $c(t) = c[X(t,\Sigma)]$, and $j(t) = j(t,\Sigma)$. The solution of the inhomogeneous equation (18) can now be obtained by the method of "variation of parameters". The result is

(27)

$$z^{(m)}(t) = z^{(m)}(t_0)\frac{c(t)}{c(t_0)}\left[\frac{j(t_0)}{j(t)}\right]^{1/2} - \frac{c(t)}{2\omega}\int_{t_0}^{t}\left[\frac{j(t')}{j(t)}\right]^{1/2} c(t')\Box z^{(m-1)}(t')\,dt' ;$$

$$m = 0,1,2,\ldots .$$

2.4. Constant coefficients. The foregoing results simplify considerably in case the coefficient functions are constant: $b = b_0$, $c = c_0$. In this case the ray equations (9) imply that k_ν, ω, g_ν, and ℓ are constant on each ray; i.e.

(28)

$$k_\nu = k_{\nu 0}(\Sigma),\ \omega = \omega_0(\Sigma),\ g_\nu = g_{\nu 0}(\Sigma) = h_{k_\nu}[k_{j0}(\Sigma)] ,$$

$$\ell = \ell_0(\Sigma) = k_{\nu 0}\,g_{\nu 0} - \omega_0 .$$

Furthermore the rays are the straight lines

$$x_\nu = x_{\nu 0}(\Sigma) + g_{\nu 0}(\Sigma)\,[t - t_0(\Sigma)] = x_{\nu 0} - t_0 g_{\nu 0} + g_{\nu 0} t \,, \tag{29}$$

and

$$s = s_0(\Sigma) + \ell_0(\Sigma)[t - t_0(\Sigma)] = s_0 - t_0 \ell_0 + \ell_0 t \,. \tag{30}$$

(25) and (29) now imply that (in general)

$$j(t,\Sigma) = \det\left[(x_{\nu 0} - t_0 g_{\nu 0})_{\sigma_i} + (g_{\nu 0})_{\sigma_i} t\right] \tag{31}$$

is a polynomial of degree μ in t, with coefficients which are functions of Σ. Hence if $\tau_1(\Sigma), \ldots, \tau_\mu(\Sigma)$ are the roots of this polynomial we may write

$$j(t,\Sigma) = a(\Sigma) \prod_{\nu=1}^{\mu} [t - \tau_\nu(\Sigma)] \,, \tag{32}$$

and (27) takes the special form

(33)

$$z^{(m)}(t) = z^{(m)}(t_0)\left[\frac{j(t_0)}{j(t)}\right]^{1/2} - \frac{c_0^2}{2\omega_0} \int_{t_0}^{t} \left[\frac{j(t')}{j(t)}\right]^{1/2} \Box z^{(m-1)}(t')\,dt' \,;$$

$$m = 0, 1, 2, \ldots \,.$$

where

$$\frac{j(t_0)}{j(t)} = \frac{(t_0 - \tau_1) \ldots (t_0 - \tau_\mu)}{(t - \tau_1) \ldots (t - \tau_\mu)} \,. \tag{34}$$

2.5. plane waves. The simplest examples of our formal expansion are the plane waves. We assume that the coefficients are constant and take the initial surface to be the hyperplane $t = 0$. For arbitrary constant $K = (k_1, \ldots, k_\mu)$ we set $s^0(\Sigma) = k_\nu \sigma_\nu$. Then (17) yields

$$k_{\nu 0}(\Sigma) = k_\nu,\ \omega_0(\sigma) = h(k_\nu) = \pm\sqrt{c_0^2 k^2 + b_0^2} \,. \tag{35}$$

We define $g_{\nu 0}$ and ℓ_0 by (28). Then (29) yields the family of parallel straight rays.

$$x_\nu = \sigma_\nu + g_{\nu 0} t \tag{36}$$

and (30) yields

$$s = k_\nu \sigma_\nu + (k_{\nu 0} g_{\nu 0} - \omega_0) t = k_\nu x_\nu - \omega_0 t \ . \tag{37}$$

From (36) we see that $j \equiv 1$. We now set $z^{(m)}$ = const. on the plane $t = 0$ for $m = 0, 1, 2, \ldots$. Then (33) implies that $z^{(m)}(t, X)$ is constant. If we insert these results in (1) we obtain

$$u(t, X) = z(\lambda) e^{i\lambda(k_\nu x_\nu - \omega_0 t)}; \ z(\lambda) \sim \sum (i\lambda)^{-m} z^{(m)} \ . \tag{38}$$

In fact (38) is an exact solution of (1.17) with arbitrary $z(\lambda)$ provided ω_0 satisfies (35).

2.6. waves. Any asymptotic series solution of (1.17) of the form (1) will be called a wave. Plane waves are a special case. We have seen that if the value of s is prescribed on a suitable μ-dimensional manifold M, two solutions s of the dispersion equation are determined (at least in a neighborhood of M). If the values of the functions $z^{(m)}$ for $m = 0, 1, 2, \ldots$ are also prescribed on M exactly two waves are completely determined. In succeeding sections we will attempt to show how a sum of one or more waves can be constructed to yield asymptotic solutions of suitable problems for (1.17).

2.7. lower dimensional initial manifolds. For some problems it will be necessary to construct waves which are determined by the values of s and $z^{(m)}$ on a manifold M of dimension $\delta < \mu$. In the extreme case, $\delta = 0$, M is a single point $(t_0, X_0) = (t_0, X_{10}, \ldots, X_{\mu 0})$, and s has the prescribed value

$$s(t_0, X_0) = s_0 \ . \tag{39}$$

We shall then require waves for which all of the associated rays pass through M . These rays are obtained by solving the ray equations with initial conditions

$$x_\nu(t_0) = x_{\nu 0}, \ k_\nu(t_0) = p_\nu, \ \omega(t_0) = h(X_0, P) = \pm h_0(X_0, P) \ . \tag{40}$$

Here $P = (p_1, \ldots, p_\mu)$ is arbitrary, and we obtain the μ-parameter family of rays, $x_\nu = x_\nu(t; P)$ for which $x_\nu(t_0; P) = x_{\nu 0}$. (In fact we obtain two such families, one corresponding to each of the two values of h). When the rays are determined, $s(t, X)$ is given on each ray by

$$s(t) = s[t, X(t;P)] = s_0 + \int_{t_0}^{t} \ell[X(t';P), P]\,dt' \quad . \tag{41}$$

Here $\ell(X, K) = k_\nu h_{k_\nu} - h$.

In solving the transport equations to determine the functions $z^{(m)}$ along the rays emanating from M, our earlier argument is valid if we replace $\Sigma = (\sigma_1, \ldots, \sigma_\mu)$ everywhere by $P = (p_1, \ldots p_\mu)$ and replace t_0 in (26) and (27) by t_1, where $t_0 < t_1$. Of course now

$$j = j(t, P) = \frac{\partial(x_1, \ldots, x_n)}{\partial(p_1, \ldots, p_n)} = \det\left[\frac{\partial x_\nu(t;P)}{\partial p_i}\right] \quad . \tag{42}$$

However it is clear that j vanishes at the point M, i.e. at $t = t_0$, hence the functions $z^{(m)}$ become singular there. If we set

$$\tilde{z} = \lim_{t_1 \to t_0} \frac{z(t_1)\,|j(t_1)|^{1/2}}{c(t_1)} \tag{43}$$

then, we may let $t_1 \to t_0$ in (27) (for $m = 0$) . Thus we obtain

$$z(t) = \tilde{z}\, c(t)\,|j(t)|^{-1/2} \quad . \tag{44}$$

Here $z(t) = z[t, X(t;P)]$, $c(t) = c[X(t;P)]$, $j(t) = j(t, P)$, $\omega = h(X_0, P)$, and $\tilde{z} = \tilde{z}(P)$. At the beginning of the preceding paragraph we stated that the waves associated with the point manifold M are determined by the values of s and $z^{(m)}$ on M . We see now that this statement must be modified, for the $z^{(m)}$ are infinite on M . In fact, the leading term of each of the two waves emanating from M is uniquely determined by the values of the number s_0 and the function $\tilde{z}(P)$.

For the case of constant coefficients, k_ν is constant on each ray, i.e. $k_\nu = k_\nu(t_0) = p_\nu$, and the rays are given by

$$x_\nu = x_{\nu 0} + (t - t_0)\, g_\nu ; \quad g_\nu = h_{k_\nu}(P) = h_{k_\nu}(K) \quad . \tag{45}$$

Furthermore (41) becomes

$$s(t) = s_0 + (t - t_0)\ell ; \quad \ell = k_\nu h_{k_\nu} - h = \ell(K) \quad , \tag{46}$$

and

$$(47)\qquad j(t,K) = \det\left|(t-t_0)h_{k_\nu k_i}\right| = (t-t_0)^\mu \det(h_{k_\nu k_i}) \;.$$

Finally, we may replace (44) by

$$(48)\qquad z(t) = c\,\tilde{z}\left|(t-t_0)^\mu \det(h_{k_\nu k_i})\right|^{-1/2} \;.$$

It is of interest to note that the discussion of this subsection is not valid for a non-dispersive equation. For such equations the rays emanating from a point all lie on the surface of the characteristic conoid determined by that point, hence the rays do not fill a region of t, X-space and the concept of a "tube" becomes meaningless. Furthermore, the factor $\det(h_{k_\nu k_i})$ in (48) vanishes in the non-dispersive case. *

3. Initial-boundary value problems for the homogeneous equation. In this section we will show how sums of one or more waves can be constructed to yield asymptotic solutions of initial and initial-boundary value problems for (1.17). We restrict our attention to the simple case of one space dimension ($\mu = 1$) and shall obtain just the leading term of the asymptotic expansion. Our examples are intended to be only illustrations of methods which are applicable to higher dimensional problems as well as to other differential equations. Therefore we shall avoid using special methods which are suitable only for the particular equation under consideration.

We consider the following initial value problem:

$$(1)\qquad c^2(x)\,u_{xx} - u_{tt} - \lambda^2 b^2(x)\,u = 0 \;,$$

$$(2)\qquad u(0,x) = u_0(x;\lambda)\,,\quad u_t(0,X) = u_1(x;\lambda) \;.$$

In some cases we shall also prescribe a homogeneous boundary condition. An interesting feature of the asymptotic method is that entirely different types of solutions are obtained, depending upon how the parameter λ appears in the initial data u_0, u_1. We consider first the initial value problem with the simplest type of initial data.

* This can be seen by differentiating the Euler equation $k_\nu \frac{\partial h}{\partial k_\nu} = h$ with respect to k_i.

3.1. oscillatory initial data. Let us choose initial data which already have the form of a wave. If $u(t,x) \sim z(t,x)\,e^{i\lambda s(t,x)}$ then $u_t(t,x) \sim i\lambda s_t z e^{i\lambda s} = -i\lambda h(s_x)\,z\,e^{i\lambda s}$ where $h(k) = \pm h_0(k) = \pm\sqrt{c^2k^2+b^2}$. Let us therefore consider the initial value problem (1, 2) with

$$u_0(x;\lambda) \sim z_0(x)\,e^{i\lambda s_0(x)}, \quad u_1(x;\lambda) \sim i\lambda h[s_0'(x)]\,z_0(x)\,e^{i\lambda s_0(x)} . \tag{3}$$

(Actually we are simultaneously considering two initial value problems, since $h(k)$ has two values.) The functions z_0 and s_0 are given.

If we attempt to solve this initial value problem by constructing a wave,

$$u(t,x) \sim z(t,x)\,e^{i\lambda s(t,x)} \tag{4}$$

we see that (3) yields the values of s and z at $t = 0$:

$$s(0,\sigma) = s_0(\sigma) \quad \text{and} \quad z(0,\sigma) = z_0(\sigma) . \tag{5}$$

Then $z(t,x)$ and $s(t,x)$ can be determined by the method of section 2. Let us carry out the details for the case of constant coefficients. From (2.17)

$$k_0(\sigma) = s_0'(\sigma)\,; \quad \omega_0(\sigma) = h[s_0'(\sigma)] . \tag{6}$$

We then solve the ray equations with $k_0(\sigma)$, $\omega_0(\sigma)$ given by (6), $t_0(\sigma) = 0$, and $x_0(\sigma) = \sigma$. From (2.30) and (2.31) we see that the ray emanating from the point $(t,x) = (0,\sigma)$ is given by

$$x = \sigma + gt; \quad g = h'[s_0'(\sigma)] \; ; \tag{7}$$

while on this ray

$$k = s_0'(\sigma), \quad \omega = h[s_0'(\sigma)], \quad s = s_0(\sigma) + \ell t; \quad \ell = kg - \omega . \tag{8}$$

Here $h' = dh/dk$.

To determine $z(t,x)$ we first compute the Jacobian,

$$j(t,\sigma) = \frac{dx}{d\sigma} = 1 + t\frac{dg}{d\sigma} = 1 + th''(s_0')\,s_0'' . \tag{9}$$

Then $j(0,\sigma) = 1$, and (2.35) yields the value of z on the ray:

$$z(t) = z_0(\sigma)[1 + th''(s_0')\,s_0'']^{-1/2} . \tag{10}$$

Thus we see that the asymptotic solution of the intial value problem is given parametrically (with parameter σ) by

$$u \sim z_0(\sigma)\left\{1 + t h''[s_0'(\sigma)]\, s_0''(\sigma)\right\}^{-1/2} \exp\left\{i\lambda\left(s_0(\sigma) + \left[s_0' h'(s_0') - h(s_0')\right] t\right)\right\},$$

$$x = \sigma + h'[s_0'(\sigma)]t; \quad h(k) = \pm h_0(k) = \pm\sqrt{c^2k^2 + b^2}\ . \tag{11}$$

Now

$$h_0'(k) = c^2(c^2k^2+b^2)^{-1/2}k; \quad h_0''(k) = c^2b^2(c^2k^2+b^2)^{-3/2} > 0\ . \tag{12}$$

Let us assume for the sake of definiteness that

$$s_0''(\sigma) \leq 0\ . \tag{13}$$

Let us also denote the solutions corresponding to the two values $h = \pm h_0$ by $u\pm$. Then for u_- we see from (12) and (13) that the Jacobian (9) vanishes only for $t < 0$, and the solution formula (11) for u_- does not become singular for $t > 0$. However it is easy to see that

$$u_-(t,x) = u_+(-t,x) \tag{14}$$

hence the representation (11) for u_+ becomes singular for certain points in the half-space $t > 0$. It is easy to show that these points lie on the caustic curve or envelope of the ray system. The singularity is a defect of the asymptotic solution (11) and must be repaired by considering a different kind of asymptotic expansion in the neighborhood of the caustic. The rays of u_- are illustrated in the following figure. The corresponding picture for u_+ is obtained by reflection in the x axis.

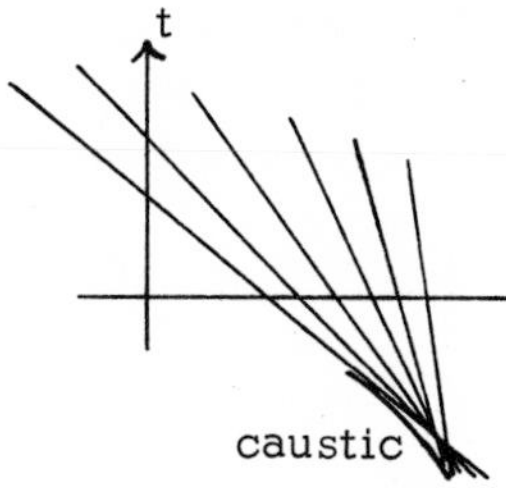

It is interesting to note that if $m = dt/dx = g^{-1}$ is the slope of a ray, then from (12) $|m| > c^{-1}$, i.e. c is an upper bound on the group speed.

Let us now set

$$z_0(x) = -\frac{y_0(x)}{h_0[s_0'(x)]} \tag{15}$$

and

$$u(t,x) = \frac{1}{2}[u_+(t,x) - u_-(t,x)] \ . \tag{16}$$

Then u is an asymptotic solution of (1) and we see from (3) that it satisfies the initial conditions

$$u(0,x) \sim 0; \quad u_t(0,x) \sim i\lambda y_0(x)\, e^{i\lambda s_0(x)} \ . \tag{17}$$

Thus the asymptotic solution of the initial value problem with initial conditions (17) consists of a sum of two waves. Finally, let us set

$$u(t,x) = u_2(t,x) + \frac{1}{i\lambda}\frac{\partial}{\partial t} u_1(t,x) \tag{18}$$

where u_1 and u_2 are solutions with initial data

$$u_j(0,x) \sim 0, \quad \frac{\partial}{\partial t} u_j(0,x) \sim i\lambda y_j(x)\, e^{i\lambda s_j(X)}; \ j = 1,2 \ . \tag{19}$$

Then u is the solution of (1) which satisfies the initial conditions

$$u(0,x) \sim y_1(x)\, e^{i\lambda s_1(x)}, \quad u_t(0,x) \sim i\lambda y_2(x)\, e^{i\lambda s_2(x)} \ . \tag{20}$$

(In deriving (20) we have used the fact that, at $t = 0$, $u_{1tt} = c^2 u_{1xx} - \lambda^2 b^2 u_1 \sim 0$.) Thus we see that the asymptotic solution of the initial value problem with oscillatory initial data (20) can, in general, be obtained as a sum of waves.

It is interesting to note the special features of our result when $b = 0$. In this case the parameter λ is absent from the partial differential equation (1) (in fact that equation becomes merely the wave equation) and appears only in the initial data. From (12) we see that the group speed $g = h'(k)$ becomes $g = \pm c$, and the rays lie on the characteristic surfaces $x \pm ct = \text{constant}$. In this case the expansion reduces to Lax's expansion [4].

3.2. the phase-shift at a caustic. In Appendix I the exact solution of the initial value problem (1, 2) (with constant coefficients) is given. Let us set $h = + h_0$ in (3) and examine the solution u_+ by the method of Appendix I. From (I.10) we see that

$$(21) \qquad u_+(t,x) \sim \frac{\lambda}{4\pi} \sum_{\pm} \int_{-\infty}^{\infty} dk \int_{-\infty}^{\infty} d\sigma \left\{ 1 \pm \frac{h_0[s_0'(\sigma)]}{h_0(k)} \right\} z_0(\sigma)\, e^{i\lambda\phi_\pm(k,\sigma)}$$

where

$$(22) \qquad \phi_\pm(k,\sigma) = k(x-\sigma) \mp h_0(k)t + s_0(\sigma) \ .$$

We now apply the stationary phase formula (II. 12) of Appendix II to obtain the asymptotic expansion of (21) for $\lambda \to \infty$. The stationary point is determined by the conditions

$$(23) \qquad \frac{\partial}{\partial k}\phi_\pm = x - \sigma \mp h_0'(k)t = 0; \quad \frac{\partial}{\partial \sigma}\phi_\pm = s_0'(\sigma) - k = 0 \ .$$

At the stationary point $h_0[s_0'(\sigma)]/h_0(k) = 1$ therefore the term corresponding to the lower sign in (21) vanishes. At the stationary point (for the term with the upper sign) (22) and (23) yield

$$(24) \qquad x = \sigma + h_0'[s_0'(\sigma)]t, \quad k = s_0'(\sigma) \ ,$$

$$(25) \qquad \phi = \phi_+ = s_0(\sigma) + \left\{ s_0'(\sigma) h_0'[s_0'(\sigma)] - h_0[s_0'(\sigma)] \right\} t \ ,$$

and

$$(26) \qquad (\phi_{\nu j}) = \begin{pmatrix} \phi_{kk} & \phi_{k\sigma} \\ \phi_{\sigma k} & \phi_{\sigma\sigma} \end{pmatrix} = \begin{pmatrix} -h_0''t & -1 \\ -1 & s_0'' \end{pmatrix} ; \quad h_0'' = h_0''[s_0'(\sigma)] \ .$$

Hence

$$(27) \qquad \det(\phi_{\nu j}) = -(1 + h_0'' s_0'' t) \ .$$

It follows now from (II. 12) that

(28)

$$u_+ \sim z_0(\sigma)\left\{\left|1+th_0''[s_0'(\sigma)]\,s_0''(\sigma)\right|\right\}^{-1/2} \exp\left\{i\lambda\left|s_0(\sigma)+[s_0'h_0'(s_0')-h_0(s_0')]t\right| + i\frac{\pi}{4}\,\mathrm{sig}(\phi_{\nu j})\right\},$$

$$x = \sigma + h_0'[s_0'(\sigma)]t, \quad h_0(k) = \sqrt{c^2k^2+b^2}\ .$$

In some neighborhood of the initial plane $t = 0$, $|1+th_0''s_0''| = 1+th_0''s_0''$, and we see that (28) agrees exactly with (11) (for $h = +h_0$) provided $\mathrm{sig}(\phi_{\nu j}) = 0$.

In order to determine $\mathrm{sig}(\phi_{\nu j})$ we compute the eigenvalues r_1, r_2 of $(\phi_{\nu j})$. They are the roots of the polynomial

(29) $$\det(\phi_{\nu j} - r\delta_{\nu j}) = (-h_0''t-r)(s_0''-r) - 1 = r^2 + (h_0''t - s_0'')r - s_0''h_0''t - 1\ .$$

Thus

(30) $$2r_{\substack{1\\2}} = (s_0'' - h_0''t) \pm \left[(s_0'' + h_0''t)^2 + 4\right]^{1/2}\ .$$

In a neighborhood of $t = 0$ it is now clear that $r_1 > 0$, $r_2 < 0$; hence $\mathrm{sig}(\phi_{\nu j}) = \mathrm{sgn}\, r_1 + \mathrm{sgn}\, r_2 = 0$. As a function of t, $\mathrm{sig}(\phi_{\nu j})$ changes discontinuously when (27) vanishes, i.e. when

(31) $$t = t_0(\sigma) = -(h_0''s_0'')^{-1}\ .$$

We recall that $h_0'' > 0$ and $s_0'' < 0$. Therefore $t_0(\sigma) > 0$. From (30) we see that at $t = t_0$,

(32)

$$2r_{\substack{1\\2}} = (s_0'' + \frac{1}{s_0''}) \pm [(s_0'' - \frac{1}{s_0''})^2 + 4]^{1/2} = (s_0'' + \frac{1}{s_0''}) \pm \left|s_0'' + \frac{1}{s_0''}\right| =$$

$$= (s_0'' + \frac{1}{s_0''}) \mp (s_0'' + \frac{1}{s_0''})\ .$$

Therefore at $t = t_0$ r_1 vanishes while r_2 remains negative. For $t > t_0$ both roots are negative. Thus

$$(33) \qquad \operatorname{sig}(\phi_{\nu j}) = \begin{Bmatrix} 0 & \text{for} & t < t_0 \\ -2 & \text{for} & t > t_0 \end{Bmatrix}$$

The result (11) for u_+ which was obtained without the use of the solution formula (I. 10) is valid in the region $t < t_0(\sigma)$. We now see that that result is verified by (28) and (33). However (28) and (33) are also valid for $t > t_0(\sigma)$. This suggests a rule for extending our general method to the region $t > t(\Sigma)$, beyond a caustic $t = t(\Sigma)$: The formula (2. 28) for the function z becomes indeterminate for $t > t(\Sigma)$ because $j(t_1)/j(t)$ becomes negative. The indeterminacy is removed by replacing j/j by $|j/j|$ and introducing the phase-shift factor $\exp\{-i\pi/2\}$. This "phase-shift rule" is identical to an analogous rule for the reduced wave equation [9].

In section 3. 1 we noted that the asymptotic formula fails (i. e. becomes infinite) at the caustic $t = t(\sigma)$. The correct expansion at $t = t(\sigma)$ could be obtained by expanding the integral (21) by means of a different stationary phase formula which is valid when $\det(\phi_{\nu j})$ vanishes at the stationary point.

3. 3. a simple initial-boundary value problem. The initial value problem for u_- required the solution of (1) with the initial conditions

$$(34) \quad u(0,x) \sim z_0(x)\, e^{i\lambda s_0(x)}, \quad \frac{\partial u}{\partial t}(0,x) \sim i\lambda h_0[s_0'(x)]\, z_0(x)\, e^{i\lambda s_0(x)} \quad .$$

The asymptotic solution was given by (11) with $h = -h_0$. Let us now modify the problem by adding the boundary condition at $x = 0$,

$$(35) \qquad u(t,0) \equiv 0 \quad .$$

The solution in the quarter-space $t \geq 0$, $x \geq 0$ is required. For consistency we must assume that $z_0(0) = 0$.

The asymptotic solution of this initial-boundary value problem is obtained by adding to u_- a reflected wave $u_r(t,x)$ which, together with u_- satisfies (35). The reflected wave must vanish at $t = 0$ so that (34) is unchanged. Thus we set

$$(36) \quad u = u_- + u_r;\ u_-(t,x) \sim z(t,x)\, e^{i\lambda s(t,x)};\ u_r(t,x) \sim z_r(t,x)\, e^{i\lambda s_r(t,x)} \quad .$$

Here z and s are given along the "incident" rays (7) by (10) and (8).

By inserting (36) in (35) we obtain

(37) $$s_r(t,0) = s(t,0) \quad ,$$

(38) $$z_r(t,0) = -z(t,0) \quad ,$$

and differentiation of (37) with respect to t yields

(39) $$\omega_r(t,0) = \omega(t,0) \quad .$$

Since both incident and reflected waves satisfy the dispersion equation $\omega^2 = c^2k^2 + b^2$ we conclude that $k_r(t,0) = \pm k(t,0)$, hence $g_r(t,0) = \pm g(t,0)$. In order that the reflected rays should not intersect the initial line,* $t = 0,\ x \geq 0$, we must take

(40) $$k_r(t,0) = -k(t,0),\ g_r(t,0) = -g(t,0) \quad .$$

It is convenient to express the boundary parametrically in terms of the same parameter, σ, used in describing the incident wave u. From (7) we see that at $x = 0$, $\sigma + g(\sigma)t = 0$. Hence the boundary is given parametrically by

(41) $$x = x_0(\sigma) = 0,\ t = t_0(\sigma) = -\sigma/g(\sigma) \quad .$$

Then, on the reflected ray emanating from the boundary at $[t_0(\sigma), 0]$, (39), (40), and (6-8) yield

(42)
$$\omega_r = \omega = -h_0[s_0'(\sigma)],\ k_r = -k = -s_0'(\sigma),\ g_r = -g = h_0'[s_0'(\sigma)],\ \ell_r = k_r g_r - \omega_r$$
$$= kg - \omega = \ell \quad .$$

From (2.31) the parametric equation of the reflected ray is

(43) $$x = g_r(t - t_0) = -g(t - t_0) = -\sigma - gt = -\sigma + th_0'[s_0'(\sigma)] \quad ,$$

while (2.32), (37), (8), and (42) yield

(44) $$s_r = s[t_0(\sigma)] + \ell_r(t - t_0) = s_0(\sigma) + \ell t_0 + \ell(t - t_0) = s_0(\sigma) + \ell t \quad .$$

---

* This condition is clearly required if $u = u_- + u_r$ is to satisfy the initial conditions, for then we must require that $u_- = 0$ at $t = 0$, $x \geq 0$.

From (43) we may now compute the Jacobian,

$$j = \frac{dx}{d\sigma} = -\left\{1 - th_0''[s_0'(\sigma)]\, s_0''(\sigma)\right\} . \tag{45}$$

Then (38), (2.28), and (10) yield

$$\begin{aligned} z^r(t) = z[t_0(\sigma)]\left[\frac{j(t_0)}{j(t)}\right]^{1/2} &= -z_0(\sigma)\left[1 - t_0 h_0'' s_0''\right]^{-1/2}\left[\frac{1-t_0 h_0'' s_0''}{1 - th_0'' s_0''}\right]^{1/2} \\ &= -z_0(\sigma)\left[1 - t\, h_0''\, s_0''\right]^{-1/2} . \end{aligned} \tag{46}$$

Summarizing our results, we see that $u = u_- + u_r$ where

$$u_r \sim -z_0(\sigma)\left[1 - th_0'' s_0''\right]^{-1/2} \exp\left\{i\lambda(s_0 + \ell t)\right\}, \quad x = -\sigma - gt \tag{47}$$

and

$$u_- \sim z_0(\sigma)\left[1 - th_0'' s_0''\right]^{-1/2} \exp\left\{i\lambda(s_0 + \ell t)\right\}, \quad x = \sigma + gt . \tag{48}$$

This completes the solution of the initial-boundary value problem.

From (47) and (48) we note that

$$u_r(t, x) = -u_-(t, -x) . \tag{49}$$

Of course (49) is easily obtained by the "image method"* which yields the solution of the initial-boundary value problem at once in terms of the solution u_- of the initial value problem. Thus this method provides a check on the construction we have used.

The above problem, though essentially trivial, suffices to illustrate the general procedure for the asymptotic solution of initial-boundary value problems: We first obtain the asymptotic solution of the initial value problem in terms of one or more waves emanating from a space-like initial surface. When these waves are "incident" on a time-like boundary, additional reflected waves are produced. Each reflected wave is uniquely determined by the incident wave and the boundary condition. Of course we must expect complications to occur when incident rays are tangent to the boundary or when boundaries are not

---

* In this case the image method would consist in extending the initial data to $x < 0$ in such a way that $u(0, x)$ and $u_t(0, x)$ are odd functions of x.

smooth. In such cases there will be "shadows" and we shall have to study "diffracted" waves in the shadow region. *

The incident and reflected rays of our simple problem are illustrated in the following figure:

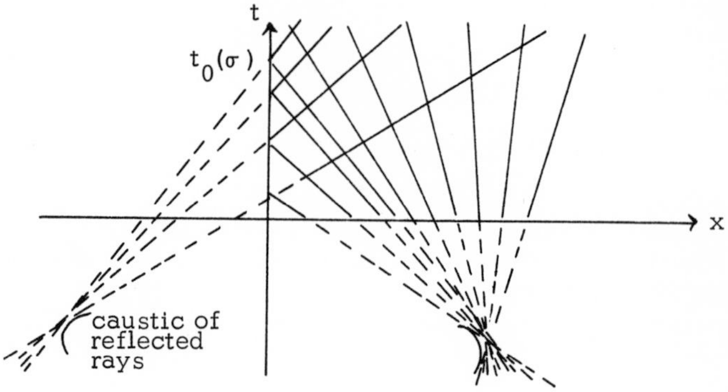

3.4. rapidly varying initial data. Our results so far have been restricted to problems with oscillatory initial data. In this, and succeeding sections, we shall consider other kinds of initial data. In each case the initial data give rise to one or more waves. Then, if the problem involves boundaries, reflected waves will be produced just as in Section 3.3. Thus the essential new features are embodied in problems without boundaries and we may restrict our attention to pure initial value problems.

In this section we consider the initial value problem for equation (1) with initial data of the form

$$u(0,x) = u_0(x;\lambda) = u_0(\lambda x), \quad u_t(0,x) = u_1(x;\lambda) = \lambda u_1(\lambda x) \quad . \tag{50}$$

Such data are called rapidly varying because of their large derivatives. In terms of the transformation (1.31) this problem is equivalent to the problem for the differential equation without a parameter,

$$(c')^2 u'_{x'x'} - u'_{t't'} - (b')^2 u' = 0 \tag{51}$$

* Such diffracted waves for elliptic problems are exhaustively treated in [1] and [2].

and with initial data of the form

(52) $$u'(0,x') = u_0(x'),\; u'_{t'}(0,x') = u_1(x')\;,$$

i.e. also independent of the parameter. Thus we see that rapidly varying initial data are quite natural for certain problems.

We assume that functions $u_0(x')$, $u_1(x')$ have compact support, i.e. vanish outside a finite region called the support of these functions. Then for $\lambda \to \infty$ the support of $u_0(\lambda x)$ and $\lambda u_1(\lambda x)$ shrinks to the point $x = 0$. This suggests that the waves produced by the rapidly varying initial data (50) emanate from the single point (0,0). In Section (2.7) we saw that a point initial manifold, in general, gives rise to two waves. Therefore we set

(53) $$u = u_+ + u_-;\quad u_\pm \sim z_\pm e^{i\lambda s_\pm}\;.$$

The functions $z_\pm$ and $s_\pm$ are given by the method of Section 2.7 except that the numbers $s_{0\pm}$ and the functions $\tilde{z}_\pm(p)$ are undetermined. In order to determine them we proceed as follows: First we complete the construction for the case of constant coefficients. Then we shall compare the result with the asymptotic expansion of the exact solution of our problem. This will determine $s_{0\pm}$ and $\tilde{z}_\pm(p)$. We then postulate that the newly determined quantities have the same values for the case of variable coefficients.*

From (2.47) the rays are given by

(54) $$x = gt;\; g = h'(k) = \pm h_0'(k)\;.$$

Then from (2.48) and (2.50) we see that $s_\pm$ and $z_\pm$ are given along the rays by

(55) $$s_\pm(t) = s_{0\pm} + \ell t;\quad \ell = kh'(k) - h\;,$$

and

(56) $$z_\pm(t) = \tilde{z}_\pm(k)\, c\, |t\, h_0''(k)|^{-1/2}\;.$$

Therefore for $t > 0$, $u(t,x)$ is given parametrically in terms of the parameter k by

---

* This is the method of comparison with the asymptotic expansion of the solution of a "canonical problem". The validity of the procedure for the problems treated here has been confirmed, as pointed out in in the introduction.

$$u \sim \sum_{\pm} c\tilde{z}_{\pm}(k)\,|th_0''(k)|^{-1/2} \exp\left\{i\lambda\left[s_{0\pm} \pm (kh_0' - h_0)t\right]\right\} ;$$

(57)

$$x = \pm h_0'(k)t \;.$$

The exact solution of the initial value problem (, 50) with constant coefficients is given by (I. 3) with $a_{\pm}$ given by (I. 9). We therefore insert (50) in (I. 9). This yields

(58)

$$a_{\pm}(k) = \frac{\lambda}{4\pi} \int \left[u_0(\lambda x) \pm \frac{i}{h_0(k)} u_1(\lambda x)\right] e^{-i\lambda kx} dx =$$

$$= \frac{1}{4\pi} \int \left[u_0(x') \pm \frac{i}{h_0(k)} u_1(x')\right] e^{-ikx'} dx' \;.$$

We note that $a_{\pm}$ is independent of λ . From (I. 3) ,

(59) $$u(t,x) = \sum_{\pm} \int a_{\pm}(k)\, e^{i\lambda\phi(k)} dk; \quad \phi = kx - ht; \; h = \pm h_0 = \pm\sqrt{c^2k^2 + b^2} \;.$$

We now apply the one-dimensional stationary phase formula (II.15) to each of the two terms in (59). The stationary point is determined by

(60) $$\phi'(k) = x - gt = 0, \quad g = h'(k) = \pm h_0'(k) \;,$$

and at the stationary point

(61) $$\phi''(k) = -h''(k)t = \mp h_0''(k)t; \quad \phi = (kg - h)t = \pm(kh_0' - h_0)t \;.$$

Therefore (II. 12) yields, for $t > 0$.

$$u \sim \sum_{\pm} \left(\frac{2\pi}{\lambda}\right)^{1/2} \left\{a_{\pm}(k)\, e^{\mp i\frac{\pi}{4}}\right\} |th_0''(k)|^{-1/2} \exp\left\{i\lambda\left[\pm(kh_0' - h_0)t\right]\right\} ;$$

(62)

$$x = \pm h_0'(k)t \;.$$

(Here we have used the fact that $h_0''(k) > 0$, hence $\operatorname{sig} \phi'' = \operatorname{sgn} \phi'' = \mp 1$ for $t > 0$.)

We now note that (57) and (62) agree exactly, provided we set

(63) $$s_{0\pm} = 0; \quad \tilde{z}_{\pm}(k) = \left(\frac{2\pi}{\lambda}\right)^{1/2} \frac{a_{\pm}(k)}{c} e^{\mp i\pi/4} \;.$$

Here $a_\pm(k)$ are the fourier transforms of the initial data, given by (58). Thus we have verified our general method, and have determined $s_{0\pm}$ and $\tilde{z}_\pm$. The asymptotic solution of the initial value problem for the case of variable coefficients $c(x)$, $b(x)$ can now be completed by the method of Section (2.7) with s_0 and $\tilde{z}_\pm(p)$ given by (63). Of course, it is clear that in that case we should replace c and b in (63) by c(0) and b(0).* The details of the construction will be omitted.

For the case of constant coefficients, the rays associated with each wave are illustrated in the following figure.

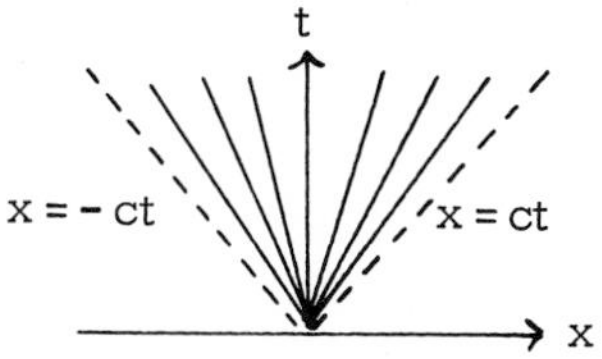

From (12) we see that for $-\infty < k < \infty$, $-c < h_0'(k) < c$ hence the rays all lie within the characteristic cone $x = \pm ct$ emanating from the origin. The origin itself is a caustic of the ray family and the asymptotic solution is singular there. From (12) we note that $[h_0''(k)]^{-1/2} = 0(|k|^{3/2})$ as $k \to \pm\infty$, therefore the asymptotic solution also becomes singular on the characteristic cone unless $a_\pm(k) = 0(|k|^{-3/2})$. Singularities of asymptotic solutions on caustics and other special manifolds (such as shadow boundaries) are well-known phenomena in the asymptotic theory of partial differential equations. The singularity on the characteristic cone appears to be another phenomenon of this type.

For the case of variable coefficients the ray picture will of course be similar to the figure except that the rays will, in general, be curves lying within the characteristic conoid.

As a special case of our method we obtain the asymptotic expansion of the Riemann function for (1) which is a solution of the initial value problem with

(64) $$u(0,x) = 0, \quad u_t(0,x) = \delta(x) \ .$$

Since $\delta(x) = \lambda\delta(\lambda x)$, we may take $u_0(x') = 0$ and $u_1(x') = \delta(x')$ in (50). Then (58) yields

(65) $$a_\pm(k) = \pm i[4\pi h_0(k)]^{-1}$$

* (63) depends on b as well as c because $h_0(k) = \sqrt{c^2k^2 + b^2}$ appears in (58).

and (63) becomes

$$(66) \qquad s_0 = 0, \; z_{\pm}(k) = \left[2(2\pi\lambda)^{1/2} c h_0(k)\right]^{-1} e^{\pm i\pi/4} \; .$$

3.5. slowly varying initial data. In view of our definition (50) of "rapidly varying" initial data, it is appropriate to refer to initial data of the form

$$(67) \qquad u(0,x) = u_0(x;\lambda) = u_0(x), \; u_t(0,x) = u_1(x;\lambda) = \lambda u_1(x)$$

as slowly varying. In terms of the transformation (1.31) the initial value problem (1, 67) is equivalent to the initial value problem for (51) with initial data

$$(68) \qquad u'(0,x') = u_0(x'/\lambda), \; u'_{t'}(0,x') = u_1(x'/\lambda) \; .$$

The asymptotic solution of the problem (1, 67) is easily obtained by observing that (67) is a special case of oscillatory initial data (20, with $s_1 = s_2 = 0$, $y_1 = u_0$, and $iy_2 = u_1$. As we saw in Section (3.1) the asymptotic solution of such problems consists of a sum of waves, each of which is generated by data of the form (3). If we set $s_0(x) = 0$ in (3) it becomes

$$(69) \qquad u_0(x;\lambda) \sim z_0(x), \; u_1(x,\lambda) \sim -i\lambda h(0)\, z_0(x)\,; h(0) = \pm|b(x)| \; .$$

For the case of constant coefficients, the asymptotic solution can be obtained from (11) by setting $s_0 = 0$. This yields

$$(70) \qquad u_{\pm}(t,x) \sim z_0(x) \exp\{\mp i\lambda|b|t\} \; .$$

The rays, in this case,are straight lines parallel to the t-axis, i.e. the group-speed is zero. If we follow the procedure outlined in (15-20) we obtain the asymptotic solution of the initial value problem (1, 67) for constant coefficients;

$$(71) \qquad u(t,x) \sim u_0(x)\cos(\lambda|b|t) + \frac{u_1(x)}{|b|} \sin(\lambda|b|t) \; .$$

3.6. discontinuous initial data. It is a characteristic feature of asymptotic solutions of differential equations that discontinuities of the data give rise to additional terms in the asymptotic expansion. In order to illustrate this phenomena, let us suppose that the function $z_0(x)$ in the initial value problem (1, 2, 3) is smooth, except for a jump discontinuity,

$$(72) \qquad [z_0] = z_0(x_0 + 0) - z_0(x_0 - 0)$$

at $x = x_0$. For definiteness we shall take $h = +h_0$ in (3).

We assume that, in addition to the wave (11) generated by the initial data, two secondary waves $\hat{u}_\pm \sim z_\pm e^{i\lambda s_\pm}$ emanate from the point of discontinuity $(0, x_0)$ on the initial line $t = 0$. The functions $z_\pm$ and $s_\pm$ are given by the method of Section 2.7 except that the numbers $s_{0\pm}$ and the functions $\tilde{z}_\pm(p)$ are undetermined. In order to determine them we proceed as in Section 3.4. The first step is to complete the construction for the case of constant coefficients.

From (2.47) the rays are given by

(73) $$x = x_0 + gt; \quad g = h'(k) = \pm h_0'(k) \quad .$$

From (2.48) and (2.50), $s_\pm$ and $z_\pm$ are given along the rays by

(74) $$s_\pm(t) = s_{0\pm} + \ell t; \quad \ell = kh' - h = \pm(kh_0' - h_0)$$

and

(75) $$z_\pm(t) = \tilde{z}_\pm(k)\, c\,|th_0''(k)|^{-1/2} \quad .$$

Thus

(76) $$\hat{u}_\pm \sim c\tilde{z}_\pm(k)\,|h_0''(k)t|^{-1/2} \exp\left\{i\lambda\left[s_{0\pm} \pm (kh_0' - h_0)t\right]\right\} \quad ;$$

$$x = x_0 \pm h_0'(k)t \quad .$$

Let us now determine $s_{0\pm}$ and $\tilde{z}_\pm$ by asymptotic expansion of the exact solution, which is given by (21). The leading term of the asymptotic expansion of the double integral (21) comes from the neighborhood of the stationary point and has already been computed (see (28, 33).) It can be shown that the next term in the asymptotic expansion comes from the neighborhood of the discontinuity line $\sigma = x_0$ of the integrand and can be determined as follows:

We first divide the integral (21) into two parts, w_2 correspond ing to the strip $x_0 - \epsilon \leq \sigma \leq x_0 + \epsilon$, and w_1 corresponding to the complementary region of the σ, k-plane. We choose ϵ small enough so that the stationary point lies in the domain of w_1. w_2 may be written in the form

(77) $$w_2 = w_+ + w_-$$

where

$$w_{\pm} = \int_{-\infty}^{\infty} v_{\pm}(k)\, e^{i\lambda[kx \mp h_0(k)t]} dk \; . \tag{78}$$

and

$$v_{\pm}(k) = \frac{\lambda}{4\pi} \int_{x_0-\epsilon}^{x_0+\epsilon} q_{\pm}(\sigma, k)\, z_0(\sigma)\, e^{i\lambda[s_0(\sigma) - k\sigma]} d\sigma \; ;$$

$$q_{\pm}(\sigma, k) = 1 \pm \frac{h_0[s_0'(\sigma)]}{h_0(k)} \; . \tag{79}$$

Next we divide each integral (79) into two parts corresponding to the intervals $x_0 - \epsilon \le \sigma \le x_0$ and $x_0 \le \sigma \le x_0 + \epsilon$, and integrate each by parts. It is easily shown (by a second integration by parts) that the resulting integrals are of order $1/\lambda$ while the boundary terms are of order 1. Of the four boundary terms, the two which come from the points $x_0 - \epsilon$ and $x_0 + \epsilon$ must be ignored for they are exactly cancelled by boundary contributions from w_1. Then the boundary terms corresponding to the points $x_0 - 0$ and $x_0 + 0$ yield

$$v_{\pm}(k) \sim \left\{ \frac{-[z_0]}{4\pi i} \; \frac{q_{\pm}(x_0, k)}{s_0'(x_0) - k} \right\} e^{i\lambda[s_0(x_0) - kx_0]} \; . \tag{80}$$

We now insert (80) in (78). This yields

$$w_{\pm} \sim \frac{-[z_0]}{4\pi i} e^{i\lambda s_0(x_0)} \int_{-\infty}^{\infty} \frac{q_{\pm}(x_0, k)}{s_0'(x_0) - k} e^{i\lambda \phi_{\pm}(k)} dk \; , \tag{81}$$

where

$$\phi_{\pm}(k) = k(x - x_0) \pm h_0(k)t \; .$$

Finally we apply the stationary phase formula to (81). The stationary point is determined by

$$\phi'(k) = x - x_0 \pm h_0'(k)t = 0 \; , \tag{83}$$

and at that point,

$$\phi'' = \mp h_0''(k)t, \quad \phi = \pm[kh_0' - h_0]t \; . \tag{84}$$

Then, for $t > 0$, (II.12) yields $w_{\pm} \sim \hat{u}_{\pm}$ where

$$\hat{u}_{\pm} = \frac{i[z_0]e^{\pm i\pi/4}}{2(2\pi\lambda)^{1/2}} \frac{\{1 \pm h_0[s_0'(x_0)]/h_0(k)\}}{s_0'(x_0) - k} |h_0''(k)t|^{-1/2}$$

(85) $$\exp\{i\lambda[s_0(x_0) \pm (kh_0' - h_0)t]\},$$

$$x = x_0 \pm h_0'(k)t .$$

Since the integral w_1 contains the stationary point, its asymptotic expansion is again given by (28, 33), and corresponds to the primary wave. Therefore the two secondary waves correspond to (85). If we now compare (85) and (76) we see that they agree exactly provided we set

(86) $$s_{0\pm} = s_0(x_0), \quad \tilde{z}_{\pm}(k) = \frac{i[z_0]e^{\pm i\pi/4}}{2(2\pi\lambda)^{1/2}c} \frac{\{1 \pm h_0[s_0'(x_0)]/h_0(k)\}}{s_0'(x_0) - k} .$$

We note that the primary wave (28) is of order 1 while the secondary waves are of order $\lambda^{-1/2}$. The rays of the primary wave are illustrated in the figure of Section 3.1. Those of the secondary waves are illustrated in the following figure:

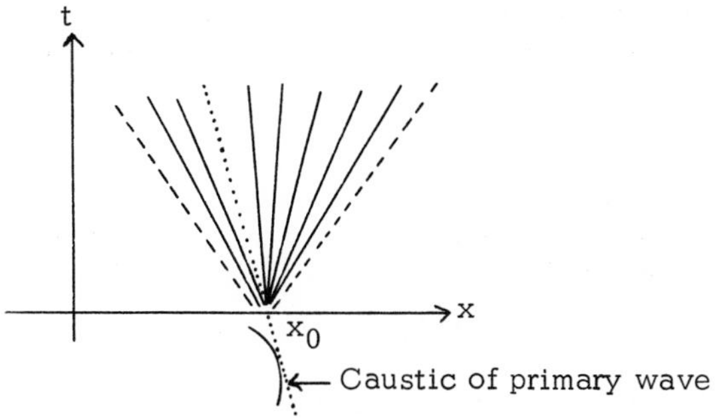

They all lie within the characteristic cone (dashed lines) emanating from the point $(0, x_0)$. One ray (dotted line) coincides with a ray of the primary wave. From (7) we see that the equation of this ray is

(87) $$x = x_0 + h_0'[s_0'(x_0)]t .$$

From (73) we see that the ray

(88) $$x = x_0 + h_0'(k)t$$

of the secondary wave $\hat{u}_+$ coincides with it, provided

(89) $$k = s_0'(x_0) \ .$$

But for this value of k we see from (86) that $\tilde{z}_+(k)$ is infinite (while $\tilde{z}_-$ is indeterminate). Thus the secondary wave $\hat{u}_+$ is infinite along the ray which coincides with a ray of the primary wave. Since $[h_0''(k)]^{-1/2} = 0(|k|^{3/2})$ as $k \to \infty$, it is easily seen that both secondary waves become singular on the characteristic cone.

As in Section (3.4), the formulas (86) for $s_0 \pm$ and $\tilde{z}_\pm(p)$ can be used to complete the construction of the secondary waves $\hat{u}_\pm$ for the case of variable coefficients. In doing so we must take $c = c(x_0)$ and $b = b(x_0)$ in (86). Once $\hat{u}_\pm$ are determined, the asymptotic solution of the initial value problem (1, 2, 3) (with z_0 discontinuous at $x = x_0$ and $h = +h_0$) is given by

(90) $$u = u_+ + \hat{u}_+ + \hat{u}_- + 0(1/\lambda) \ .$$

Here u_+ is given by (11) for the case of constant coefficients. For the case of variable coefficients $\hat{u}_\pm$ can be determined by the method of Section 2, using (86).

4. Initial-boundary value problems for the inhomogeneous equation.

In this section we shall develop methods for obtaining the asymptotic solution of initial-boundary value problems for the inhomogeneous equation

(1) $$c^2(x)\, u_{xx} - u_{tt} - \lambda^2 b^2(x)\, u = \lambda^2 f(t, x; \lambda) \ .$$

Without loss of generality, we may assume that the initial data, which we prescribe at $t = t_1 < 0$, is homogeneous, i.e.

(2) $$u(t_1, x) = u_t(t_1, x) = 0 \ .$$

(The solution of the problem for (1) with inhomogeneous initial data is then given by $u_1 + u_2$ where u_1 is the solution of (1, 2) and u_2 is a solution of the problem (3.1, 2) for the homogeneous equation.)

We shall assume that the source term $\lambda^2 f$ gives rise to one or more waves. The sum of these waves provides the asymptotic solution of the initial value problem. For initial-boundary value problems we assume that a secondary reflected wave is produced (as in Section 3.3) when a primary wave is incident on the boundary. Since we have already examined this phenomenon, at least in a simple case, we shall restrict our attention here to problems without boundaries.

In the following subsections we shall construct the waves produced by several different types of sources.

4.1. rapidly varying source. The source-function will be said to be rapidly-varying if it is of the form

$$\lambda^2 f(t, x; \lambda) = \lambda^2 g(\lambda t, \lambda x) \quad . \tag{3}$$

In terms of the transformation (1.16) the initial-value problem (1, 2, 3) is then equivalent to the problem

$$(c')^2 u'_{x'x'} - u'_{t't'} - (b')^2 u' = g(t', x'), \tag{4}$$

$$u'(\lambda t_1, x') = u'_{t'}(\lambda t_1, x') = 0 \quad . \tag{5}$$

Hence we see that this type of source is quite natural for the problem without a parameter in the differential equation and with homogeneous initial conditions in the "distant past", i.e. at $t' = \lambda t_1$ $(t_1 < 0, \lambda \to \infty)$.

Let us assume that the function $g(t', x')$ has compact support.* Then for $\lambda \to \infty$ the support of $g(\lambda t, \lambda x)$ shrinks to the point $(t, x) = (0, 0)$. Therefore we assume that the source (3) gives rise to waves emanating from this point. If we set

$$u = u_+ + u_-; \; u_\pm \sim z_\pm e^{i\lambda s_\pm} \quad , \tag{6}$$

then the functions $z_\pm$ and $s_\pm$ are given by the method of Section (2.7) except that the numbers $s_{0\pm}$ and the functions $\tilde{z}_\pm(p)$ are undetermined. As in Section (3.4), we shall carry out the construction for the case of constant coefficients, and then shall determine $s_{0\pm}$ and $\tilde{z}_\pm$ by comparison with the asymptotic expansion of the exact solution.

The asymptotic solution for the case of constant coefficients is the same as that of Section (3.4) except for the values of $s_{0\pm}$ and $\tilde{z}_\pm$. Therefore $u_\pm$ is given along the rays

$$x = \pm h_0'(k) t \tag{7}$$

by

$$u_\pm = c\tilde{z}_\pm(k) \, |t h_0''(k)|^{-1/2} \exp\{i\lambda[s_{0\pm} \pm (k h_0' - h_0) t]\} \quad . \tag{8}$$

The exact solution of the initial value problem (1, 2) is given by (I.23) of Appendix I. We insert (3) in that equation and then introduce the transformation $x' = \lambda y$, $t' = \lambda s$. The result is

---

* Actually it is sufficient to assume that the decay at infinity of $g(t', x')$ is sufficiently rapid for the integral (11) to exist.

(9)

$$u(t,x;\lambda) = \sum_{\pm} \frac{1}{4\pi i} \int_{-\infty}^{\infty} dk \int_{-\infty}^{\infty} dx' \int_{\lambda t_1}^{\lambda t} dt' \, \frac{g(t',x')}{h(k)} e^{-i[kx'-ht']+i\lambda[kx-ht]} \, .$$

Here $h = \pm h_0(k)$. For $\lambda \to \infty$ it is clear from (9) that

$$u \sim \sum_{\pm} \frac{1}{4\pi i} \int_{-\infty}^{\infty} \frac{a(k,h)}{h} e^{i\lambda\phi(k)} dk \, , \tag{10}$$

where

$$a(k,h) = \int_{-\infty}^{\infty} dx' \int_{-\infty}^{\infty} dt' \, g(t',x') e^{-i[kx'-ht']} \, , \tag{11}$$

and

$$\phi(k) = kx-ht \, . \tag{12}$$

We now apply the method of stationary phase (Appendix II) to (10). The stationary point is determined by

$$\phi'(k) = x-h't = 0 \, , \tag{13}$$

and at the stationary point,

$$\phi = (kh'-h)t = \pm(kh_0' - h_0)t; \quad \phi'' = -h''t = \mp h_0'' t \, . \tag{14}$$

According to (3.12) $h_0'' > 0$ therefore for $t > 0$ sgn $\phi'' = \mp 1$. It follows from (II.12) that $u \sim u_+ + u_-$, where

$$u_\pm \sim \frac{a(k,\pm h_0)}{2(2\pi\lambda)^{1/2} h_0} |th_0''(k)|^{-1/2} \exp\{i\lambda[\pm(kh_0' - h_0)t] \mp 3i\,\pi/4\} \, ;$$

(15)

$$x = \pm h_0'(k)t \, .$$

This equation agrees exactly with (8) if we set

$$s_{0\pm} = 0, \quad \tilde{z}_\pm(k) = \frac{a[k,\pm h_0(k)]}{2(2\pi\lambda)^{1/2} c h_0(k)} e^{\mp 3i\pi/4}; \; h_0 = \sqrt{c^2k^2+b^2} \, . \tag{16}$$

Here $a(k,h)$ is given by (11). (16) can be used to complete the asymptotic solution of the problem with variable coefficient functions. In so doing we must set $c = c(0)$ and $b = b(0)$ in (16).

Two special cases of the results of this section are of some interest. One is the point source with

$$(17) \qquad g(t', x') = g(t')\delta(x') \ .$$

The other is the source

$$(18) \qquad g(t', x') = \delta(t')\,\delta(x')$$

which determines the Green's function of the initial value problem. For the point source, we see from (11) that

$$(19) \qquad a(k, h) = a(h) = \int_{-\infty}^{\infty} g(t')\, e^{iht'}\, dt' \ ,$$

while, for the Green's function

$$(20) \qquad a(k, h) \equiv 1 \ .$$

4.2. source with rapid time variation. Let us now consider a source function of the form

$$(21) \qquad f(t, x; \lambda) = g\{\lambda[t - t_0(x)], x\} \ .$$

If the function $g(t', x)$ has compact support* then as $\lambda \to \infty$ the support of f shrinks to the curve $t = t_0(x)$. In order to conform to the notation of Section 2, we express this curve in the parametric form

$$(22) \qquad t = t_0(\sigma), \quad x = x_0(\sigma) \equiv \sigma \ .$$

To simplify our subsequent work it is convenient to assume that $t_0(\sigma)$ is a monotonic function, and for definiteness we shall take

$$(23) \qquad t_0'(\sigma) \geq 0 \ .$$

We assume that two waves are produced by the source (21) and that they emanate from the curve (22). We also assume that on this curve, $s(t, x)$ is constant for each wave, i.e.

$$(24) \qquad s[t_0(\sigma), \sigma] = s_{0\pm} = \text{const.} \ .$$

Differentiation of (24) with respect to σ yields the condition

$$(25) \qquad -\omega t_0' + k = 0 \text{ or } \omega/k = 1/t_0' = \frac{dx}{dt} \ .$$

---

* It is sufficient to assume that the integral (44) exists.

(The condition (25) may be stated as follows: The "phase speed" ω/k is equal to the speed dx/dt of the source.) By squaring (25) we obtain $k^2 = (t_0')^2 h^2(k,\sigma)$, and since h depends on k only as a function of k^2 this equation has two solutions

$$k = \pm k_0(\sigma) \quad . \tag{26}$$

(By using the formula (2.6) for the Hamiltonian h it is easy to find the solutions (26) explicitly. However, since we wish to keep our methods as general as possible we shall not make use of the explicit expression for k_0.)

We now impose the condition that the solutions (26) be real, and we take $k_0(\sigma) \geq 0$. For the case of equation (1) it is easy to show that this condition is equivalent to

$$|c(\sigma)\, t_0'(\sigma)| < 1 \quad \text{or} \quad |c| < \left|\frac{dx}{dt}\right| \ , \tag{27}$$

i.e. the source speed must be greater than the characteristic speed $|c|$. (Geometrically, the condition is that the curve (22) should be space-like.) From (25) and (2.6)

$$\omega = \pm\omega_0(\sigma) = \pm k_0(\sigma)/t_0' = \pm h_0[k_0(\sigma), \sigma] \tag{28}$$

and from (2.8)

$$g = g_0(\sigma) = \pm \frac{\partial h_0}{\partial k}(\pm k_0, \sigma) = \frac{\partial h_0}{\partial k}(k_0, \sigma) \ . \tag{29}$$

The value of the function z for each wave is determined by its value

$$z[t_0(\sigma), \sigma] = z_{\pm}(\sigma) \tag{30}$$

on the curve (22). If $z_{\pm}(\sigma)$ and the constants $s_{0\pm}$ were known, the construction of the two waves could be completed by the methods of Section 2. We shall determine $z_{\pm}$ and $s_{0\pm}$ by completing the construction for the case of constant coefficients and comparing the result with the asymptotic expansion of the exact solution.

If the coefficients are constant, the rays are given by*

$$x = \sigma + g_0(\sigma)\,[t - t_0(\sigma)] = \sigma + h_0'[k_0(\sigma)]\,[t - t_0(\sigma)] \tag{31}$$

and s is given along the rays by

---

* We note that $g_0(\sigma)$ is the same for both waves, therefore the rays are the same.

(32) $$s = s_{0\pm} + (t-t_0) \quad ,$$

where

(33) $$\ell = kg-\omega = \pm[k_0(\sigma)h_0'(k_0) - h_0(k_0)] \quad .$$

From (2.35) and (30), z is given along the rays by

(34) $$z(t) = z_{\pm}(\sigma)\,[j(t_0)/j(t)]^{1/2} \quad ,$$

where $j(t,\sigma) = dx/d\sigma$. In order to calculate this derivative, using (31), we shall need the value of $k_0'(\sigma) = dk_0/d\sigma$. This is obtained by differentiating implicitly the equation

(35) $$h_0(k_0)\,t_0' = k_0$$

which is a consequence of (25), (26), and (28). The result is

(36) $$k_0'(\sigma) = h_0 t_0''/(1-h_0' t_0') \quad .$$

Then

(37) $$j(t,\sigma) = dx/d\sigma = 1-h_0't_0' + (t-t_0)\,h_0''h_0t_0''/(1-h_0't_0') \quad .$$

It follows that

(38) $$j(t_0,\sigma) = 1-h_0't_0' \quad ,$$

and (34) yields

(39) $$z(t) = z_{\pm}(\sigma)\,[(1-h_0't_0')^2 + (t-t_0)\,h_0''h_0t_0'']^{-1/2} \quad .$$

If we denote the two waves by u_+ and u_-, then the asymptotic solution of the initial value problem (1, 2, 21) is given by $u = u_+ + u_-$, where

$$u_{\pm} \sim z_{\pm}(\sigma)[(1-h_0't_0')^2 + (t-t_0)\,h_0''h_0t_0'']^{-1/2}\exp\{i\lambda[s_{0\pm} \pm (k_0h_0'-h_0)(t-t_0)]\} \; ;$$

(40) $$x = \sigma + h_0'(t-t_0) \quad .$$

Here, the argument of h_0, h_0', h_0'' is $k_0(\sigma)$.

The exact solution of the problem is given by (I. 23). We insert (21) in that equation, change y to σ, and introduce the transformation $t' = \lambda[s-t_0(\sigma)]$ in the inner integral. This yields

(41)

$$u = \sum_{\pm} \frac{\lambda}{4\pi i} \int_{-\infty}^{\infty} dk \int_{-\infty}^{\infty} d\sigma \int_{\lambda[t_1-t_0(\sigma)]}^{\lambda[t-t_0(\sigma)]} dt' \frac{g(t',\sigma)}{h(k)} \exp\{i\lambda[k(x-\sigma)-h(t-t_0)]+iht'\}$$

Here $h = \pm h_0(k)$. We assume that

(42) $$t_1 < t_0(\sigma) < t .$$

Then, for $\lambda \to \infty$,

(43) $$u \sim \sum_{\pm} \frac{\lambda}{4\pi i} \int_{-\infty}^{\infty} dk \int_{-\infty}^{\infty} d\sigma \, \frac{a(h,\sigma)}{h(k)} e^{i\lambda\phi(k,\sigma)} ,$$

where

(44) $$a(h,\sigma) = \int_{-\infty}^{\infty} g(t',\sigma) e^{iht'} dt'$$

and

(45) $$\phi(k,\sigma) = k(x-\sigma) - h[t-t_0(\sigma)] .$$

We now apply the method of stationary phase to (43). The stationary point is determined by the conditions

(46) $$\phi_k = x-\sigma-h'[t-t_0(\sigma)] = 0, \quad \phi_\sigma = -k+ht_0'(\sigma) = 0 .$$

By comparison with (25) we see that (46) implies that

(47) $$k = \pm k_0(\sigma) ,$$

and

(48) $$x = \sigma + h_0'[k_0(\sigma)][t-t_0(\sigma)] .$$

Here we have used the fact that $\pm h_0'(\pm k_0) = h_0'(k_0)$. (45) and (48) now yield

(49) $$\phi = \pm[k_0 h_0' - h_0][t-t_0] .$$

In order to apply (II.12) we require the second derivatives,

(50) $$\phi_{kk} = -h''[t-t_0], \quad \phi_{k\sigma} = -1+h't_0', \quad \phi_{\sigma\sigma} = ht_0'' .$$

The derivatives are evaluated at the stationary point, $[k,\sigma] = [\pm k_0(\sigma),\sigma]$. We set

$$(51)\qquad (\phi_{\nu j}) = \begin{pmatrix} \phi_{kk} & \phi_{k\sigma} \\ \phi_{\sigma k} & \phi_{\sigma\sigma} \end{pmatrix} .$$

Then (50) and (51) yield

$$(52)\qquad \det(\phi_{\nu j}) = -\,[(1-h't_0')^2 + (t-t_0)h''\,h\,t_0'']$$

$$= -\,[(1-h_0't_0')^2 + (t-t_0)h_0''\,h_0t_0''] .$$

Again we have used the fact that $\pm h_0'(\pm k_0) = h_0'(k_0)$.

For $t = t_0$ we note that $\det(\phi_{\nu j}) = -1$. Therefore, in a neighborhood of $t = t_0$ (and in fact until the ray reaches a caustic), $\operatorname{sig}(\phi_{\nu j}) = 0$. Therefore we see from (II.12) that $u \sim u_+ + u_-$, where

(53)

$$u_\pm \sim \frac{\pm a(\pm h_0,\sigma)}{2ih_0}[(1-h_0't_0')^2 + (t-t_0)h_0''h_0t_0'']^{-1/2}\exp\{i\lambda[\pm(k_0h_0'-h_0)(t-t_0)]\};$$

$$x = \sigma + h_0'(t-t_0) .$$

We see that (53) and (40) agree exactly if we set

$$(54)\qquad s_{0\pm} = 0,\quad z_\pm(\sigma) = \frac{\pm a(\pm h_0,\sigma)}{2ih_0} .$$

Here $h_0 = h_0[k_0(\sigma)]$, and $a(h,\sigma)$ is given by (44). For the case of variable coefficients (54) supplies the values of $s_{0\pm}$ and $z_\pm(\sigma)$ necessary to complete the construction of the asymptotic solution. In that case we must set $h_0 = h_0[k_0(\sigma),\sigma]$ in (54).

An interesting special case of the results of this subsection is a source function of the form

$$(55)\qquad f(t,x;\lambda) = \delta[\lambda(t-t_0)]\,\gamma(x) = \frac{1}{\lambda}\,\delta[t-t_0(x)]\,\gamma(x) .$$

In this case $g(t',\sigma) = \delta(t')\gamma(\sigma)$ and $a(h,\sigma) = \gamma(\sigma)$. It follows that $z_{\pm}(\sigma) = \pm\gamma(\sigma)/2ih_0$ and

(56)

$$u \sim u_+ + u_- = \frac{\gamma(\sigma)}{h_0}[(1-h_0't_0')^2 + (t-t_0)h_0''h_0t_0'']^{-1/2}\sin[\lambda(k_0h_0'-h_0)(t-t_0)] ;$$

$$x = \sigma + h_0'(t-t_0) .$$

If f is of the form (55) where t_0 is a constant, then (25) implies that $k_0(\sigma) = 0$. Hence $h_0 = |b|$, $x = \sigma$, and (56) becomes

(57) $$u \sim -\frac{\gamma(x)}{b}\sin[\lambda b(t-t_0)] .$$

A source function of the form (21) is said to have rapid time variation. One of the form

(58) $$f(t,x;\lambda) = g\{t, \lambda[x-x_0(t)]\}$$

is said to have rapid space variation. Since the treatment of (58) is similar to that of (21) we shall not examine it further. A special case of (58) is the moving point source,

(59) $$f(t,x;\lambda) = \gamma(t)\,\delta[\lambda(x-x_0)] = \frac{1}{\lambda}\gamma(t)\,\delta[x-x_0(t)] .$$

4.3. oscillatory point source. A source function of the form

(60) $$\lambda^2 f(t,x;\lambda) = \lambda^2\delta(\lambda x)\,p(t)\,e^{-i\lambda q(t)} = \lambda\delta(x)\,p(t)\,e^{-i\lambda q(t)}$$

will be said to represent an oscillatory point source located at the origin.

In constructing the asymptotic solution of (1, 2, 60) it is natural to assume that waves emanate from the t-axis: $x = 0$, $t = \tau(t_1 \le \tau)$ with a phase given at $x = 0$ by

(61) $$s(\tau,0) = s_0(\tau) = -q(\tau) .$$

Differentiation of (61) with respect to τ leads to

(62) $$\omega = h(k) = \pm h_0(k) = q'(\tau) ; \quad h_0 = \sqrt{c^2k^2+b^2} .$$

This equation has real solutions k if and only if $[q'(\tau)]^2 > b^2(0)$.

For definiteness we shall assume that*

(63) $$q'(\tau) > b(0) \quad .$$

If (63) is satisfied then (62) has real solutions k only for

(64) $$h = + h_0 \quad ,$$

and then

(65) $$k = \pm k_0(\tau) \quad .$$

As in the preceding section, the explicit formula for $k_0(\tau)$ is easily obtained but will not be used. The corresponding values of g at the source are clearly given by

(66) $$g = h_0'(\pm k_0) = \pm h_0'(k_0) \quad .$$

The value of the function z is determined by its value

$$z(\tau, 0) = z_\pm(\tau)$$

at the source. If $z_\pm(\tau)$ were known the solution could be completed by the methods of Section (2). As usual, we shall determine the value of $z_\pm(\tau)$ by completing the construction for the case of constant coefficients and by comparison with the expansion of the exact solution.

If the coefficients are constant, the rays are given by

(67) $$x = \pm h_0'[k_0(\tau)](t-\tau), \quad t_1 \leq \tau \leq t \quad ;$$

and are illustrated in the following figure. Those corresponding to the upper (lower) sign in (67) proceed to the right (left) with increasing t. As usual, s is given along each ray by

(68) $$s = s_0(\tau) + \ell(t-\tau) = -q(\tau) + (t-\tau)[k_0(\tau) h_0'(k_0) - q'(\tau)] \quad .$$

(Here we have made use of the equations $\pm h_0'(\pm k_0) = h_0'(k_0)$ and $h_0(k_0) = q'(\tau)$.) The function z is given along each ray by

(69) $$z(t) = z_\pm(\tau)[j(\tau)/j(t)]^{1/2}$$

* In terms of the physical interpretation of (1) given in the introduction, the condition (63) is that the frequency of the source should be greater than the plasma frequency ϕ. It is well-known that waves of frequency less than ϕ are exponentially damped in a plasma.

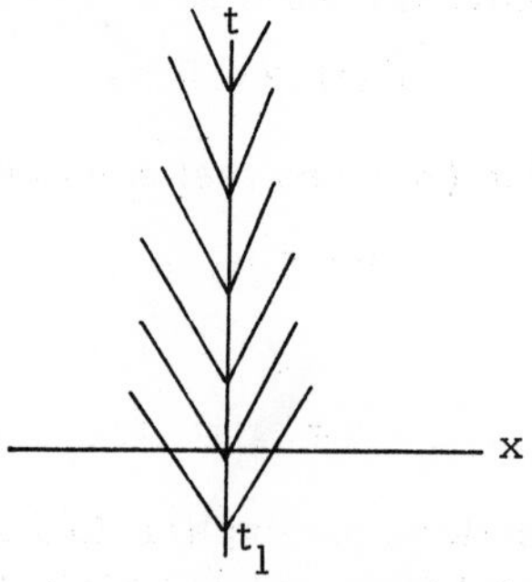

where $j(t) = j(t,\tau) = dx/d\sigma$. In order to calculate j, using (67) we first obtain the value of $k_0'(\tau)$. This is easily obtained by implicit differentiation of (62) with $h = +h_0$. The result is

(70) $$k_0'(\tau) = q''(\tau)/h_0'(k_0) \; .$$

Then

(71) $$j(t,\tau) = \pm[h_0'(k_0)]^{-1}\{h_0''(k_0)\,q''(\tau)\,(t-\tau) - [h_0'(k_0)]^2\}$$

and

(72) $$j(\tau,\tau) = +h_0'(k_0) \; .$$

(69) now yields

(73) $$z(t) = z_{\pm}(\tau)\left[1 - \frac{(t-\tau)\,q''(\tau)\,h_0''(k_0)}{[h_0'(k_0)]^2}\right]^{-1/2} ,$$

hence the asymptotic solution of the initial-value problem (1, 2, 60) is given parametrically in terms of τ by

$$u \sim z_{\pm}(\tau)\left[1 - \frac{(t-\tau)\,q''(\tau)\,h_0''(k_0)}{[h_0'(k_0)]^2}\right]^{-1/2}$$

(74) $$\exp\left[i\lambda\{-q(\tau) + (t-\tau)\,[k_0(\tau)\,h_0'(k_0) - q'(\tau)]\}\right];$$

$$x = \pm\, h_0'[k_0(\tau)]\,(t-\tau) \quad ; \quad t_1 \leq \tau \leq t \; .$$

The exact solution of the problem is given by (I. 23). We set

(75) $$\hat{p}(\tau) = \begin{cases} p(\tau), & t_1 \leq \tau \leq t \\ 0, & \text{otherwise} \end{cases} .$$

Then if we insert (60) into (I. 23) we obtain

(76) $$u(t,x) = \frac{\lambda}{4\pi i} \sum_{h=\pm h_0} \int_{-\infty}^{\infty} dk \int_{-\infty}^{\infty} d\tau \frac{\hat{p}(\tau)}{h(k)} e^{i\lambda\phi(k,\tau)} .$$

Here

(77) $$\phi(k,\tau) = -q(\tau) + kx - (t-\tau)h(k) .$$

We now apply the method of stationary phase to (76). Stationary points are determined by the conditions

(78) $$\phi_k = x - (t-\tau)h'(k) = 0; \quad \phi_\tau = -q'(\tau) + h(k) = 0 .$$

Again assuming that (63) is satisfied, we see that (78) is satisfied only for $h = +h_0$ and then $k = \pm k_0(\tau)$. Thus only one term of (76) yields a stationary point, and at this point

(79) $$x = (t-\tau)h_0'[\pm k_0(\tau)] = \pm(t-\tau)h_0'[k_0(\tau)] .$$

It is now an easy matter to compute the matrix

(80) $$(\phi_{\nu j}) = \begin{pmatrix} \phi_{kk} & \phi_{k\tau} \\ \phi_{\tau k} & \phi_{\tau\tau} \end{pmatrix}$$

at the stationary point. Then

(81)

$$\det(\phi_{\nu j}) = (t-\tau)q''(\tau)h_0''[\pm k_0] - [h_0'(\pm k_0)]^2 = (t-\tau)q''(\tau)h_0''(k_0) - [h_0'(k_0)]^2 .$$

In a neighborhood of $t = \tau$ the determinant is negative, hence $\text{sig}(\phi_{\nu j}) = 0$. The stationary phase formula, (II. 12) now yields

$$u \sim \frac{1}{2i} \{[h_0'(k_0)]^2 - (t-\tau)\, q''(\tau)\, h_0''[k_0]\}^{-1/2} \frac{p(\tau)}{q(\tau)}$$

(82) $$\exp\left[i\lambda\{-q(\tau) + (t-\tau)\,[k_0(\tau)\, h_0'(k_0) - q'(\tau)]\}\right];$$

$$x = \pm h_0'[k_0(\tau)]\,(t-\tau)\;; \qquad t_1 \leq \tau \leq t\;.$$

Comparison of (74) and (82) shows that they agree exactly if we set

(83) $$z_\pm(\tau) = \frac{p(\tau)}{2ih_0'[k_0(\tau)]\, q'(\tau)}\;.$$

For the case of variable coefficients, (83) supplies the formula for $z_\pm(\tau)$ necessary to complete the construction of the asymptotic solution. Important special cases of the results of this section are obtained by setting

(84) $$q(t) = \nu t \qquad [\nu > b(0)]$$

and

(85) $$q(t) = \nu t \quad [\nu > b(0)]\;; \qquad p(t) \equiv p_0\;.$$

(86) yields a time-harmonic point source of frequency $\lambda\nu$, and (84) may be interpreted as an amplitude-modulated time-harmonic source.

4. 4. slowly varying source. As a final example of our method of solving the initial value problem (1, 2) we consider the slowly varying source function

(87) $$\lambda^2 f(t, x; \lambda) = g(t, x)\;.$$

We assume that $g(\tau, x) \equiv 0$ for $t_2 < \tau$ where t_2 is a constant, and we examine the solution $u(t, x)$ for $t_2 < t$. By virtue of (2) we may define $g(\tau, x) \equiv 0$ for $\tau < t_1$. Thus

(88) $$g(t, x) \equiv 0 \quad \text{for } t < t_1 \text{ or } t_2 < t\;.$$

Then, in general, $g(t, x)$ will have a discontinuity on the line $t = t_1$, and perhaps on other curves of the form

(89) $$t = t_0(\sigma), \quad x = \sigma\;.$$

As in Section (4. 2) we take $t_0'(\sigma) \geq 0$, for simplicity.

We assume that each discontinuity curve (95) produces two waves and that on the curve s is constant for each wave. We shall calculate the waves produced by one discontinuity curve (95). The calculation is identical to that of Section 4.2 and we obtain the two waves $u_{\pm}$ given by (40). Again we must impose the condition (27) and $z_{\pm}(\sigma)$, $s_{0\pm}$ are undetermined. In order to determine them we use the exact solution (I.23). By virtue of (88) we may write it in the form

(90)

$$u = \sum_{\pm} \frac{1}{4\pi i} \int_{-\infty}^{\infty} dk \int_{-\infty}^{\infty} d\sigma \int_{-\infty}^{\infty} d\tau \frac{g(\tau,\sigma)}{h} e^{i\lambda[k(x-\sigma)-(t-\tau)h]} \; ; \; h = \pm h_0(k) .$$

Now let

(91) $$\gamma(\sigma) = [g] = g[t_0(\sigma)+0,\sigma] - g[t_0(\sigma)-0,\sigma]$$

be the magnitude of the jump discontinuity of g. Then by integration by parts

(92) $$\int_{-\infty}^{\infty} \frac{g(\tau,\sigma)}{i\lambda h} e^{i\lambda\tau h} d\tau \sim -\gamma(\sigma) e^{i\lambda t_0(\sigma) h} .$$

Next we insert (92) in (90). The result is

(93) $$u \sim \sum_{\pm} -\frac{\lambda}{4\pi} \int_{-\infty}^{\infty} dk \int_{-\infty}^{\infty} d\sigma \; \gamma(\sigma) e^{i\lambda\phi(k,\sigma)}$$

where

(94) $$\phi(k,\sigma) = k(x-\sigma) - h[t-t_0(\sigma)] .$$

The integral (93) may be evaluated asymptotically by the method of stationary phase. Since (93) is of the same form as (43), we may obtain the result at once by replacing $\frac{a(h,\sigma)}{ih} = \frac{\pm a(\pm h_0,\sigma)}{ih_0}$ by $-\gamma(\sigma)$ in (53). We may then determine $s_{0\pm}$ and $z_{\pm}(\sigma)$ by comparison with (40). In this way we obtain

(95) $$s_{0\pm} = 0, \quad z_{\pm}(\sigma) = -\frac{\gamma(\sigma)}{2} = -\frac{1}{2}[g] ,$$

and these results may be used to obtain the asymptotic solution of the initial value problem with variable coefficients.

Appendix I. <u>Exact solution of the initial value problem for constant coefficients</u>. We first consider the initial value problem for the homogeneous equation,

(1) $$c^2 u_{xx} - u_{tt} - \lambda^2 b^2 u = 0 \ ,$$

(2) $$u(0,x) = u_0(x;\lambda), \quad u_t(0,x) = u_1(x;\lambda) \ .$$

We consider a solution of (1) in the form of a superposition of plane waves,

(3) $$u(t,x) = \sum_{\pm} \int_{-\infty}^{\infty} a_{\pm}(k,\lambda)\, e^{i\lambda(kx \pm h_0 t)}\, dk; \quad h_0 = \sqrt{c^2 k^2 + b^2} \ .$$

In order to satisfy the initial conditions (2) we set

(4) $$u(0,x) = \sum \int a_{\pm} e^{i\lambda kx} dk = u_0(x;\lambda) \ ,$$

(5) $$u_t(0,x) = \sum \int \mp i\lambda h_0 a_{\pm} e^{i\lambda kx} dk = u_1(x;\lambda) \ .$$

Then, by means of the Fourier transform formulas,

(6) $$g(x,\lambda) = \int a(k,\lambda)\, e^{i\lambda kx} dk; \quad a(k,\lambda) = \frac{\lambda}{2\pi} \int g(x,\lambda)\, e^{-i\lambda kx} dx \ ,$$

we may invert (4) and (5). This yields

(7) $$a_+ + a_- = \frac{\lambda}{2\pi} \int u_0(x;\lambda)\, e^{-i\lambda kx} dx \ ,$$

(8) $$a_+ - a_- = \frac{i}{2\pi h_0} \int u_1(x;\lambda)\, e^{-i\lambda kx} dx \ ,$$

and therefore

(9) $$a_{\pm}(k,\lambda) = \frac{1}{4\pi} \int [\lambda u_0(x;\lambda) \pm \frac{i}{h_0} u_1(x;\lambda)]\, e^{-i\lambda kx} dx \ .$$

Finally the solution of (1, 2) is obtained by inserting (9) in (3). This yields

(10)

$$u(t,x) = \frac{1}{4\pi} \sum_{\pm} \int_{-\infty}^{\infty} dk \int_{-\infty}^{\infty} d\sigma \left[\lambda u_0(\sigma;\lambda) \pm \frac{i}{h_0(k)} u_1(\sigma;\lambda) \right] e^{i\lambda[k(x-\sigma) \pm h_0 t]} \ .$$

The solution of the initial value problem for the inhomogeneous equation can be reduced to the solution of (1, 2) and the solution of the problem for the inhomogeneous equation with zero initial data. Therefore we consider the problem,

$$c^2 u_{xx} - u_{tt} - \lambda^2 b^2 u = \lambda^2 f(t, x; \lambda) \tag{11}$$

$$u(t_1, x) = u_t(t_1, x) = 0 \ . \tag{12}$$

Here t_1 is a constant. In order to solve (11, 12) we set

$$u(t, x) = \int a(t, k)\, e^{i\lambda kx} dk; \quad f(t, x; \lambda) = \int \phi(t, k; \lambda)\, e^{i\lambda kx} dk \ . \tag{13}$$

Then (11) yields

$$a_{tt} + \lambda^2 h_0^2 a = -\lambda^2 \phi \ , \tag{14}$$

and from (12),

$$a(t_1, k) = a_t(t_1, k) = 0 \ . \tag{15}$$

To solve the initial value problem (14, 15) for the inhomogeneous linear ordinary differential equation (14) we apply the method of "variation of parameters" to the two linearly independent solutions $\exp\{\pm i\lambda h_0 t\}$ of the homogeneous equation; i.e. we set

$$a = v_1 e^{i\lambda h_0 t} + v_2 e^{-i\lambda h_0 t} \tag{16}$$

and insert (16) in (14). In so doing we require that

$$v_{1t} e^{i\lambda h_0 t} + v_{2t} e^{-i\lambda h_0 t} = 0 \tag{17}$$

and we obtain

$$i\lambda h_0 v_{1t} e^{i\lambda h_0 t} - i\lambda h_0 v_{2t} e^{-i\lambda h_0 t} = -\lambda^2 \phi \ . \tag{18}$$

(17) and (18) may now be solved for v_{1t} and v_{2t} and then integrated to obtain

$$(19)\quad v_1 = \frac{\lambda^2}{2i\lambda h_0}\int_{t_1}^{t} e^{-i\lambda h_0 s}\,\phi(s)\,ds;\quad v_2 = \frac{\lambda^2}{2i\lambda h_0}\int_{t_1}^{t} e^{i\lambda h_0 s}\,\phi(s)\,ds\ .$$

We now insert (19) in (16). This yields

$$(20)\qquad a = \sum \pm \frac{\lambda}{2ih_0}\int_{t_1}^{t} e^{\pm i\lambda h_0(t-s)}\,\phi(s,k;\lambda)\,ds\ ,$$

and it is easily seen that (15) is satisfied. By inverting the Fourier transform (13) we see that

$$(21)\qquad \phi(s,k;\lambda) = \frac{\lambda}{2\pi}\int f(s,y;\lambda)\,e^{-i\lambda ky}\,dy\ .$$

Then

$$(22)\qquad a = \sum \pm \frac{i\lambda^2}{4\pi h_0}\int_{-\infty}^{\infty} dy \int_{t_1}^{t} ds\, e^{i\lambda[-ky\pm(t-s)h_0]}\,f(s,y;\lambda)$$

and by inserting (22) in (13) we obtain the solution of (11, 12),

(23)

$$u(t,x;\lambda) = \sum \frac{\lambda^2}{4\pi i}\int_{-\infty}^{\infty} dk \int_{-\infty}^{\infty} dy \int_{t_1}^{t} ds\,\frac{f(s,y;\lambda)}{h}\,e^{i\lambda[k(x-y)-(t-s)h]}\ .$$

Here $h(k) = \pm h_0(k)$.

Appendix II. <u>The method of stationary phase in n dimensions.</u> In this appendix we derive a simple formula for the leading term of the asymptotic expansion (for $\lambda\to\infty$) of a function $f(\lambda)$ defined by a certain type of n-dimensional integral. The method we use is the method of <u>stationary phase</u>. Although numerous references for this method exist, the n-dimensional formula we require is not readily available. We will derive it by a method which is, if not entirely rigorous, relatively simple. Let

$$(1)\quad f(\lambda) = \int_D g(t_1,\dots,t_n)\,e^{i\lambda\phi(t_1,\dots,t_n)}\,dt_1\dots dt_n = \int_D g(T)\,e^{i\lambda\phi(T)}\,dT\ .$$

A stationary point is a point $T = S = (s_1, \ldots, s_n)$ for which the real-valued phase function $\phi(T)$ is stationary, i.e. $\phi_\nu(S) = \phi_{t_\nu}(S) = 0$; $\nu = 1, \ldots, n$. We assume that the domain of integration D in Euclidean n-space E^n contains exactly one stationary point, and that this point lies in the interior of D . (If D contains several stationary points it can be subdivided into sub-domains each containing one.) A Taylor expansion of $\phi(T)$ about the stationary point then yields

$$(2) \qquad \phi(T) = \phi(S) + \frac{1}{2}(t_\nu - s_\nu)(t_j - s_j)\phi_{\nu j} + 0\left[|T - S|^3\right] .$$

Here $\phi_{\nu j} = \phi_{t_\nu t_j}(S)$, and the summation convention with respect to repeated indices from 1 to n is employed.

We now introduce a translation and rotation of T-space so that the point T = S is the origin and the matrix $(\phi_{\nu j})$ is diagonal. Then

$$(3) \qquad \phi_{\nu j} = r_\nu \delta_{\nu j} .$$

Here $r_1, \ldots, r_n$ are the (real) eigenvalues of $(\phi_{\nu j})$. It is assumed that $(\phi_{\nu j})$ is non-singular. Hence no eigenvalues vanish. We now set $\gamma = \lambda^{-1/2}$ and introduce the transformation

$$(4) \qquad x_k = \gamma t_k .$$

Then

$$(5) \qquad \lambda(t_\nu - s_\nu)(t_j - s_j)\phi_{\nu j} = \gamma^2 t_\nu t_j r_\nu \delta_{\nu j} = x_\nu x_j r_\nu \delta_{\nu j} = x_\nu^2 r_\nu$$

and from (2)

$$\exp\left\{i\lambda\phi(T)\right\} = \exp\left\{i\lambda\phi(S) + \frac{i}{2}r_k x_k^2 + 0(\lambda^{-1/2})\right\} =$$

$$(6) \qquad \exp\left\{i\lambda\phi(s) + \frac{i}{2}r_k x_k^2\right\}\left[1 + 0(\lambda^{-1/2})\right] .$$

Furthermore g(T) has the expansion

$$(7) \qquad g(t) = g(S) + 0(\lambda^{-1/2}) = g(s)\left[1 + 0(\lambda^{-1/2})\right]$$

and

$$(8) \qquad \frac{dX}{dT} = \gamma^n = \lambda^{n/2}$$

We now insert (6), (7) and (8) in (1). This yields

(9) $$f(\lambda) \sim g(S)\, e^{i\lambda\phi(S)} f' \; ; \quad f' = \lambda^{-n/2} \int_{D'} e^{\frac{i}{2} r_k x_k^2}\, dX \; .$$

Here D' is the image of D under (4). We assume that a negligible error is introduced if we replace D' by the infinite X-space. Then

(10) $$f' \sim \lambda^{-n/2} \prod_{k=1}^{n} \int_{-\infty}^{\infty} e^{(i/2) r_k z^2}\, dz \; .$$

We now apply to (10) the standard integral formula

(11) $$\int_{-\infty}^{\infty} e^{i/2\, r z^2}\, dz = \left(\frac{2\pi}{|r|} \right)^{1/2} e^{i\pi/4 \,\mathrm{sgn}\, r} \; .$$

Here $\mathrm{sgn}\, r = \pm 1$ if $r \gtrless 0$. Then (9), (10), and (11) yield the required formula

(12) $$f(\lambda) \sim \left(\frac{2\pi}{\lambda} \right)^{n/2} \left[|\det(\phi_{\nu j})| \right]^{-1/2} g(S)\, e^{i\lambda\phi(S) + i\pi/4\, \mathrm{sig}(\phi_{\nu j})} \; ; \lambda \to \infty \; .$$

In (12), $\mathrm{sig}(\phi_{\nu j})$ denotes the "signature" of the matrix $(\phi_{\nu j})$ defined by

(13) $$\mathrm{sig}\, (\phi_{\nu j}) = \sum_{k=1}^{n} \mathrm{sgn}\, r_k \; ,$$

where $r_1, \ldots, r_n$ are the eigenvalues of $(\phi_{\nu j})$. We have also used the identity,

$$|\det(\phi_{\nu j})| = \left| \prod_{k=1}^{n} r_k \right| = \prod_{k=1}^{n} |r_k| \; .$$

We note that both $|\det(\phi_{\nu j})|$ and $\mathrm{sig}(\phi_{\nu j})$ are invariant under translation and rotation of the coordinate system, hence the result (12) is valid for the original coordinates.

REFERENCES

1. Keller, J. B. The Geometrical Theory of Diffraction, Proceedings of the Symposium on Microwave Optics, McGill University (1953), or J. Opt. Soc. Amer., 52, 116 (1962).

2. Lewis, R. M. and Keller, J. B., Asymptotic Methods for Partial Differential Equations: The Reduced Wave Equation and Maxwell's Equations, N.Y.U. Research Report No. EM-194, (1964).

3. Lewis, R. M., Asymptotic Expansion of Steady-state Solutions of Symmetric Hyperbolic Linear Differential Equations. J. Math. and Mech., 7, 593 (1958).

4. Lax, P. D., Asymptotic Solutions of Oscillatory Initial Value Problems, Duke Math. J., 24, 627 (1957).

5. Courant, R. and Hilbert, D., Methods of Mathematical Physics, Vol. II, Interscience Publishers (1962).

6. Whitham, G. B., Group Velocity and Energy Propagation for Three Dimensional Waves, Comm. Pure Appl. Math. 14, 675 (1961).

7. Budden, K. G., Radio Waves in the Ionosphere, Cambridge Univ. Press (1961).

8. Landau, L. D. and Lipshitz, E. M., Electrodynamics of Continuous Media, Pergamon Press (1960).

9. Kay, I. and Keller, J. B., Asymptotic Evaluation of the Field at a Caustic, J. Appl. Phys., 25, 876 (1954).

The research reported in this paper has been sponsored by the Air Force Cambridge Research Laboratories, Office of Aerospace Research, under Contract No. AF 19(628) 3868. Reproduction in whole or in part is permitted for any purpose of the United States Government.

ROBERT W. McKELVEY

Asymptotic Solutions and Indefinite Boundary Value Problems

§1. In this lecture I wish to examine several differential boundary value problems, all of them in a certain sense self-adjoint relative to an indefinite inner product. I shall begin by describing briefly the salient features revealed in each case by asymptotic studies. Then I shall describe an abstract vector space setting for the problems, providing an explanation for their common properties. I shall also show the significance in the abstract setting of certain individual features which are observed. Finally I shall point out phenomena, seen in the special cases, which are as yet unexplained by any general theory.

§2. Our point of departure is an article [1] by R. E. Langer, which appeared in the Transactions of the American Mathematical Society in January 1929. In it Professor Langer undertook an analysis of a certain differential boundary value problem of the Sturm-Liouville type

$$(1) \qquad -u'' + r(t)u = \lambda\sigma(t)u\ ; \qquad U_1(u) = U_2(u) = 0\ ,$$

on a finite interval $\alpha \leq t \leq \beta$. The principal point of interest is the function $\sigma(t)$, which is assumed to vanish within the interval. Thus the problem is one involving a turning point.

In our considerations we shall assume that the functions $r(t)$ and $\sigma(t)$ are real and continuous on $\alpha \leq t \leq \beta$. The eigenvalue parameter λ is complex and unrestricted. $U_1(u)$ and $U_2(u)$ are a pair of two point boundary conditions applied at α and β and relative to which the differential equation is formally self-adjoint.

Let us note some characteristics of a boundary-value problem of type (1). In general, despite the formal self-adjointness of the problem, it can have some non-real eigenvalues. Eigenvectors corresponding to distinct eigenvalues will be orthogonal with respect to the indefinite weight function $\sigma(t)$:

$$\int_\alpha^\beta u_n(t)\bar{u}_m(t)\sigma(t)\,dt = 0 \qquad (\lambda_n \neq \lambda_m),$$

while the corresponding quadratic expression

$$(2) \qquad \int_\alpha^\beta |u_n(t)|^2 \sigma(t)\,dt$$

may be of either sign or may vanish. However, under a certain special assumption of "definiteness", the eigenvalues are all real and the expression (2) is non-vanishing [2]. In this case, the eigenfunction series for an integrable function $f(t)$ is

$$\Sigma c_n u_n(t), \quad \text{where } c_n = \frac{\int_\alpha^\beta f(\tau)\bar{u}_n(\tau)\sigma(\tau)\,d\tau}{\int_\alpha^\beta |u_n(\tau)|^2 \sigma(\tau)\,d\tau}.$$

Taking account of the symmetrizability of the problem, one may in this definite case prove convergence to $f(t)$ of the series [3]. One assumes, e.g. that $f(t) \in C^2$ and satisfies the boundary conditions.

Langer's approach was to select for detailed analysis a specific boundary problem of type (1), namely

$$(3) \qquad -u'' = \lambda t^s u; \qquad u(\alpha) = u(\beta) = 0 \qquad (\alpha < 0 < \beta;\ s \geq 0).$$

In particular, when s is an odd integer the function $\sigma(t) = t^s$ is real, and changes sign across the origin. The differential equation in (3) is explicitly solvable, in terms of Bessel functions, and this fact makes possible a detailed analysis unavailable in the generality of (1). Employing techniques which have since become widely familiar, Langer was able to obtain asymptotic formulas for the eigenvalues and eigenfunctions of the problem, and to give criteria for the convergence to $f(t)$ of its eigenfunction series. The results obtained are of course specifically for equation (3) but, as we know from Langer's later work [4], this equation is entirely representative of a wide class of equations (1) with the same turning point structure as (3). Only in exceptional cases are such boundary problems definite.

Langer's formulas show that the eigenvalues of (3) are asymptotically distributed at points

$$(4a) \qquad \lambda_{1,m} k^2 \beta^{-2k}[(m-1/4)^2\pi^2 + c] + O(m^{-2})$$

and

$$(4b) \qquad \lambda_{2,m} = -k^2|\alpha|^{-2k}[(m-1/4)^2\pi^2 + c] + O(m^{-2})$$

where $k = (s+2)/2$, $c = \Gamma(1/2k + 3/2) / \Gamma(1/2k - 1/2)$ and m takes on large positive integral values.

The eigenfunctions corresponding to the large positive eigenvalues have the asymptotic form

$$(5) \qquad U_{1,m}(t) = \begin{cases} t^{-s/4}[\sin(\rho_m t^k + \frac{\pi}{4}) + \frac{O(1)}{\rho_m t^k}], & (t > 0,\ \rho_m t^k \geq N), \\ \rho^{(k+1)/2k} O(1), & (\rho_m |t|^k \leq N), \\ |t|^{-s/4} e^{-\rho_m |t|^k} O(1), & (t < 0,\ \rho_m |t|^k \geq N), \end{cases}$$

where $\rho_m = \lambda_{1,m}^{1/2}$ and N is a sufficiently large fixed positive number. The eigenfunctions corresponding to the negative eigenvalues are given by a similar formula, but with the sense of the interval reversed: that is, the eigenfunctions are oscillatory to the left of the origin, and exponentially damped to the right.

This remarkable behavior of the eigenfunctions has no counterpart in classical Sturm-Liouville theory (where $\sigma(t) > 0$), but seems to be typical for turning point problems. For example one knows, by another later study of Langer's [5], the asymptotic behavior of solutions of the differential equation in (1) whenever $\sigma(x)$ has two simple zeros in the interval $\alpha < t < \beta$: there then exists an asymptotic solution of the equation which is oscillatory between the zeros and is exponentially damped outside this subinterval. A second solution is oscillatory outside and exponentially damped between the zeros. If one imposes vanishing boundary conditions on the differential equation and calculates the asymptotic eigenvalues, one finds that these now form <u>three</u> sequences, associated with the three subintervals of $[\alpha, \beta]$. The eigenvalues are asymptotically real, and have the same sign as has $\sigma(t)$ on the associated subinterval. (For details, see [6]).

In 1956 there appeared in the Pacific Journal an article [7] by B. Friedman and L. I. Mishoe investigating the boundary value problem

$$(6) \qquad -u'' + r(t)u = \lambda[iu' + q(t)u]; \qquad u(0) = u(1) = 0 \quad .$$

I have written their equation in a form which emphasizes its formal self-adjointness whenever $r(t)$ and $q(t)$ are real. Virtually the same remarks made about the system (1) - existence of non-real eigenvalues, etc. - apply here also. The orthogonality relation is now

$$\int [iu'_n + q(t)u_n]\bar{u}_m \, dt = 0 \qquad (\lambda_n \neq \lambda_m)$$

and the corresponding quadratic expression for $n = m$ is real-valued but, as before, may be of either sign or may vanish. Note that by (6) the orthogonality relation may also be written

$$\int [-u''_n + r(t)u_n]\bar{u}_m \, dt = 0 \ .$$

The differential equation in (6) involves no turning points hence its asymptotic solutions are classically known. Using these, Friedman and Mishoe showed that the eigenvalues of the problem are asymptotically real and uniformly distributed on positive and negative axes. The corresponding eigenvectors are oscillatory on $0 \leq t \leq 1$ and

$$\int_0^1 [iu'_n + q(t)u_n]\bar{u}_m \, dt \neq 0 \qquad (\text{large } |\lambda_n|).$$

The most interesting feature here is the behavior of the eigenfunction expansion. For the boundary problem (3), Langer had shown that the eigenfunction expansion[1] of a function $f(t)$ of bounded variation converges pointwise to $f(t)$ at each interior point of the interval[2]. This is, of course, in accord with classical results, e.g. for Fourier series. Friedman and Mishoe found by contrast that the corresponding series for boundary problem (6) converges, but not in general to $f(t)$. Its pointwise sum within the interval is

$$(7) \qquad f(t) - 1/2[f(0) + f(1)\exp -i\int_0^1 q(\tau)\,d\tau]\exp i\int_0^t q(\tau)\,d\tau \ .$$

---

[1] Defined in general by the residues of the Green's function for the boundary problem.

[2] I am assuming the normalization $f(t) = 1/2[f(t-0) + f(t+0)]$ for $\alpha < t < \beta$ and $f(\alpha) = f(\alpha + 0)$, $f(\beta) = f(\beta - 0)$.

Thus the series represents $f(t)$ iff[3] that function satisfies the boundary condition

$$(8) \qquad f(0) + f(1)\exp -i\int_0^1 q(\tau)\,d\tau = 0 \ .$$

Note that the function

$$\exp i\int_0^t q(\tau)\,d\tau$$

is one which causes the right side of equation (6) to vanish, but which satisfies neither the original boundary conditions nor condition (8).

A similar behavior can be expected of more general boundary problems, for example,

$$-u'' + r(t)u = i\lambda[2\sigma(t)u' + \sigma'(t)u]; \qquad u(\alpha) = u(\beta) = 0 \ ,$$

which is formally self-adjoint when $r(t)$ and $\sigma(t)$ are real. If $\sigma(t)$ changes sign, the equation involves a turning point, so that a variety of asymptotic forms are possible. I have examined the special case where

$$\sigma(t) = t^{k-1} \quad (k \geq 1), \qquad r(t) \equiv 0 , \qquad \alpha < 0 < \beta ,$$

which is closely related to Langer's boundary problem (3). It turns out in this case [8] that the eigenfunction series for $f(t)$ converges in (α, β) to

$$f(t) - \frac{1}{2} f(\beta)\cdot\left|\frac{\beta}{t}\right|^{\frac{k-1}{2}} - \frac{1}{2}\left|\sin\frac{k\pi}{2}\right|\cdot\sin\frac{\pi}{2k}\cdot f(\alpha)\cdot\left|\frac{\alpha}{t}\right|^{\frac{k-1}{2}}$$

when $t > 0$ and to

$$f(t) - \frac{1}{2}\left|\sin\frac{k\pi}{2}\right|\cdot\sin\frac{\pi}{2k}\cdot f(\beta)\cdot\left|\frac{\beta}{t}\right|^{\frac{k-1}{2}} - \frac{1}{2} f(\alpha)\cdot\left|\frac{\alpha}{t}\right|^{\frac{k-1}{2}}$$

when $t < 0$. Thus when $k > 1$ the series converges to $f(t)$ iff that function satisfies the boundary conditions

[3] In this chapter the symbol "iff" is used as an abbreviation for the phrase "if and only if".

$$f(\alpha) = f(\beta) = 0 .$$

§3. The natural setting for treating boundary value problems of the types I have described is a vector space with an indefinite inner product. Such spaces, without special assumptions of semifiniteness, were first investigated by R. Nevanlinna [9], and it seems appropriate to affix to them his name. More recently, the geometry of these spaces has been studied by E. Scheibe [19]. (See also [20].)

By a Nevanlinna space $\mathfrak{n}$ we shall understand a complex vector space V with a topology $\mathfrak{T}$ and inner product $[x, y]$ such that:

1) The topology $\mathfrak{T}$ is given by any member of a family of equivalent quadratic norms. Thus typically $\|x\|^2 = (x, x)$ where (x, y) is a positive-definite inner product on V.

2) V is complete in $\mathfrak{T}$; that is, V is a Hilbert space $\mathfrak{H}$ relative to (x, y).

3) $[x, y]$ is a symmetric bilinear form on V representable by $[x, y] = (Jx, y)$ where J is a bounded self-adjoint operator having bounded inverse on $\mathfrak{H}$. This inner product $[x, y]$ is in general indefinite, i.e. the (real) quantity $[x, x]$ can be positive, negative or zero.

By a Nevanlinna subspace (or simply subspace) will be meant a closed linear manifold of $\mathfrak{n}$ which is itself a Nevanlinna space under the topology and inner product inherited from $\mathfrak{n}$.

All topological or metrical properties of $\mathfrak{n}$ are to be taken as usual relative to the norm $\|x\|$: such notions as e.g. the closedness of a manifold or the boundedness of an operator.

On the other hand, those notions which derive from inner product are taken relative to the indefinite $[x, y]$. So, for instance, the orthogonal complement $M^{\perp}$ of a manifold M is the closed manifold consisting of those vectors y such that $[x, y] = 0$ for all $x \in M$.

In contrast to the situation in a definite space, a closed manifold M may be degenerate relative to the inner product, i.e. the intersection $M \cap M^{\perp}$ may contain non-zero vectors - vectors which are at the same time in M and orthogonal to it. On the other hand, $M^{\perp\perp} = M$ still holds for closed M. Consequently M is degenerate iff $M^{\perp}$ is. Because of the assumption above that J^{-1} exists, the space itself is non-degenerate and so too is any subspace.

Also defined relative to the indefinite inner product is the notion of the adjoint of an operator. In particular, an operator A defined on $\mathfrak{n}$ is self-adjoint iff $[Ax, y] = [x, Ay]$ holds for all $x, y \in \mathfrak{n}$. An operator of particular importance is an orthogonal projector P which 1) is self-adjoint on $\mathfrak{n}$ and 2) satisfies $P^2 = P$. An orthogonal projector is automatically bounded. Its range and null space are orthogonal complements and their direct sum is $\mathfrak{h}$. Indeed:

Theorem. For a (closed) linear manifold M these are equivalent:

1) M is the range of an orthogonal projector
2) $\mathfrak{h} = M + M^{\perp}$ (automatically a direct sum)
3) M is a Nevanlinna subspace.

We note the corollary that a closed manifold M is a subspace iff $M^{\perp}$ is.

Among the decompositions of $\mathfrak{h} = \mathfrak{h}^{+} \dot{+} \mathfrak{h}^{-}$ as an orthogonal direct sum are in particular those where the inner product is positive definite on $\mathfrak{h}^{+}$ and negative definite on $\mathfrak{h}^{-}$. We shall call such a decomposition a primary decomposition, and the corresponding orthogonal projectors a pair of primary projectors.

Returning to the operator J acting in $\mathcal{H}$, let E_t be its resolution of the identity and set

$$E^{-} = \int_{-\infty}^{0} dE_t \;, \qquad E^{+} = \int_{0}^{\infty} dE_t \;.$$

Then E^{+} and E^{-} are a pair of primary projectors. Conversely every pair of primary projectors has this representation relative to a suitable quadratic norm.

The numbers $\delta^{-} = \dim \mathfrak{h}^{-}$ and $\delta^{+} = \dim \mathfrak{h}^{+}$ are independent of the particular primary decomposition, and are characteristic of the space $\mathfrak{h}$. They are called the negative and positive signatures of the space. A space having at least one signature finite is called a Pontryagin space: such spaces have been extensively studied by the Russian school, beginning with Pontryagin himself. (A survey article by Iokvidov and Krein [10] may be found in the AMS Translation series.) If one of the signatures is zero then of course the space reduces to ordinary Hilbert space.

In any orthogonal decomposition $\mathfrak{h} = \mathfrak{h}_1 \dot{+} \mathfrak{h}_2$ we have $\delta^{\pm} = \delta_1^{\pm} + \delta_2^{\pm}$. In particular, subspaces of a Pontryagin space are themselves Pontryagin spaces.

We note that Pontryagin space is in many ways simpler to handle than general Nevanlinna space. For example, in Pontryagin space any non-degenerate closed manifold is automatically a subspace.

As is usual, the span $\vee M_n$ of a collection $\{M_n\}$ of closed manifolds is defined as the smallest closed manifold containing all of them. Since the usual complementation formulas hold between span and intersection one finds that $\vee M_n$ is a subspace iff $\cap (M_n^{\perp})$ is.

Suppose now that $\{M_n\}$ is a sequence of mutually orthogonal subspaces of $\mathfrak{h}$, with $\{P_n\}$ the corresponding orthogonal projectors. We shall say that $M = \vee M_n$ is the Cartesian sum of $\{M_n\}$ whenever

a) M is a subspace and

b) Every $x \in M$ is given by $x = \Sigma P_n x$, the series being convergent unconditionally in the topology on $\mathfrak{h}$.

Let us note that neither (a) nor (b) holds automatically, even when $\mathfrak{h}$ is a Pontryagin space. However, in some circumstances (a) implies (b): this is true if M is a Pontryagin subspace, and in particular when M is a Hilbert subspace, of Nevanlinna space $\mathfrak{h}$.

I intend to give elsewhere a more detailed account of the theory of orthogonal projectors and Cartesian sums.

Turning from the geometry of space, we now examine briefly linear operator theory. The spectral theory for self-adjoint operators in Pontryagin space has reached a highly perfected state in [10], in the paper [11] by Aronszajn, and in the recently announced work [12] of M. G. Krein and Heinz Langer.

Let A be self-adjoint in Π, where $\delta = \min(\delta^+, \delta^-)$ is finite. Then A may have non-real points in its spectrum: isolated eigenvalues placed symmetrically about the real axis. But the total dimension of the root manifolds corresponding to eigenvalues in either upper or lower half-plane is $\leq \delta$. Root manifolds for either real or complex eigenvalues may contain Jordan chains of length greater than one, but the total length of any chain cannot exceed $2\delta + 1$, and the total number of such chains from all sources cannot exceed 2δ. By considering separately the chains of various types one may in fact give much more precise estimates.

The root manifold corresponding to an isolated real point of the spectrum is a subspace, in fact a reducing subspace for A. The span of the root manifolds corresponding to a pair of conjugate complex eigenvalues is likewise a reducing subspace, although each root manifold taken alone is totally degenerate in the inner product.

We turn to the question of the total reduction of A. For simplicity assume that A is completely continuous with countably many eigenvalues tending to zero. With each non-zero real eigenvalue γ_n (or conjugate complex pair $\gamma_n, \overline{\gamma}_n$) we associate the corresponding root manifold (or span of manifolds) M_n and the orthogonal P_n onto M_n. Then $\{M_n\}$ are mutually orthogonal and their span $M = \vee M_n$ is precisely the orthogonal complement of M_0, the root manifold corresponding to $\gamma = 0$. M is the Cartesian sum of $\{M_n\}$ iff M_0 is non-degenerate, and in this case only is the eigenfunction series $\sum_0^\infty P_n x$ unconditionally convergent to x.

§4. Our task is now to place the differential problems in the abstract setting. The procedure outlined in this paragraph is only a variant of one in common use for positive definite elliptic partial differential boundary value problems. (See [11], [13], [14]).

Let

$$\mathring{A}u = (-1)^{\nu}[p(t)u^{[\nu]}]^{[\nu]} + r_{2\nu-1}(t)u^{[2\nu-1]} + \ldots + r_0(t)u \quad ,$$

and

$$\mathring{B}u = q_{\mu}(t)u^{[\mu]} + q_{\mu-1}(t)u^{[\mu-1]} + \ldots + q_0(t)u\,, \quad (\mu \leq \nu) \quad ,$$

be formal differential operators on $\alpha \leq t \leq \beta$. We shall suppose that $q_\kappa(t)$ and $r_\kappa(t)$ belong to C^κ and that $p(t) > 0$ and $q(t) \neq 0$. The boundary value problem is

$$(9) \qquad \mathring{A}u = \lambda \mathring{B}u \quad ; \qquad U_1(u) = .. = U_{2\nu}(u) = 0$$

where U_κ are linear two-point boundary conditions involving derivatives up to order $2\nu-1$. A basic assumption is that both $\mathring{A}$ and $\mathring{B}$ are formally self-adjoint with respect to the boundary conditions, i.e. that

$$\int_\alpha^\beta \mathring{A}u\cdot \bar{v}dt = \int_\alpha^\beta u\cdot \overline{\mathring{A}v}\, dt \quad ; \qquad \int_\alpha^\beta \mathring{B}u\, \bar{v}dt = \int_\alpha^\beta u\cdot \overline{\mathring{B}v}\, dt$$

when $u, v \in C^{2\nu}$ and satisfy the boundary conditions.

The formal operator $\mathring{A}$ may be realized as a self-adjoint operator A in $\mathfrak{L}_2$. Let $D^{2\nu}$ be the manifold of functions $u(t)$ with $2\nu-1$ absolutely continuous derivatives and $u^{[2\nu]} \in \mathfrak{L}_2$. Then D_A consists of the functions of $D^{2\nu}$ which satisfy the 2ν boundary conditions of (9). By the dominance of its leading term, A is semibounded below, with spectrum consisting of discrete eigenvalues $\theta_0 \leq \theta_1 \leq \ldots$. The first few of these may be negative, but we assume that none is zero. (This last can usually be achieved by adding a small multiple of $\mathring{B}u$ to both sides of equation (9).)

Utilizing the semiboundedness of A, we may realize the differential boundary problem as a spectral problem in a Pontryagin space. One takes as indefinite inner product the expression

$$[u, v] = \int_\alpha^\beta Au\cdot \bar{v}dt \quad ,$$

defined at first on D_A but then extended to a complete space Π.

The appropriate vector space is $V = D(|A|^{\frac{1}{2}})$ with quadratic norm $\int ||A|^{\frac{1}{2}}u|^2 dt$. As is known (see [14], [15]), V consists of the functions of class D^ν which satisfy the stable boundary conditions of order up to $\nu-1$ which are implied by the boundary conditions of (9). An equivalent quadratic norm on V is

$$\|u\|^2 = \sum_{\kappa=0}^{\nu} \int_\alpha^\beta |u^{[\kappa]}|^2 dt .$$

The space Π obtained in this way is indeed a Pontryagin space; its negative signature is the sum of the dimensions of the eigenspaces belonging to negative eigenvalues of A. In case all eigenvalues of A are positive, the space is an ordinary Hilbert space - this is the case of definiteness of §1.

The formal operator $\overset{\circ}{B}$ is now realized as an operator B in $\mathcal{L}_2$ by setting $D_B = V$. So defined, B is a symmetric operator, in the technical Hilbert space sense, and is closed iff $\mu = \nu$.

The boundary value problem (9) is realized in Π as the spectral problem for $H = A^{-1}B$. This operator has the integral representation

$$Hu = \int_\alpha^\beta G(t,\tau)Bu(\tau)\,d\tau = \int_\alpha^\beta \{B_\tau G(t,\tau)\}\; u(\tau)\,d\tau \;,$$

where G is the Green's function for the operator A. Hence H is a completely continuous self-adjoint operator in Π. Its non-zero eigenvalues γ_n are the reciprocals of those of (9), and the corresponding root spaces coincide with those of (9). The expansion $\Sigma P_n x$ in spectral projections is identical with the eigenfunction series for a function $x(t)$ in V.

The question arises as to the unconditional convergence of this eigenfunction series and, by the general theory, is settled through an examination of the root space M_0 of H. We note that the null space of H coincides with that of B. Hence when B is one-to-one, then $M_0 = \{0\}$ and is a fortiori a subspace. This happens to be the case in both the boundary-value problem of Langer and that of Friedman-Mishoe. Hence in both these cases the eigenfunction series of $f(t) \in V$ converges to f in the topology of Π - and so also uniformly.

In other cases M_0 can actually be degenerate for a differential boundary value problem - even for one of second order. This possibility was first recognized by N. Aronszajn. (Private communication). In Appendix A we analyze some circumstances in which M_0 may degenerate, and we give an example.

§5. The construction in Pontryagin space goes far to explain the similarities observed in the examples of §1. The theory is general: its results are quite independent of special characteristics of a problem, as for example turning point structure.

Nevertheless, it seems that these special features really do derive from the indefinite character of the problems, and they re-emerge when one takes into account not only the indefiniteness of $\int Au\cdot\bar{u}dt$ but also the indefiniteness of $\int Bu\cdot\bar{u}dt$.

As the first illustration of this remark let us examine again the Sturm-Liouville equation (1), with turning points, and in particular Langer's equation (3). Let $\mathcal{L}_2(|\sigma|)$ denote the space of functions complete in the quadratic norm

$$\|u\|^2 = \int_\alpha^\beta |u(t)|^2 \cdot |\sigma(t)|dt \quad .$$

This space becomes a Nevanlinna space $\mathfrak{h}_\sigma$ when one introduces the inner product

$$[u, v] = \int_\alpha^\beta u(t)\bar{v}(t)\sigma(t)dt \quad ;$$

however, both signatures of $\mathfrak{h}_\sigma$ are infinite.

The eigenspaces M_n of the boundary problem (9) remain orthogonal as subspaces of $\mathfrak{h}_\sigma$; their span is all of $\mathfrak{h}_\sigma$.

Our principal assertion is:

Theorem: For the boundary problem (3), $\mathfrak{h}_\sigma$ is the Cartesian sum of $\{M_n\}$. Thus the eigenfunction expansion of a function in $\mathcal{L}_2(|\sigma|)$ converges in norm unconditionally to that function.

To prove this proposition, we examine the closed manifolds in $\mathfrak{h}_\sigma$

$$M^+ = \vee M_{1,m} \, , \quad M^- = \vee M_{2,m}$$

which correspond to the asymptotic sequences $\{\lambda_{1,m}\}$ and $\{\lambda_{2,m}\}$ of eigenvalues (4). Evidently $\pm[x,x] \geq 0$ on $M^\pm$. The theorem is proved by showing that M^+ and M^- are Hilbert subspaces of $\mathfrak{h}_\sigma$. But M^+ is a Hilbert subspace iff

$$\text{(10)} \qquad \sup \frac{\Sigma\Sigma c_n \bar{c}_m \int_\alpha^0 u_{1,n}(t)\overline{u_{1,m}(t)}\,|\sigma(t)|\,dt}{\Sigma |c_k|^2 \int_\alpha^\beta |u_{1,k}(t)|^2 \sigma(t)\,dt} < \infty ,$$

the supremum being taken over all finite sequences $c_1, c_2, \ldots$; a similar expression applies to M^-. (See Appendix B).

The condition (10) is a very stringent one. It is satisfied in the present circumstances by virtue of the estimates, based on (5), that

$$\text{(11)} \qquad \begin{aligned} &\int_0^\beta |u_{1,m}(t)|^2 \sigma(t)\,dt = \frac{1}{2}\beta^k + \frac{O(1)}{\rho_m} \\ &\int_\alpha^0 u_{1,n}(t)\bar{u}_{1,m}(t)\sigma(t)\,dt = \frac{O(1)}{\rho_n}\left[\frac{\rho_m}{\rho_n}\right]^{\frac{k-1}{2k}} , \quad m \le n , \end{aligned}$$

These formulas again reflect the concentration of the eigenfunctions on one side of the turning point, so that we may look upon the theorem as still another manifestation of this remarkable circumstance.

For further details we refer to Appendix B.

Evidently the above procedure may be applied to a study of other boundary value problems. The key step is the formation of a Nevanlinna space with indefinite inner product $\int Bu \cdot \bar{u}\,dt$. When B is self-adjoint and has trivial null space, one takes as v the manifold $D_{|B|^{\frac{1}{2}}}$ with quadratic norm $\int \| |B|^{\frac{1}{2}} u|^2\,dt$. When B is symmetric without being self-adjoint, but is semibounded below, one bases the construction on the Friedrichs' extension B_F of B. By a special property of the Friedrichs' extension, D_B is dense in the Nevanlinna space so obtained.

For example, if A is a fourth order operator with boundary conditions $u(\alpha) = u'(\alpha) = u(\beta) = u'(\beta) = 0$ and if B is the second order operator

$$Bu = -u'' + q(t)u \qquad (q(t) \ge q_0 > 0) ,$$

then D_B will consist of the functions of class D^2 which satisfy these four boundary conditions. B^* is given by the same expression but $D_{B^*} = D^2$, i.e. no boundary conditions are imposed. Applying the construction described above we find that

$$V = \{u: u \in D^1, \quad u(\alpha) = u(\beta) = 0\}$$

Let u_1 and u_2 be the null vectors of B^* determined by

$$u_1(\alpha) = 1, \quad u_1'(\alpha) = 0, \quad u_2(\alpha) = 0, \quad u_2'(\alpha) = 1$$

Then any function $f \in D^1$ has a unique representation

$$f = f_0 + c_1u_1 + c_2u_2 \qquad \text{with } f_0 \in V,$$

and in fact the coefficients c_1 and c_2 are given by

$$c_1 = f(\alpha), \qquad c_2 = f'(\alpha) \quad .$$

It would seem that the phenomena observed by Friedman-Mishoe should have a similar explanation, with the space V begin delimited by the single boundary condition (8). The difficulty in verifying this arises from the fact that the operator B in (6) is not semi-bounded, and therefore the theories of Friedrichs and Krein no longer can be applied.

§6. Of various open questions, I shall point out only two. First, we have insisted throughout the discussion that the boundary value problem be self-adjoint. But the asymptotic methods assure us that this should not be necessary: if for example in (1) or (6) the functions $r(t)$ and $q(t)$ are non-real, the asymptotic formulas will be unchanged in their dominant terms, the eigenvalues will remain asymptotically real and the eigenfunction expansion will still converge. These considerations suggest that the perturbation methods developed by J. Schwartz and others [17, 18] might be applicable here to refer the mildly non-self-adjoint cases back to the self-adjoint ones which we have been describing. An interesting feature of these perturbation methods is that while they are "abstract" in character, still they rely for application upon special knowledge of the asymptotic structure of the problems in question - e.g. one needs to know the asymptotic distribution of eigenvalues.

Our second remark is in connection once more with the turning point problem of Langer. In his development Langer found no added difficulty in carrying through the calculations for $\sigma(t) = t^s$ with <u>any</u> positive exponent, not merely with s an integer. In the general case the problem probably cannot be thought of as "self-adjoint":

specifically, the eigenvalues are asymptotically distributed along two rays emanating at some angle from the origin. It would seem that a general approach must handle an inner product $[x, x]$ which is not only indefinite but is even non-real. To my knowledge, the necessary theory still awaits discovery.

Appendix A. Degeneracy of M_0. We have seen that $M_0 = \{0\}$, whenever $N_B = \{0\}$. Let us now suppose that $N_B \neq \{0\}$, and that $x_1, \dots x_n$ is a maximal chain in M_0:

$$Hx_1 = 0, \qquad Hx_2 = x_1, \dots, \qquad Hx_n = x_{n-1}, \qquad x_n \notin R_H .$$

we note that since $H = A^{-1}B$ therefore $Ax_1, \dots Ax_{n-1}$ belong to R_B, and so are orthogonal in $\mathcal{L}_2$ to N_{B*}. In particular,

$$[x_j, x_1] = \int Ax_j \cdot \bar{x}_1 dt = 0 \qquad (j = 1, 2, \dots n-1).$$

Hence necessary and sufficient for degeneracy of the inner product on the chain is the condition that $[x_n, x_1] = 0$.

Since the chain is maximal ($x_n \notin R_H$) we have either:

I. $\qquad x_n \notin D_A$

or

II. $\qquad x_n \in D_A \quad$ but $\quad Ax_n \notin R_B$.

Note that case I would normally not be considered in a study of the concrete boundary problem (9). When $\mu = \nu$ (so that B has a closed range), case II is equivalent to:

II'. $\qquad x_n \in D_A$; Ax_n is not orthogonal in $\mathcal{L}_2$ to N_{B*}.

We may therefore conclude that: <u>When $\mu = \nu$ and $N_{B*} = N_B = \{x_1\}$ then degeneracy cannot occur for a type II chain</u>. In particular case II degeneracy is ruled out whenever B is a first order operator.

We now give an example of degeneracy arising from a type I chain.

Let $q(t)$ be continuous on $0 \leq t \leq 1$ with the following properties

a) $q'(t) \notin \mathcal{L}_2$,

b) $\int_0^1 q(\tau)\,d\tau = 2\pi$,

c) $\eta \equiv \int_0^1 q^2(\tau)\,d\tau \neq n^2\pi^2$ $(\eta = 1, 2, \ldots)$.

For the operator A we take

$$Au = -u'' - \eta u \;; \qquad u(0) = u(1), \quad u'(0) = u'(1).$$

By condition (c), zero is not an eigenvalue of A. V consists of functions of class D^1 which satisfy $u(0) = u(1)$, and the indefinite inner product on V is

$$[u, v] = \int_0^1 [u'(t)\overline{v}'(t) - \eta u(t)\overline{v}(t)]\,dt .$$

For the operator B we take

$$Bu = iu' + q(t)u, \qquad (D_B = V).$$

By condition (b), the equation $Bx_1 = 0$ has the solution in V

$$x_1(t) = \exp i \int_0^t q(\tau)\,d\tau \;;$$

however, by (a), $x_1(t) \notin D_A$. Hence M_0 consists of a single chain of length 1 :

$$Hx_1 = 0, \qquad x_1 \notin D_A .$$

Furthermore a calculation shows that $[x_1, x_1] = 0$ so that M_0 is degenerate.

Appendix B. The eigenfunction expansion in $\mathcal{L}_2(|\sigma|)$. We asserted above that M^+ is a Hilbert subspace iff (10) holds. In fact, for M^+ to be a subspace it is necessary and sufficient that the representation on M^+ of the indefinite inner product

$$[x, y] = (J_1 x, y), \quad x, y \in M^+ ,$$

shall involve an operator J_1 with bounded inverse. That is,

$$\inf_{x \in M'} \frac{[x, x]}{\|x\|^2} > 0 ,$$

where M' is a dense set in M^+.

Let $x = E^+x + E^-x$ be the primary decomposition

$$E^+x(t) = \begin{cases} x(t) & x > 0 \\ 0 & x < 0 \end{cases} ,$$

$$E^-x(t) = \begin{cases} 0 & x > 0 \\ x(t) & x < 0 \end{cases} .$$

Then $\|x\|^2 = [x, x] + 2(E^-x, x)$, $\|x\|^2/[x, x] = 1 + 2(E^-x, x)/[x, x]$, and the necessary and sufficient condition becomes

$$\sup_{x \in M'} \frac{(E^-x, x)}{[x, x]} < \infty .$$

If one now chooses as M' the finite linear combinations $x = \Sigma x_j u_{1,j}$, then, because of the orthogonality of the $\{u_{1,j}\}$, the condition takes the form (10).

The calculation of the estimates (11) from (5) is entirely straight-forward. One begins by decomposing

$$\int_\alpha^0 = \int_\alpha^{\xi_m} + \int_{\xi_m}^{\xi_n} + \int_{\xi_n}^0 ,$$

where ξ_n and ξ_m are such that

$$\rho_n |\xi_n|^k = N ; \quad \rho_m |\xi_m|^k = N .$$

One obtains for the three integrals the respective estimates

$$\frac{O(1)}{\rho_n} \left(\frac{\rho_m}{\rho_n}\right)^{\frac{k-1}{2k}} , \quad \frac{O(1)}{\rho_n^2} \left(\frac{\rho_m}{\rho_n}\right)^{\frac{k-1}{2k}} \left[e^{-N} - e^{-\frac{\rho_n}{\rho_m} N}\right], \quad \frac{O(1)}{\rho_m + \rho_n} e^{-\frac{\rho_n}{\rho_m} N} .$$

Thus the dominant contribution comes from the vicinity of the turning point. But this may reflect only the relative inprecision of the formulas for $u_{1,j}$ at that point.

The integral on $0 \leq t \leq \beta$ is handled similarly.

In order to deduce (10) from the estimates (11), we apply an inequality of I. Schur [16, p. 238] which asserts that

$$\frac{\sum_m \sum_n K_{nm} c_n \bar{c}_m}{\sum_j |c_j|^2} \leq \sup_n \sum_m |K_{nm}|$$

for any symmetric infinite matrix K. In the present case, with $n, m \geq n_0$,

$$\sum_m |K_{nm}| = \sum_m \left| \int_\alpha^0 u_{1,n}(t) \bar{u}_{1,m}(t) |\sigma(t)| dt \right.$$

$$= \frac{O(1)}{n^{1+(k-1)/2k}} \sum_{m=m_0}^{n} m^{\frac{k-1}{2k}} + n^{\frac{k-1}{2k}} O(1) \sum_{m=n+1}^{\infty} \frac{1}{m^{1+(k-1)/2k}} = O(1).$$

REFERENCES

1. R. E. Langer, The boundary problem associated with a differential equation in which the coefficient of the parameter changes sign. Trans. A. M. S. v 31 (1929) pp. 1-24.

2. E. L. Ince, Ordinary differential equations, Dover (1956).

3. W. T. Reid, A boundary value problem for the calculus of variations. Amer. J. of Math. v 54 (1932) pp. 769-790.

   ___________, Symmetrizable completely continuous transformations in Hilbert space. Duke J. Math v18 (1951) pp. 41-56.

4. R. E. Langer, On the asymptotic solutions of ordinary differential equations with an application to the Bessel functions of large order. Trans. A. M. S. v 33 (1931) pp. 23-64.

5. R. E. Langer, The asymptotic solutions of a linear differential equation of the second order with two turning points. Trans. A. M. S. v 90 (1959) pp. 113-142.

6. R. McKelvey, A boundary value problem involving an ordinary differential equation with two turning points. PEC Corp. Report, Boulder, Colo. (1960).

7. B. Friedman and L. I. Mishoe, Eigenfunction expansions associated with a non-self-adjoint differential equation. Pac. J. Math 6(1956) pp. 249-270.

8. R. McKelvey, A class of indefinite boundary value problems, PEC Corp. Report, Boulder, Colo. (1960).

9. R. Nevanlinna, Uber metrische lineare Räume II-V. Ann. Acad. Sci. Fennicae AI, 113 (1952), 115(1952), 163(1954), 222(1956).

10. I. S. Iokvidov and M. G. Krein, Spectral theory of operators in spaces with an indefinite metric, I. Trans. A. M. S. Ser. 2 v 13, pp. 105-175.

11. N. Aronszajn, Quadratic forms on vector spaces. Proc. International Symposium on Linear Spaces, Jerusalem (1960), Pergamon Press.

12. M. G. Krein and H. K. Langer, The spectral function of a self-adjoint operator in a space with indefinite metric. Soviet Math 4 (1963) pp. 1236-1239.

13. A. Pleijel, Eigenfunction distribution of certain indefinite differential problems. University of Kansas Technical Report I (1959).

14. K. T. Smith, Functional spaces, functional completion, and differential problems. Conference on Partial Differential Equations, Univ. of Kansas (1954) pp. 59-75.

15. M. Krein, The theory of self-adjoint extensions of semi-bounded Hermitian transformations and its applications II, Mat. Sboynik N. S. 21(63)(1947), pp. 365-404.

16. Angus Taylor, Introduction to Functional Analysis, Wiley, 1961.

17. J. Schwartz, Perturbations of spectral operators and applications I, Pacific J. Math. v 4 (1954) pp. 415-458.

18. Robert Turner, Perturbations of compact operators. N.Y.U. Thesis (1963).

19. E. Scheibe, Über Hermitische Formen in Topologichen Vecterräumen. Ann. Acad. Sci. Fenn. AI 294 (1960).

20. Yu P. Ginzberg, I. S. Iokividov, Investigations in the geometry of infinite dimensional spaces with a bilinear metric. Russian Math. Surveys v17 no. 4 (1962) (Translated by Lond. Math. Soc.)

C. C. LIN

Some Examples of Asymptotic Problems in Mathematical Physics

1. Introduction. In this paper, I propose to discuss a few problems in mathematical physics, where the theory of asymptotic solutions plays an important role. I wish especially to comment on those points where the solution of the problem is not yet entirely satisfactory in the hope that this might stimulate further mathematical investigations. It is in the nature of Applied Mathematics that one should be concerned not only with the application of existing mathematical theories and methods, but also with the stimulation of new mathematical problems through the study of interesting problems in science, and the attempts to solve these problems. In honor of Professor R. E. Langer, the problems selected for this discussion will especially be related to the theory of turning points in ordinary differential equations.

The physical problems that led to the asymptotic studies are the following:

1. motion in a stratified atmosphere,
2. instability of shear flows,
3. spiral structure of disc galaxies.

Before we proceed with these problems, let me first make a brief observation on the significance of asymptotic solutions: it is not only convenient for approximate calculations of details, but often it has fundamental physical significance. One of the most important classical cases is the asymptotic solution of the Schrödinger equation. The method yields the classical theory of mechanics in its first approximation. If we take Schrödinger's equation in the stationary form:

$$\nabla^2\psi + \lambda^2(E - V)\psi = 0\,, \tag{1}$$

where $\lambda = (2m)^{\frac{1}{2}}/\hbar$ is a large parameter, and attempt to solve it with the formal asymptotic expression

(2) $$\psi = \Phi \exp(i\lambda S), \quad \Phi = \Phi_0(\underline{x}) + \lambda^{-1}\Phi_1(\underline{x}) + \dots$$

we obtain

(3) $$(\nabla S)^2 + V(\underline{x}) = E$$

which is the well-known Hamilton-Jacobi partial differential equation (in the time-independent form). The classical theory has a meaning only in the domain where $E - V > 0$. There is then a "turning surface" defined by

(4) $$E - V(\underline{x}) = 0$$

where the particle must turn back, according to classical mechanics. The behavior of the solution near the "turning point" in the one-dimensional case is the well-known problem * that gives occasion to this conference, for Professor Langer developed the rigorous mathematical theory for it in 1931 and subsequent papers. The general three-dimensional problem is however not yet fully solved.

The problem just mentioned is associated with physical phenomena that occur at atomic dimensions of the order of 10^{-8} cm. and at a time scale of the order of 10^{15} sec. (period of oscillation of visible light). In the galactic problem to be discussed, the linear dimensions are of the order of 10^{22} cm. (about ten thousand light years), and the time scale is of the order of 10^{-15} sec. (about thirty million years). The other two problems occur at intermediate scales of length and time. Yet despite these differences and despite the fact that all these phenomena are quite different from one another, we are capable of using similar mathematical methods. This reassures our firm belief in the basic existence of harmony and order in the universe. To put it in more poetical terms: we believe that God is a mathematician.

2. Motion in a stratified atmosphere. Professor Langer also solved the problem involving two turning points (1935), as well as the problem involving a turning point where the coefficient function may also have a pole of the second order; thus,

---

* The formal method usually goes by the name of W-K-B method, as it was developed by Wentzel, Kramers, and Brillouin in 1926 for the solution of the quantum mechanical problem mentioned here. More recently, it has often been referred to as the WKBJ method in honor of the work of Harold Jeffreys (1923) in connection with a hydrodynamical problem prior to the discovery of Schrödinger's equation.

(5) $$\frac{d^2u}{dx^2} + [\lambda^2 P(x,\lambda) + x^{-2}Q(x,\lambda)]u = 0$$

where $P(z,\lambda)$ and $Q(z,\lambda)$ both have asymptotic expansions of the form

(6) $$P(x) = P_0(x) + \lambda^{-1} P_1(x) + \lambda^{-2} P_2(x) + \ldots$$

where $P_n(x)$ are continuous and may even be analytic, and $P_0(x)$, but not $Q_0(x)$, has a simple zero at $x = 0$. This problem arises in a recent study by Steven Rosencrans on the motion of a stratified atmosphere for the understanding of the problem of the heating of the solar corona. Indeed, two such turning points naturally occur in his problem.

The physical problem is roughly as follows. Although the local temperature near the solar surface may be as low as 4500 °K, and the "effective temperature" of the solar surface is about 5800 ° K, the kinetic temperature of the solar corona is of the order of one million degrees, at a distance of (say) two solar radii from the center.* The mechanism for the heating of the solar corona has been investigated by many astrophysicists. It is quite likely that the energy is propagated by gravity waves generated by the convective motion near the solar surface. This leads to the study of small disturbances in a stratified atmosphere which is partly stable and partly unstable. The mathematical problem mentioned above then arises. For further details, the reader is referred to the dissertation by Rosencrans (1964).

The mechanism for the heating of the solar corona is intimately connected with the ejection of solar plasma from the sun, which is then observed at the earth as the "solar wind".

3. Instability of shear flows. For the study of the basic mechanism of transition from laminar flow to turbulent flow (which occurs abundently in the atmosphere around us) one first considers the possible growth of small disturbances in a two-dimensional parallel flow through a channel, under the influence of a gradient of pressure. This problem has been studied by a number of mathematicians and

* The sun has a mass of 1.9866×10^{33} gm., and a linear diameter of 1.3914×10^6 km. Its "effective temperature" T_e is defined by means of the relation $L = 4\pi R^2 \sigma T^4$, where L is the observed total energy out put of the sun in ergs per second, R is its radius, and σ is the Stefan-Boltzmann constant, 5.672×10^{-5} erg/cm. deg. sec. The temperature at the center is calculated to be about 14 million degrees.

physicists, including Heisenberg (1924), Langer (1940), Lin (1945), Meksyn and Stuart (1951). The mathematical problems associated with it have been investigated by Wasow (1953), by Langer (1957) and by Lin and Rabenstein (1960). The problem associated with small disturbances is now essentially solved, and current studies are mainly concerned with the nonlinear effects. (See Benney and Lin, 1962). However, there are certain features in the method of solution which make it difficult to generalize the theory to other cases, e.g., the closely related problem of the stability of boundary layers in a compressible gas (Lees and Lin, 1946; Morawetz, 1954; Dunn and Lin, 1955). So far, this latter problem has only been treated by the older method of outer and inner expansions. I wish therefore to report on the current status of this type of problems, and to make some suggestions in the hope of stimulating further work in this direction.

The mathematical problem (in the incompressible case) is to deal with the asymptotic behavior of the solutions of the following differential equation of the fourth order when the absolute value of the parameter λ is large:

$$\frac{d^4\varphi}{dx^4} + \lambda^2 \left[P(x,\lambda) \frac{d^2\varphi}{dx^2} + Q(x,\lambda)\frac{d\varphi}{dx} + R(x,\lambda)\varphi \right] = 0 \tag{7}$$

where $P(x,\lambda)$, $Q(x,\lambda)$ and $R(x,\lambda)$ are generic symbols for functions with asymptotic expansions of the form (6). The initial term $P_o(x)$ has a simple zero at $x = 0$, but $Q_o(x)$, and $R_o(x)$ may or may not have a zero there. All the functions $P_n(x), \ldots$ $(n = 1, 2, \ldots)$ are at least continuous, and may even be analytic.

The heuristic approach to the problem divides itself into the following three steps:

(a) First, we look for outer solutions, which are asymptotically valid for finite values of x (not approaching zero). These may be found in the following forms

$$\phi = \phi^{(0)}(x) + \lambda^{-2}\phi^{(1)}(x) + \ldots \tag{8}$$

$$\phi = \{\exp(\pm\lambda S)\} \cdot \{f^{(0)}(x) + \lambda^{-1} f^{(1)}(x) + \ldots\}, \tag{9}$$

where

$$S(x) = \int_0^x \{P_o(x)\}^{\frac{1}{2}}\, dx = \frac{2}{3} z^{\frac{3}{2}} . \tag{10}$$

There are two solutions each of the forms (8) and (9). The variable z is introduced for convenience in the next step.

(b) Next, we look for four inner solutions of the form

$$\phi = \psi(\zeta, \epsilon) = \psi_o(\zeta) + \epsilon\psi_1(\zeta) + \dots \tag{11}$$

where

$$\epsilon = \lambda^{-\frac{2}{3}}, \qquad \zeta = z/\epsilon . \tag{12}$$

These solutions are expected to be asymptotically valid for finite values of ζ and small values of ϵ .

(c) Finally, we attempt to "join" or "identify" the outer and inner solutions by considering such large values of ζ that still correspond to small values of z, and assuming that both forms of the solution are valid. Apart from complications in practice, this procedure raises some questions in principle. Since the two types of solutions are originally established for strictly disjoint domains (finite z versus finite ζ), is it possible to extend their domains of asymptotic validity so that the heuristic process can be shown to be legitimate?

One therefore attempts to resolve the difficulty by using the method of comparison equations, in terms of whose solution one attempts to find a uniformly valid representation of the solution for a finite z-domain including the point $z = 0$. This is the method used by Langer in the case of the Schrödinger equation. In short, one tries to represent the solution of the given equation (7) in the form

$$\Phi = TU \tag{13}$$

where Φ is a fundamental solution matrix of the linear system corresponding to (7), and U is that for a simpler differential equation

$$\frac{dU}{dz} = A_o(z)U \tag{14}$$

which can be solved explicitly, and which (hopefully) contains the essentially characteristics of the equation (7). The matrix function $T(z,\lambda)$ has the asymptotic expansion

$$T(z,\lambda) = T_o(z) + \lambda^{-1}T_1(z) + \dots \tag{15}$$

The various authors differ mainly in the choice of the basic reference equation:

(16) Wasow: $$u^{iv} + \lambda^2(zu'' + \alpha u) = 0 ,$$

(17) Langer: $$u^{iv} + \lambda^2(zu'' + \alpha u') = 0 ,$$

(18) Lin and Rabenstein: $$u^{iv} + \lambda^2(zu'' + \alpha u' + \beta u) = 0 .$$

Langer actually used the third order equation

$$u''' + \lambda^2(zu' + \alpha u) = 0 ,$$

which yields, upon differentiation, the equation (17) with α replaced by $\alpha + 1$.

The choice of a third order equation is at least partly motivated by a desire to represent the solution in terms of those of simpler reference equations, so that one does not have to construct a new reference equation for each equation to be solved. Unfortunately, for the hydrodynamical problem at hand, where the reduced equation of the second order has indices 0 and 1, which differ by an integer, it was found necessary to use the more general form (18) to reproduce all the characteristics of the solutions. Even then it was found necessary to include fractional powers in the expansion (15), with the exact power dependent on the detailed form of (7) in an involved manner (Lin and Rabenstein, 1960). The reference equation (16) can yield adequate approximations to the lowest order, but it is difficult to formulate a general scheme for obtaining the higher approximations based on it.

There thus appears to be a need for the proliferation of basic reference systems of equations, each to be properly chosen for each equation given. This is of course extremely undesirable. Indeed, it has not yet been found possible to construct such a reference system for the sixth order system occurring in the stability equations for compressible flow (Lees and Lin, 1946). On the other hand, the original heuristic method depends only on the reference equations

(19) $$u^{iv} + \lambda^2 zu'' = 0 \quad \text{and} \quad u^{iv} + \lambda^2 zu'' = 1 ,$$

which are essentially the Airy equation and its inhomogeneous variation, the Lommel equation. If the heuristic procedure of joining the inner and outer solutions could be established in a rigorous manner (allowing for some possible extensions of the ideas), it would then be a far more desirable approach to the general theory.

We observe that the method initiated by Langer is a multiple-scale process, since functions of both z and ζ are simultaneously used in the same expression to represent the solution. Thus, it might be a natural step to develop the general theory from such an approach. This was especially suggested by David J. Benney in connection with all problems in hydrodynamic stability, as he found that other scales must also simultaneously enter in the nonlinear problems. Much work remains to be done.

4. Spiral structure of disc galaxies. The stars in the universe are grouped together into galaxies by their mutual gravitational attraction. Because of the large angular momentum of the system, most galaxies are in the form of a very flat disc. Figure 1 shows the side view of a version of the model of our galaxy, the Milky Way. (From Struve, 1962, p. 76.) It shows our sun at a distance of about 10,000 parsecs (about 30,000 light years) from the center, where there is a bulge caused by the random velocity of the stars. When the galaxy is viewed face-on, it shows a spiral structure. (Figure 2, from Struve, 1962, p. 36). This spiral structure is observed in many other disc galaxies, but its cause is still not well understood.

In trying to understand this spiral structure, Lin and Shu (1964) found it convenient to integrate the differential equations of stellar dynamics by means of an asymptotic process. In reality, the partial differential equations involved can be reduced to an ordinary integro-differential equation. The solution obtained so far has some characteristics similar to those associated with turning points, but the mathematical theory of the asymptotic solution is as yet unclear. In this short account, we shall merely outline the problem and some of the results. For further details, the reader is referred to the paper cited above.

Consider now our own galaxy in some detail. It consists of 200 billion stars with a total mass of about 4×10^{44} gm. The linear dimension is of the order of 3×10^{22} cm. Our sun is a typical star moving about the galactic center at a period of about 200 million years, or 6×10^{15} sec. To visualize the relative importance of gravity versus centrifugal forces, it is convenient to adopt the following units:

galactic unit of mass $= 10^{44}$ gm. (mass of Milky Way $\cong 4$)

galactic unit of length $= 10^{22}$ cm. (radius of Milky Way $\cong 3$)

galactic unit of time $= 10^{15}$ sec. (period at the sun $\cong 6$)

In these units, the gravitational constant has a value 6.7 (instead of 6.7×10^{-8} in c.g.s. units). Thus, all of the quantities involved are of the order of magnitude of 1 - 10. Essentially, the gravitational and the centrifugal forces are in balance, dominating over all of the other effects.

The stars themselves are small indeed, compared with galactic distances. They are even much smaller than the distance between stars. (Our immediate neighbor, the alpha centauri, is at a distance of about 4 light years away.) Since the relative velocity of the stars are only of the order of 30 km./sec., they seldom make close encounters. Thus, a galaxy may be regarded as an isolated system* of particles which resemble the molecules of a rarefied gas, except that the particles attract each other according to the inverse square law of gravitational attraction. Thus, if we consider an idealized system with all stars having the same mass m, and let $\Psi(\underline{x}, \underline{v}, t)$ denote the distribution function in the sense usually used in the kinetic theory of gases, we have the following equation of the Boltzmann type:

$$\frac{\partial \Psi}{\partial t} + (\underline{v} \cdot \nabla)\Psi + (\underline{f} \cdot \nabla_v)\Psi = 0 , \tag{20}$$

where $\underline{f}$ is the gravitational acceleration, and is given in terms of the gravitational potential $\mathcal{V}$ by

$$\underline{f} = - \nabla \mathcal{V} . \tag{21}$$

The gravitational potential is related to the spacial density ρ,

$$\rho(\underline{x}, t) = m \int \Psi(\underline{x}, \underline{v}, t)\, d\tau(\underline{v}) , \tag{22}$$

by the Poisson equation

$$\nabla^2 \mathcal{V} = 4\pi G \rho . \tag{23}$$

Equations (20) to (23) are the basic equations of stellar dynamics. (Cf. Chandrasekhar, 1942).

In the following analysis, we consider the idealized case of a flat disk of infinitesimal thickness. We adopt a cylindrical system of coordinates (r, θ, z) with origin at the center of the disc. In a first approximation, we neglect the random velocity of the stars. Then the continuum concept can be conveniently used; there is indeed no pressure in the "gas". The collective gravitational forces are the only forces of interaction. The basic equations of motion are then as follows:

$$\mu_t + r^{-1}[(r\mu u)_r + (\mu v)_\theta] = 0 , \tag{24}$$

* See also legend of Figure 2.

(25) $$u_t + u u_r + (v/r) u_\theta - v^2/r = \mathcal{V}_r ,$$

(26) $$v_t + u v_r + (v/r) v_\theta + uv/r = \mathcal{V}_\theta ,$$

(27) $$\mathcal{V}_{rr} + \mathcal{V}_r/r + \mathcal{V}_{\theta\theta}/r^2 + \mathcal{V}_{zz} = -4\pi G \mu(r, \theta)\, \delta(z) .$$

In these equations, u and v denote the velocity components in the directions of increasing r and θ respectively; and μ is the surface density of mass distribution over the galactic disk.

To a first approximation, the mass distribution is symmetrical. (The large variations of luminosity in the disk pattern corresponds to a minor variation of mass, e. g., one per cent. The contrast observed is mainly determined by the difference in the amount of brilliant young stars.) In this symmetrical approximation,

(28) $$u = 0 , \quad \text{and} \quad v = V(r) ,$$

and the density distribution $\mu(r)$ must be such that the centrifugal force

(29) $$V^2/r = \Omega^2 r$$

is balanced by gravitational attraction at every point. In our galaxy, as in most other galaxies, the angular velocity Ω is not a constant.

Because of this differential rotation (shear), the spiral patterns cannot be associated with a given body of matter, for they would then be rapidly modified. Statistically, there would not be, in that case, so many spirals with the type of spacing actually observed. It is therefore more plausible to associate the pattern with a density wave propagating around the galactic disc. Such a picture was suggested by B. Lindblad (1961, 1963) and P. O. Lindblad (1962). Their analysis, however, suggests certain requirements which are not actually fulfilled in our galaxy (and not likely to be fulfilled in other galaxies). Our method, supported by an asymptotic calculation, is free from their special restriction. Indeed, it is based on a very simple idea. We inquire whether the galactic disc is stable with respect to disturbances that propagate around its center in much the same way as a hydrodynamic disturbance. For the analysis of small disturbances, we substitute

(30) $$u = 0 + u'(r, \theta, t)$$

(31) $$v = V(r) + v'(r, \theta, t)$$

$$\mu = \mu_o(r) + \mu'(r, \theta, t) \tag{32}$$

into the set of equations (24)-(27), and neglect terms quadratic in the disturbance quantities. We then obtain the following set of equations:

$$\mu'_t + \Omega\mu'_\theta + r^{-1}(r\mu_o u')_r + (\mu_o/r)v'_\theta = 0 , \tag{33}$$

$$u'_t + \Omega\, u'_\theta - 2\Omega v' = \mathcal{V}'_r , \tag{34}$$

$$v'_t + \Omega v'_\theta + (k^2/2\Omega)u' = r^{-1}\mathcal{V}'_\theta , \tag{35}$$

$$\mathcal{V}'_{rr} + r^{-1}\mathcal{V}'_r + r^{-2}\mathcal{V}'_{\theta\theta} + \mathcal{V}'_{zz} = -4\pi G\mu'\delta(z) , \tag{36}$$

where κ is the epicyclic frequency defined by $\kappa^2 = 4\Omega^2[1 + \frac{r}{2\Omega}\frac{d\Omega}{dr}]$. Clearly, this set allows solutions of the form

$$q'(r, \theta, t) = \hat{q}(r) \exp\{i(\omega t - n\theta)\} \tag{37}$$

where q' is a generic symbol for any one of the quantities u', v', μ', etc., and n is an integer. If we write

$$\hat{q}(r) = Q(r) \exp\{i\,\Phi(r)\} , \tag{38}$$

then we have a spiral distribution of q' if $\Phi(r)$ varies fairly rapidly with r, while $Q(r)$ varies slowly. The form of the spiral is given by

$$n\theta = \Phi(r) + \text{constant}.$$

Spirals with $\Phi'(r) > 0$ are designated as leading, those with $\Phi'(r) < 0$, trailing. Attempts to find $\Phi(r)$ by asymptotic integration gives

$$\pm\Phi'(r) = [\kappa^2 - (\omega - n\Omega)^2]/2\pi G\mu_o \tag{39}$$

if and only if the real part of $\kappa^2 - (\omega - n\Omega)^2$ is positive, and the form of the spiral is given by the formula

$$\pm n(\theta - \theta_o) = \int_{r_o}^{r} (2\pi G\mu_o)^{-1}[\kappa^2 + \omega_i^2 + (\omega_r - 2\Omega)^2]\, dr \tag{40}$$

where we have written $\omega = \omega_r + i\omega_i$, and the integrand in the right-hand side of (40) is positive. Thus, both leading and trailing arms are permitted by this analysis, and their difference has to be resolved by more careful investigations. In the region where the above condition is not satisfied, the asymptotic method fails. This is a rather curious situation. Numerical solution of certain examples shows that there is a generally exponential variation of the quantities $q(r)$ with radial distance. Further investigations of this and other problems (e.g., the effect of random velocities) are still in progress.

The spiral form given by (40) shows reasonable agreement with observations concerning our own galaxy. This is an encouraging feature in favor of the wave pattern theory proposed here. It is clear that much work remains to be done on both the mathematical problems and the physical problems in order to arrive at a clear understanding of the spiral structure of disc galaxies.

5. Concluding remarks. We have briefly surveyed a number of physical problems where the asymptotic solution of the differential equations involved leads to turning points or some issue akin to the turning point problem. Many facets of the problems are not yet fully understood. For the purposes of these future investigations, Professor Langer's work on the Schrödinger equation will always remain a classical example and a guide, as it concerns a fundamental physical phenomenon and it involves many of the essential features common to all similar problems.

Legend of Figures

Figure 1. Structure of the Milky Way. The units of distance are parsecs. The large spots are globular star clusters; the small dots are stars. (A parsec is the distance at which the radius of the earth orbit (1.4964×10^{13} cm.) subtends an angle of one second. More recent analysis indicates that the distance of the sun from the galactic center is about 8,000 parsecs instead of 10,000).

Figure 2. The Whirlpool Nebula (spiral galaxy M51), which resembles the Milky Way in structure; seen face-on. At the lower right corner of the picture, there is a companion galaxy. Galaxies are generally separated from each other by distances of the order of ten times their average sizes.

Figure 1.

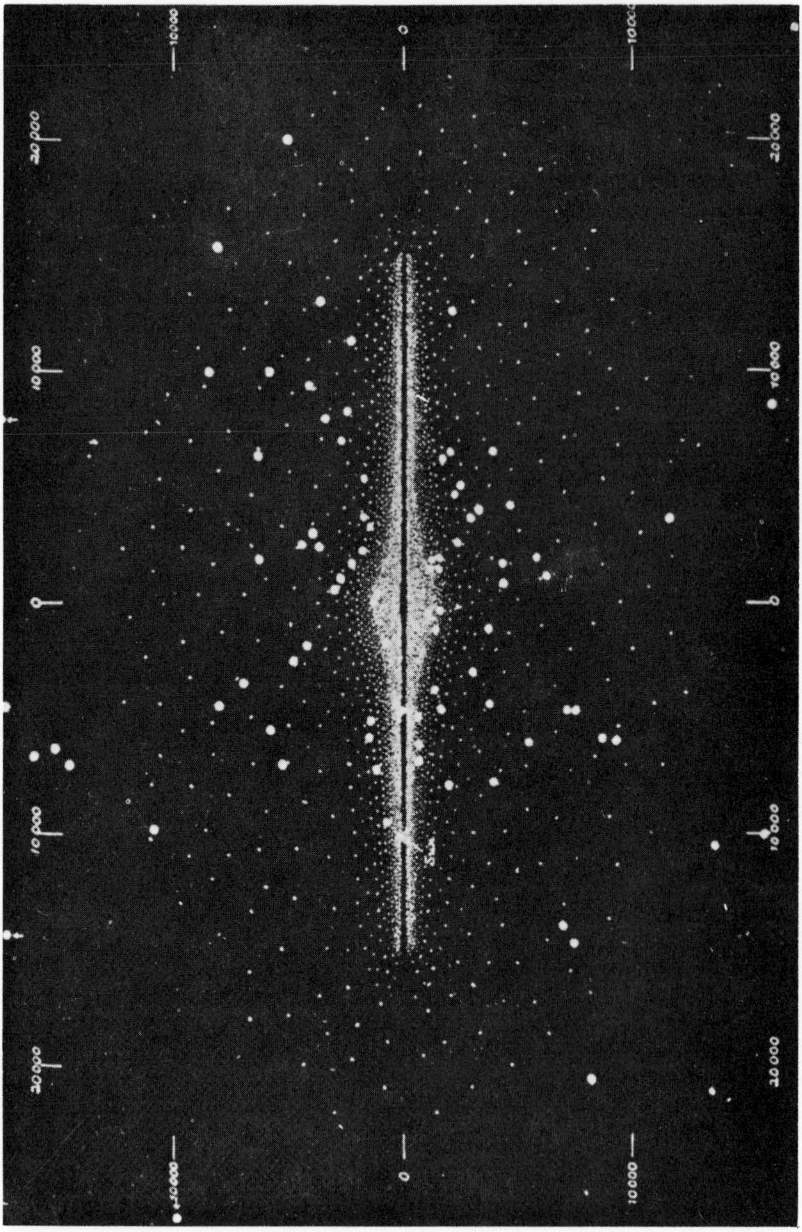

Figure 2.

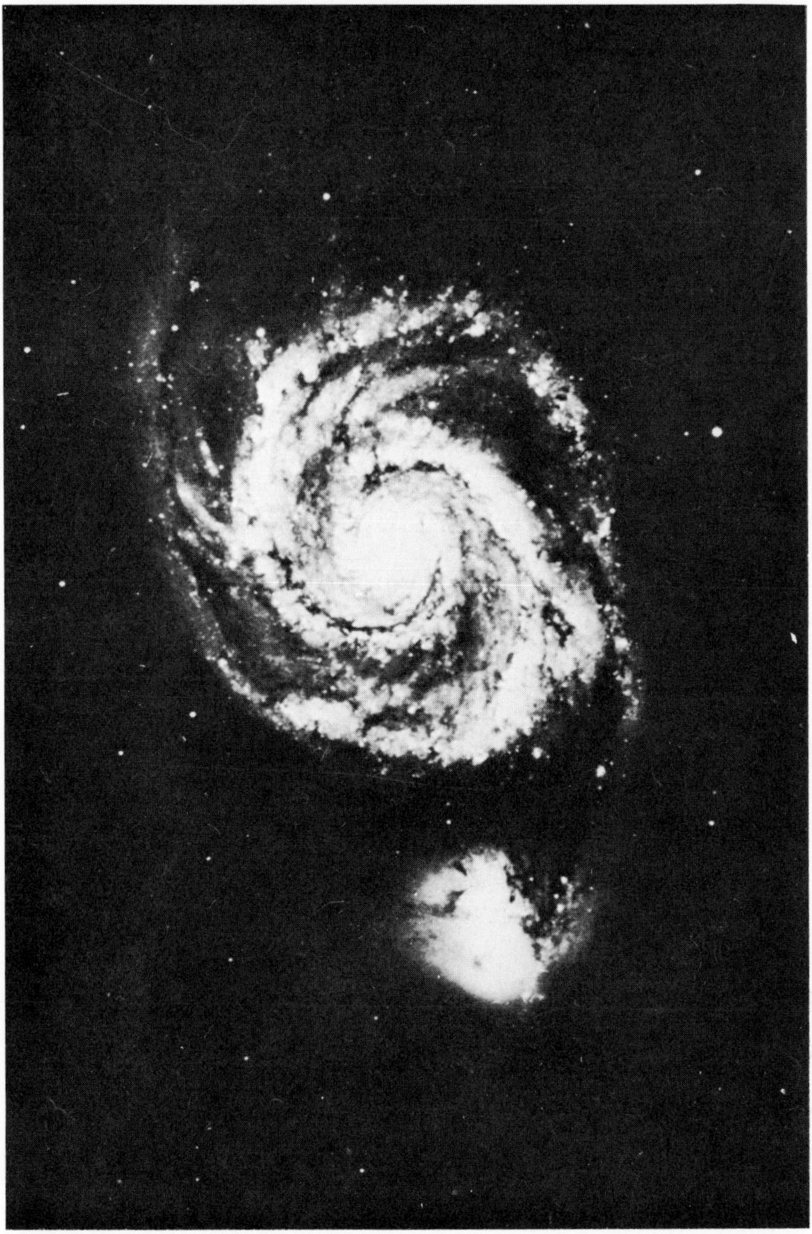

REFERENCES

1. Chandrasekhar, S. (1942). "Principles of Stellar Dynamics." University of Chicago Press, p. 184.

2. Dunn, D.W. and Lin, C.C. (1955). J. Aero. Sci. 22, pp. 455-477.

3. Heisenberg, W. (1924). Am. Phys., Lpz., (4) 74, 577-627.

4. Jeffreys, H. (1924). Proc. Lond. Math. Soc. (2) 23, pp. 426-436.

5. Langer, R.E. (1931). Trans. Amer. Math. Soc. 33, pp. 23-64.

6. ___________ (1935). Trans. Amer. Math. Soc. 37, pp. 397-416.

7. ___________ (1940). Bull. Amer. Math. Soc. 46, pp. 257-263.

8. ___________ (1957). Trans. Amer. Math. Soc. 84, pp. 144-191.

9. Lees, L. and Lin, C. C. (1946). Tech. Notes Nat. Adv. Comm. Aero., Washington No. 1115, 83 pp.

10. Lin, C.C. (1945). Quart. Appl. Math. 3, pp. 117-142, 218-234, 277-301.

11. __________ (1955). "The Theory of Hydrodynamic Stability." Cambridge University Press.

12. Lin, C.C. and Rebanstein, A.L. (1960). Trans. Amer. Math. Soc. 94, pp. 24-57.

13. Lin, C.C. and Shu, F.H. (1964). Astrophys. J., August issue (in press).

14. Lindblad, B. (1961). Stockholm Obs. Ann. 21, pp. 8-36.

15. ___________ (1963). Stockholm Obs. Ann. 22, 5, 20 pp.

16. Lindblad, P. O. (1962). "Interstellar Matter in Galaxies." (edited by L. Woltjer, Benjamin, New York), pp. 222-233.

17. Meksyn, D. and Stuart, J.T. (1951). Proc. Roy. Soc. A, 208, 517-26.

18. Morawetz, C.S. (1954). J. Math. Phys. 33, 1-26.

19. Rosencrans, S. (1964). Ph. D. Dissertation, Department of Mathematics, Massachusetts Institute of Technology, entitled: "Energy Propagation in a Stratified Gas."

20. Struve, O. (1962). "The Universe." The M. I. T. Press.

21. Wasow, W. (1953). Ann of Math. 58, pp. 222-252.

This work is supported in part by the Office of Naval Research and The National Science Foundation

YASUTAKA SIBUYA

On the Problem of Turning Points for Systems of Linear Ordinary Differential Equations of Higher Orders

1. Introduction. Previously, we have studied a linear ordinary differential equation of the n-th order of the form: [11, 12]

$$\epsilon^{n-m} L_n(y) + L_m(y) = 0 ,$$

where $n - 2 \geqq m$ and

$$L_n(y) = y^{(n)} + \sum_{h=m+1}^{n-1} R_h(z, \epsilon) y^{(h)} ,$$

$$L_m(y) = (z + \epsilon R_m(z, \epsilon)) y^{(m)} + \sum_{h=0}^{m-1} (P_h(z) + \epsilon R_h(z, \epsilon)) y^{(h)} .$$

Here ϵ is a small parameter, z is a complex independent variable, y is an unknown function of z, P_h are holomorphic functions of z, and R_h are power series in ϵ with coefficients holomorphic in z. In order to show that similar results may be obtained even in the case when y is a vector and P_h and R_h are matrices, we shall study, in this paper, a system of the following form:

$$(1.1) \qquad \epsilon^2 \{y'' + R_1(z, \epsilon) y' + R_2(z, \epsilon) y\} = z D y ,$$

where y is a two-dimensional vector, and R_h are two by two matrices whose components are holomorphic with respect to z and ϵ for

$$(1.2) \qquad |z| \leqq \delta_o , \quad |\epsilon| \leqq \epsilon_o ,$$

while D is a nonsingular constant diagonal matrix. Our purpose is to study the behavior of solutions of (1.1) as ϵ tends to zero. To do this, we shall reduce the system (1.1) to another system of a simpler form, and then we shall study the simpler system.

2. Formal transformation. First of all we shall consider a linear transformation of the form:

$$u = A_{00}(z,\epsilon)\,y + A_{01}(z,\epsilon)\,\epsilon y',$$
$$\epsilon u' = A_{10}(z,\epsilon)\,y + A_{11}(z,\epsilon)\,\epsilon y', \tag{2.1}$$

where u is a two-dimensional vector and A_{jk} are two by two matrices whose components are formal power series of ϵ with coefficients holomorphic in z for

$$|z| \leqq \delta_0, \tag{2.2}$$

and the four by four matrix

$$\begin{bmatrix} A_{00}(0,0) & A_{01}(0,0) \\ A_{10}(0,0) & A_{11}(0,0) \end{bmatrix} \tag{2.3}$$

is nonsingular. We shall construct such a transformation so that u satisfies a system of the following form:

$$\epsilon^2\{u'' + C_1(\epsilon)u' + C_2(\epsilon)u\} = zDu, \tag{2.4}$$

where C_h are two by two matrices whose components are formal power series of ϵ with constant coefficients. Namely we shall prove the following theorem.

THEOREM 1. We can construct a formal transformation (2.1) so that u satisfies a system of the form (2.4). Furthermore, we can reduce the diagonal components of C_h to zero. In case $D = \sigma 1_2$, where σ is a scalar and 1_2 is the two by two unit-matrix, we can construct the transformation (2.1) so that u satisfies the system

$$\epsilon^2 u'' = \sigma z u. \tag{2.4'}$$

The proof of this theorem in case $D = \sigma 1_2$ is the same as the proof of the corresponding result obtained by R. E. Langer [3] for a scalar second order differential equation. Therefore, in our proof, we shall assume that the diagonal components of D are distinct.

Put

$$\epsilon^2 u'' = A_{20} y + A_{21} \epsilon y' . \tag{2.5}$$

Since the system of equations (1.1) and the relation

$$\epsilon^k u^{(k)} = A_{k0} y + A_{k1} \epsilon y'$$

imply

$$\epsilon^{k+1} u^{(k+1)} = (\epsilon A'_{k0} + z A_{k1} D - \epsilon^2 A_{k1} R_2) y + (A_{k0} + \epsilon A'_{k1} - \epsilon A_{k1} R_1) \epsilon y' ,$$

we have the following relations

$$\begin{aligned} A_{k+1\,0} &= \epsilon A'_{k0} + z A_{k1} D - \epsilon^2 A_{k1} R_2 , \\ A_{k+1\,1} &= A_{k0} + \epsilon A'_{k1} - \epsilon A_{k1} R_1 . \end{aligned} \tag{2.6}$$

Put

$$C_3 = - \epsilon C_2 . \tag{2.7}$$

Then the system (2.4) can be written as

$$\epsilon^2 \{u'' + C_1 u'\} = (z D + \epsilon C_3) u . \tag{2.4''}$$

The relations (2.1), (2.5) and (2.4'') imply

$$\begin{aligned} A_{20} + \epsilon C_1 A_{10} &= (z D + \epsilon C_3) A_{00} , \\ A_{21} + \epsilon C_1 A_{11} &= (z D + \epsilon C_3) A_{01} . \end{aligned} \tag{2.8}$$

We shall determine $A_{00}, A_{01}, A_{10}, A_{11}, C_1$ and C_3 by (2.6) and (2.8).

The relations (2.6) imply

$$A_{20} + \epsilon C_1 A_{10} = z A_{00} D + \epsilon(2zA'_{01} D + A_{01} D - zA_{01} R_1 D + zC_1 A_{01} D) - \epsilon^2 E_0,$$

$$A_{21} + \epsilon C_1 A_{11} = zA_{01} D + \epsilon(2A'_{00} - A_{00} R_1 + C_1 A_{00}) - \epsilon^2 E_1$$

where E_0 and E_1 are polynomials with integral coefficients of D, $C_1, z, A_{00}, A_{01}, R_1, R_2$ and their derivatives with respect to z. Hence the relations (2.8) can be written as

$$\text{(2.9)} \quad \begin{aligned} &z(A_{00} D - DA_{00}) + \epsilon(2zA'_{01} D + A_{01} D - zA_{01} R_1 D \\ &\qquad + zC_1 A_{01} D - C_3 A_{00}) = \epsilon^2 E_0, \\ &z(A_{01} D - DA_{01}) + \epsilon(2A'_{00} - A_{00} R_1 + C_1 A_{00} - C_3 A_{01}) \\ &\qquad = \epsilon^2 E_1 . \end{aligned}$$

We shall determine A_{00}, A_{01} by (2.9) and then we shall determine A_{10}, A_{11} by (2.6). Put

$$A_{0k}(z, \epsilon) = \sum_{\nu=0}^{\infty} \epsilon^{\nu} A_{0k\nu}(z) \qquad (k = 0, 1),$$

$$R_h(z, \epsilon) = \sum_{\nu=0}^{\infty} \epsilon^{\nu} R_{h\nu}(z) \qquad (h = 1, 2),$$

$$E_k(z, \epsilon) = \sum_{\nu=0}^{\infty} \epsilon^{\nu} E_{k\nu}(z) \qquad (k = 0, 1),$$

$$C_h(\epsilon) = \sum_{\nu=0}^{\infty} \epsilon^{\nu} C_{h\nu} \qquad (h = 1, 3),$$

where $E_{k\nu}(z)$ are polynomials with integral coefficients of D, $C_{1\nu'}$, z, $A_{00\nu'}$, $A_{01\nu'}$, $R_{1\nu'}$, $R_{2\nu'}$ $(\nu' \leqq \nu)$ and their derivatives with respect to z.

Setting $\epsilon = 0$, we get from (2.9) the following equations

$$z(A_{000}(z)D - D A_{000}(z)) = 0 ,$$

(2.10)

$$z(A_{010}(z)D - D A_{010}(z)) = 0 .$$

Thus we conclude that the off-diagonal components of $A_{000}(z)$ and $A_{010}(z)$ are identically equal to zero.

By identifying the coefficients of ϵ on both members of (2.9), we get

$$z(A_{001}(z)D - D A_{001}(z)) + 2z A'_{010}(z)D + A_{010}(z)D$$

$$- z A_{010}(z)R_{10}(z)D + z C_{10}A_{010}(z)D - C_{30}A_{000}(z) = 0 ,$$

(2.11)

$$z(A_{011}(z)D - D A_{011}(z))$$

$$+ 2 A'_{000}(z) - A_{000}(z)R_{10}(z) + C_{10}A_{000}(z) - C_{30}A_{010}(z) = 0 .$$

By use of (2.11) we shall determine the off-diagonal components of $A_{001}(z)$ and $A_{011}(z)$, the diagonal components of $A_{000}(z)$ and $A_{010}(z)$, and C_{10} and C_{30}. First of all, setting $z = 0$, we get

$$A_{010}(0)D - C_{30}A_{000}(0) = 0 ,$$

(2.12)

$$2A'_{000}(0) - A_{000}(0)R_{10}(0) + C_{10}A_{000}(0) - C_{30}A_{010}(0) = 0 .$$

Then, putting

(2.13) $A_{000}(0) = 1_2, \quad C_{30} = 0, \quad A_{010}(0) = 0 ,$

we have the first equation of (2.12) satisfied. On the other hand, if we choose the diagonal components of $A'_{000}(0)$ and the off-diagonal components of C_{10} in a suitable manner, we have the second equation of (2.12) satisfied. Since the diagonal components of

$$A_{001}(z)\ D - D A_{001}(z), \quad A_{011}(z)\ D - D A_{011}(z)$$

are zero, we shall determine the diagonal components of $A_{000}(z)$ and $A_{010}(z)$ by considering the diagonal components of

$$2z A'_{010}(z) D + A_{010}(z) D - z A_{010}(z) R_{10}(z) D$$

$$+ z C_{10} A_{010}(z) D - C_{30} A_{000}(z)$$

and

$$2 A'_{000}(z) - A_{000}(z) R_{10}(z) + C_{10} A_{000}(z) - C_{30} A_{010}(z) \ .$$

Put

$$A_{000}(z) = M_0(z) + N_0(z) \ ,$$

$$A_{010}(z) = M_1(z) + N_1(z) \ ,$$

where $M_0(z)$ and $M_1(z)$ are the diagonal parts of $A_{000}(z)$ and $A_{010}(z)$ respectively, while $N_0(z)$ and $N_1(z)$ are the off-diagonal parts of $A_{000}(z)$ and $A_{010}(z)$ respectively. Actually, $N_0(z)$ and $N_1(z)$ are identically equal to zero. Then we get the following equations

$$2z M'_1(z) D + M_1(z) D - z M_1(z) R_{10}(z) D$$

$$(2.14) \qquad + z C_{10} M_1(z) D - C_{30} M_0(z) = F_0(z) \ ,$$

$$2 M'_0(z) - M_0(z) R_{10}(z) + C_{10} M_0(z) - C_{30} M_1(z) = F_1(z) \ ,$$

where $F_0(z)$ and $F_1(z)$ are known quantities. Since $M_0(0)$, $M'_0(0)$ and $M_1(0)$ have been already determined, we can determine $M_0(z)$ and $M_1(z)$ as power series of z. These power series converge for $|z| \leqq \delta_0$, since $z = 0$ is a regular singular point and there is no other singular point in this domain. Finally, since the equations (2.12) are satisfied, the off-diagonal components of $A_{001}(z)$ and $A_{011}(z)$ can be determined by (2.11).

The coefficients $A_{00\nu}(z)$, $A_{01\nu}(z)$, $C_{1\nu}$, $C_{2\nu}$ can be determined in a similar manner successively. Since

$$A_{00}(0, 0) = A_{000}(0) = 1_2 \qquad ,$$

$$A_{01}(0, 0) = A_{010}(0) = 0 \qquad ,$$

$$A_{11}(z,\epsilon) = A_{00}(z,\epsilon) + O(\epsilon) \quad ,$$

the matrix (2.3) is nonsingular. This completes the proof of Theorem 1.

3. Analytic transformation. Now we shall prove the existence of an analytic transformation which admits the formal transformation as the asymptotic representation as ϵ tends to zero in a sector. First of all, we shall consider the case when the diagonal components of D are distinct. Put

$$(3.1) \qquad D = \begin{bmatrix} \sigma_1 & 0 \\ 0 & \sigma_2 \end{bmatrix} .$$

Then put

$$\lambda_1 = \sigma_1^{\frac{1}{2}}, \quad \lambda_2 = -\sigma_1^{\frac{1}{2}}, \quad \lambda_3 = \sigma_2^{\frac{1}{2}}, \quad \lambda_4 = -\sigma_2^{\frac{1}{2}},$$

$$\lambda_{jk} = \lambda_j - \lambda_k \qquad (j \neq k) \quad ,$$

$$\omega_{jk} = \arg \lambda_{jk} \quad ,$$

$$\omega_- = \min_{(j,k)} \omega_{jk} , \qquad \omega_+ = \max_{(j,k)} \omega_{jk} .$$

Assume that in a domain

$$(3.3) \quad \ell_1 \leqq \arg z \leqq \ell_2 , \qquad \rho_1 \leqq \arg \epsilon \leqq \rho_2 ,$$

we have

$$-\frac{3}{2}\pi - \omega_- < \frac{3}{2} \arg z - \arg \epsilon < \frac{3}{2}\pi - \omega_+ .$$

This implies that

$$\frac{3}{2}\ell_1 - \rho_2 > -\frac{3}{2}\pi - \omega_- , \quad \frac{3}{2}\ell_2 - \rho_1 < \frac{3}{2}\pi - \omega_+ .$$

Although the components of the matrices C_1 and C_2 are formal power series of ϵ with constant coefficients, they can be regarded as holomorphic functions of ϵ in the sector

$$(3.4) \quad \rho_1 \leqq \arg \epsilon \leqq \rho_2 .$$

This is due to the Borel-Ritt theorem [1].

Then we can prove the following theorem.

THEOREM 2. Assume that the diagonal components of D are distinct. Then there exists two by two matrices $B_{00}(z, \epsilon)$, $B_{01}(z, \epsilon)$, $B_{10}(z, \epsilon)$, $B_{11}(z, \epsilon)$ such that

(i) their components are holomorphic for

$$|z| \leqq \delta_0, \quad 0 < |\epsilon| \leqq \epsilon_1 \ (\leqq \epsilon_0), \quad \rho_1 \leqq \arg \epsilon \leqq \rho_2 ,$$

(ii) they admit uniformly asymptotic expansions

$$B_{jk}(z, \epsilon) \cong A_{jk}(z, \epsilon)$$

for $|z| \leqq \varphi(\arg z)$, $\ell_1 \leqq \arg z \leqq \ell_2$ as ϵ tends to zero in the sector (3.4), where $\varphi(\theta)$ is a positive continuous function for $\ell_1 \leqq \theta \leqq \ell_2$.

(iii) the transformation

$$(3.5) \quad \begin{aligned} u &= B_{00}(z, \epsilon) y + B_{01}(z, \epsilon)\, \epsilon y' , \\ \epsilon u' &= B_{10}(z, \epsilon) y + B_{11}(z, \epsilon)\, \epsilon y' \end{aligned}$$

reduces the system (1.1) to the system (2.4).

This theorem can be proved by the use of one of our previous results [10]. In fact, put

$$u = u_1 , \quad \epsilon u' = u_2 .$$

Then the system (2.4) can be written as

$$\epsilon\, du_1/dz = u_2$$

(3.6)

$$\epsilon\, du_2/dz = (zD - \epsilon^2 C_2)u_1 - \epsilon C_1 u_2 .$$

If we put

$$\rho = \epsilon^{\frac{1}{3}}, \qquad z = (\rho\eta)^2 ,$$

$$u_1 = w_1 , \qquad u_2 = (\rho\eta) w_2 ,$$

we have

$$dw_1/d\eta = 2\eta^2 w_2 ,$$

$$dw_2/d\eta = 2\eta^2 \left[(D - \frac{\rho^4}{\eta^2} C_2) w_1 - (\frac{\rho^2}{\eta} C_1 + \frac{1}{2\eta^3}) w_2 \right].$$

Since the four by four matrix

$$\begin{bmatrix} 0 & 1_2 \\ D & 0 \end{bmatrix}$$

has distinct eigenvalues λ_1, λ_2, λ_3, λ_4 our previous results can be used to prove Theorem 2 [10].

A result similar to Theorem 2 can be obtained in the case when $D = \sigma 1_2$.

4. Relations between the systems (1.1) and (2.4).

Let us put

$$Y = \begin{bmatrix} y \\ \epsilon y' \end{bmatrix} \quad \text{and} \quad U = \begin{bmatrix} u \\ \epsilon u' \end{bmatrix} .$$

Then the systems (1.1) and (2.4) can be written as

(4.1) $$\epsilon\, dY/dz = A(z, \epsilon) Y$$

and

(4.2) $$\epsilon\, dU/dz = B(z, \epsilon) U$$

respectively, where

$$A(z, \epsilon) = \begin{bmatrix} 0 & 1_2 \\ zD - \epsilon^2 R_2(z, \epsilon) & -\epsilon R_1(z, \epsilon) \end{bmatrix},$$

$$B(z, \epsilon) = \begin{bmatrix} 0 & 1_2 \\ zD - \epsilon^2 C_2(\epsilon) & -\epsilon C_1(\epsilon) \end{bmatrix}.$$

Put

$$Q(z, \epsilon) = \begin{bmatrix} A_{00}(z, \epsilon), & A_{01}(z, \epsilon) \\ A_{10}(z, \epsilon), & A_{11}(z, \epsilon) \end{bmatrix}$$

and

$$P(z, \epsilon) = \begin{bmatrix} B_{00}(z, \epsilon) & B_{01}(z, \epsilon) \\ B_{10}(z, \epsilon) & B_{11}(z, \epsilon) \end{bmatrix}.$$

Then, the transformation (3.5) can be written as

(4.3) $$U = P(z, \epsilon)Y,$$

and the matrix P has an asymptotic expansion

(4.4) $$P(z, \epsilon) \cong Q(z, \epsilon)$$

for $|z| \leqq \varphi(\arg z)$, $\ell_1 \leqq \arg z \leqq \ell_2$ as ϵ tends to zero in the sector (3.4). The system (4.1) is reduced to (4.2) by the transformation (4.3).

There are many ways of choosing the values of ω_{jk} and, for each choice of their values, we can determine a domain of the form

(3.3) so that the statement of Theorem 2 corresponding to this domain holds.

Let us consider two sectors $\mathcal{D}_1$ and $\mathcal{D}_2$ with the common vertex at $z = 0$. Assume that they have a nonempty common part. Assume further that there are four by four matrices $P^{(1)}(z,\epsilon)$ and $P^{(2)}(z,\epsilon)$ such that they are holomorphic for

(4.5) $$|z| \leqq \delta_0, \qquad 0 < |\epsilon| \leqq \epsilon_1, \qquad \rho_1 \leqq \arg \epsilon \leqq \rho_2 ,$$

and they admit uniformly asymptotic expansions

(4.6)
$$P^{(1)}(z,\epsilon) \cong Q(z,\epsilon) ,$$
$$P^{(2)}(z,\epsilon) \cong Q(z,\epsilon)$$

respectively for $z \in \mathcal{D}_1$ and $z \in \mathcal{D}_2$ as ϵ tends to zero in the sector

(4.7) $$0 < |\epsilon| \leqq \epsilon_1, \qquad \rho_1 \leqq \arg \epsilon \leqq \rho_2 .$$

Let $\Psi(z,\epsilon)$ be a four by four matrix such that its components are holomorphic functions in the domain (4.5), and it satisfies the differential equation

(4.8) $$\epsilon\, d\Psi(z,\epsilon)/dz = B(z,\epsilon)\Psi(z,\epsilon)$$

and the inequalities

(4.9) $$\|\Psi(0,\epsilon)\| \leqq K|\epsilon|^{\tau}, \qquad \|\Psi(0,\epsilon)^{-1}\| \leqq K|\epsilon|^{\tau} ,$$

where K is a positive constant and τ is a real constant; $\|A\|$ denotes a norm of a matrix A.

Put

$$\Phi^{(1)}(z,\epsilon) = P^{(1)}(z,\epsilon)^{-1}\,\Psi(z,\epsilon) ,$$

$$\Phi^{(2)}(z,\epsilon) = P^{(2)}(z,\epsilon)^{-1}\,\Psi(z,\epsilon) .$$

Then $\Phi^{(1)}$ and $\Phi^{(2)}$ satisfy the differential equation

$$\epsilon\, d\Phi/dz = A(z,\epsilon)\Phi .$$

Hence there exists a four by four matrix $S(\epsilon)$ such that

$$\Phi^{(2)}(z,\epsilon) = \Phi^{(1)}(z,\epsilon)\ S(\epsilon)\ . \tag{4.10}$$

Then we can prove the following

THEOREM 3. $S(\epsilon) \cong 1_4$ as ϵ tends to zero in the sector (4.7).

In fact, putting $z = 0$ in (4.10), we have

$$\Phi^{(2)}(0,\epsilon) = \Phi^{(1)}(0,\epsilon)\, S(\epsilon)\ .$$

Hence

$$S(\epsilon) = \Psi(0,\epsilon)^{-1}\ P^{(1)}(0,\epsilon)\ P^{(2)}(0,\epsilon)^{-1}\Psi(0,\epsilon)\ .$$

Since $P^{(1)}$ and $P^{(2)}$ satisfy the asymptotic relations (4.6), we have

$$P^{(1)}(0,\epsilon)\ P^{(2)}(0,\epsilon)^{-1} \cong 1_4\ .$$

Putting

$$P^{(1)}(0,\epsilon)\ P^{(2)}(0,\epsilon)^{-1} - 1_4 = R(\epsilon)\ ,$$

the matrix $S(\epsilon)$ can be written as

$$S(\epsilon) = 1_4 + \Psi(0,\epsilon)^{-1}\ R(\epsilon)\,\Psi(0,\epsilon)\ .$$

Since $R(\epsilon) \cong 0$ and Ψ satisfies the inequalities (4.9), we have $S(\epsilon) \cong 1_4$. This completes the proof of Theorem 3.

By choosing ω_{jk} in various ways, we can construct sectors where the statements of Theorem 2 hold. These sectors form a covering of the domain $|z| \leqq \delta_0$. Therefore, if we can construct an asymptotic solution of the system (4.2) in this neighborhood of $z = 0$, we can also construct an asymptotic solution of the system (4.1) by the use of this covering and Theorem 3.

5. Study of the system (4.2). Now let us study the system (4.2):

$$\epsilon\, dU/dz = B(z,\epsilon)U = \begin{bmatrix} 0 & 1_2 \\ zD - \epsilon^2 C_2 & -\epsilon C_1 \end{bmatrix} U\ . \tag{4.2}$$

Hereafter, we shall regard the components of C_1 and C_2 as parameters instead of functions of ϵ. Put

$$\rho = \epsilon^{\frac{1}{3}}, \quad z = \rho^2 \zeta, \quad U = \begin{bmatrix} 1_2 & 0 \\ 0 & \rho 1_2 \end{bmatrix} V .$$

Then the system (4.2) becomes

$$(5.1) \qquad dV/d\zeta = \{ B_0(\zeta) + \mu B_1 + \mu^2 B_2 \} V \quad ,$$

where

$$B_0(\zeta) = \begin{bmatrix} 0 & 1_2 \\ \zeta D & 0 \end{bmatrix} ,$$

$$(5.2) \qquad B_1 = \begin{bmatrix} 0 & 0 \\ 0 & -C_1 \end{bmatrix} ,$$

$$B_2 \quad \begin{bmatrix} 0 & 0 \\ -C_2 & 0 \end{bmatrix}$$

and

$$(5.3) \qquad \mu = \rho^2 \quad .$$

We shall construct a global expression of a fundamental set of solutions of (5.1). For the system (5.1), $\zeta = \infty$ is the only singular point, and it is an irregular singular point. If we sepcify a sector in the ζ-plane suitably, we can construct a set of four independent solutions $V_k(\zeta, \mu)$ $(k = 1, 2, 3, 4)$ of (5.1) so that they admit certain asymptotic expansions in this sector as ζ tends to ∞. Their asymptotic expansions may be computed without any difficulty. Since $\zeta = \infty$ is the only singular point, the solutions

V_k are entire functions of ζ. If we can find a method for computing the values of V_k at $\zeta = 0$, then we can construct the global expressions of these independent solutions V_k, because we can express them in powers of ζ for the finite values of ζ, while we know already their asymptotic expansions in a prescribed sector at $\zeta = \infty$.

Bearing this scheme in mind, first of all, we shall construct the independent solutions V_k of (5.1) so that they admit asymptotic expansions in a suitably prescribed sector at $\zeta = \infty$ and that they are also holomorphic with respect to μ and the components of C_1 and C_2 in the full neighborhood of $\mu = 0$, $C_1 = 0$, $C_2 = 0$. Such a theorem can be established in the general theory of regular perturbations of linear differential equations at an irregular singular point. Actually, to do this, it is sufficient to modify one of our previous results [9] at certain points. We shall present this modification elsewhere. Then, by expanding the solutions V_k in powers of μ, we shall determine the coefficients of their expansions step by step. Namely, put

$$(5.4)\quad V_k(\zeta, \mu) = \sum_{h=0}^{\infty} V_{kh}(\zeta)\mu^h .$$

Then

$$dV_{k0}(\zeta)/d\zeta = B_0(\zeta)V_{k0}(\zeta),$$

$$(5.5)\quad dV_{k1}(\zeta)/d\zeta = B_0(\zeta)V_{k1}(\zeta) + B_1V_{k0}(\zeta),$$

$$dV_{kh}(\zeta)/d\zeta = B_0(\zeta)V_{kh}(\zeta) + B_1V_{kh-1}(\zeta) + B_2V_{kh-2}(\zeta)$$

$$(h = 2, 3, \ldots).$$

We can derive the asymptotic expansions of V_{kh} at $\zeta = \infty$ from the asymptotic expansions of V_k. Furthermore, if the prescribed sector is large enough, the quantities $V_{kh}(\zeta)$ can be determined uniquely by their asymptotic expansions in this sector at $\zeta = \infty$. In particular, we know a global expression of a fundamental set of solutions of the system

$$(5.6)\quad dW/d\zeta = B_0(\zeta)W .$$

Hence we can give a method of construction of $V_{kh}(\zeta)$ in terms of the independent solutions of the system (5.6) by the use of the method of variation of parameters.

For example, let us consider the case when $\sigma_1 > \sigma_2 > 0$. Let $\mathcal{S}_0$ be the sector defined by

(5.7) $-\frac{\pi}{3} + \gamma \leqq \arg \zeta \leqq \pi - \gamma$,

where γ is a sufficiently small positive constant. Then by the method explained above, we can construct a set of independent solutions $V_k(\zeta, \mu)$ so that they admit certain asymptotic expansions as ζ tends to ∞ in $\mathcal{S}_0$ and we can compute $V_k(0, \mu)$ as power series of μ. Furthermore put

$$\zeta = e^{i\omega}\hat{\zeta} ,$$

(5.8)
$$V = \begin{bmatrix} 1_2 & 0 \\ 0 & e^{-i\omega}1_2 \end{bmatrix} \hat{V} ,$$

where $e^{i3\omega} = 1$. Then we derive from (5.1) the system

(5.9) $d\hat{V}/d\hat{\zeta} = \{B_0(\hat{\zeta}) + e^{i\omega}\mu B_1 + (e^{i\omega}\mu)^2 B_2\} \hat{V}$.

Hence

(5.10)
$$V = \begin{bmatrix} 1_2 & 0 \\ 0 & e^{i\omega}1_2 \end{bmatrix} V_k(e^{-i\omega}\zeta, \ e^{i\omega}\mu) \qquad (k = 1, 2, 3, 4)$$

are also solutions of (5.1). These independent solutions (5.10) admit asymptotic expansions in the sector

(5.11) $(-\frac{\pi}{3} + \omega) + \gamma \leqq \arg \zeta \leqq (\pi + \omega) - \gamma$.

By choosing $\omega = 0, \frac{2}{3}\pi, -\frac{2}{3}\pi$ we get three sectors $\mathcal{S}_0, \mathcal{S}_+, \mathcal{S}_-$. These sectors form a covering of the ζ-plane. By the use of these three fundamental sets of solutions of (5.1), we can study the behavior of solutions of (4.2) as ϵ tends to zero.

6. Equations of the third order. A similar method can be used in the study of a system of equations of third order of the following form:

(6.1) $\epsilon^2\{y''' + R_1y'' + R_2y' + R_3y\} = zDy' + P(z)y$, where y is a two-dimensional vector, and R_h are two by two matrices whose components are holomorphic with respect to z and ϵ for (1.2), while D is a nonsingular constant diagonal matrix and $P(z)$ is a two by two matrix whose components are holomorphic functions of z for $|z| \leqq \delta_0$. If we put $\epsilon = 0$, the system is reduced to the system

$$(6.2) \qquad 0 = zDy' + P(z)y \quad .$$

For this system, $z = 0$ is a regular singular point. This problem may be regarded as a problem of a turning point as well as a problem of singular perturbations of linear differential equations at a regular singular point. P. F. Hsieh [2] studied the system (6.1) by the use of our method. Assuming that the difference of two characteristic values of the matrix $D^{-1}P(0)$ is not an integer, he reduced the system (6.1) to the system

$$(6.3) \qquad \epsilon^2\{u''' + C_1u'' + C_2u'\} = zDu' + \{P(0) + \epsilon C_3\}\, u \ ,$$

where C_h are two by two matrices whose components are functions of ϵ and independent of z. He also studied the system (6.3) by a method similar to that explained in Section 5. In Section 5, the system (5.6) played an essential role. Similarly, in the study of (6.3), the extensive study of the system

$$(6.4) \qquad d^3u/d\zeta^3 = \zeta D du/d\zeta + P(0)\, u$$

was required.

The condition on the characteristic values of $D^{-1}P(0)$ may be removed by introducing a suitable fractional power of ϵ as C.C. Lin and A. L. Rabenstein did in one of their papers [7].

L. Lees and C.C. Lin [6] and C.S. Morawetz [8] studied a system of the following form:

$$(6.5) \qquad \begin{aligned} &\epsilon^2\{x'' + R_1x' + R_2x + R_3y\} = zDx + \widetilde{P}(z)y \ , \\ &y' = R_4x + R_5y + \epsilon^2 R_6x' \ , \end{aligned}$$

where x and y are two-dimensional vectors, R_h and $\widetilde{P}$ are two by two matrices with properties similar to those of R_h and P of (6.1), while D is a diagonal matrix whose components are functions of z. If D is constant and if either $\widetilde{P}(z)$ or R_4 is nonsingular as $z = \epsilon = 0$, then the system (6.5) can be reduced to the system (6.1) by a suitable change of variables.

Lees, Lin, and Morawetz did not construct asymptotic expansions of solutions of (6.5) in the immediate neighborhood of $z = 0$, while Hsieh constructed such expansions for the system (6.1). On the other hand, Hsieh assumed the conditions on D and P(0) which were not assumed by Lees, Lin and Morawetz. Therefore any definite comparison between the results of Lees and Lin, and Morawetz, and those of Hsieh may not be given here.

On the other hand, the results of Hsieh are generalizations of the results of Langer [4, 5] for a scalar third order differential equation.

REFERENCES

1. Friedrichs, K. O., Special topics in analysis, Lecture notes, New York Univ., 1953-1954.

2. Hsieh, P. F., A turning point problem for a system of linear ordinary differential equations of the third order, Dissertation, University of Minnesota, 1964.

3. Langer, R. E., The asymptotic solutions of ordinary linear differential equations of the second order, with special reference to a turning point, Trans. Amer. Math. Soc., 67(1949), 461-490.

4. Langer, R. E., The solutions of the differential equation $v''' + \lambda^2 z v' + 3\mu\lambda^2 v = 0$, Duke Math. J., 22(1955), 525-542.

5. Langer, R. E., The solutions of a class of ordinary linear differential equations of the third order in a region containing a multiple turning point, ibid., 23(1956), 93-110.

6. Lees, L. and Lin, C. C., Investigation of the stability of the laminar boundary layer in a compressible fluid, NACA Technical Note No. 1115, 1946.

7. Lin, C. C., and Rabenstein, A. L., On the asymptotic solutions of a class of ordinary differential equations of the fourth order, Trans. Amer. Soc., 94(1960), 24-57.

8. Morawetz, C. S., Asymptotic solutions of the stability equations of a compressible fluid, J. of Math. and Phys., 33(1954), 1-26.

9. Sibuya, Y., Simplification of a system of linear ordinary differential equations about a singular point, Funkcialaj Ekvacioj, 4(1962), 29-56.

10. Sibuya, Y., Asymptotic solutions of a system of linear ordinary differential equations containing a parameter, ibid., 83-113.

11. Sibuya, Y., Formal solutions of a linear ordinary differential equation of the n-th order at a turning point, ibid., 115-139.

12. Sibuya, Y., Simplification of a linear ordinary differential equation of the n-th order at a turning point, Arch. for Rat. Mech. and Anal., 13(1963), 206-221.

This work is supported in part by the Contract of the Office of Naval Research Nonr-3776(00).

FRANK W. J. OLVER

Error Bounds for Asymptotic Expansions, with an Application to Cylinder Functions of Large Argument

1. Introduction. In 1886, Poincaré [14] introduced the notion of an asymptotic expansion

$$f(x) \sim f_0 + \frac{f_1}{x} + \frac{f_2}{x^2} + \ldots \tag{1.01}$$

of an arbitrary function $f(x)$. According to his definition the coefficients f_s are independent of x, and

$$f(x) = \sum_{s=0}^{m-1} \frac{f_s}{x^s} + \epsilon_m(x), \tag{1.02}$$

where, for each m, $\epsilon_m(x) = o(1/x^{m-1})$ as $x \to \infty$. This concept admitted a large class of divergent series expansions to the realm of analysis, enabling them to be manipulated in much the same way as convergent power series. In turn, this has led to the development of a new calculus, later called "pure asymptotics" by van der Corput [2]. A feature of this development has been the generalization of the original definition of Poincaré. Schmidt [15] showed that the restriction to power-series form is quite unnecessary. More recently, Erdélyi [6] has extended the concept still further, and, with Wyman, applied it to the asymptotic evaluation of certain integrals [6], [7], [20]. Erdélyi's generalization is given in §3 below.

For some time, however, many numerical mathematicians have been aware that in quite another way, the Poincaré definition is not restrictive enough. To understand this point of view, consider for example the well-known asymptotic expansion for the Hankel function $H_\nu^{(1)}(z)$ for large $|z|$ and fixed ν, given by

$$H_\nu^{(1)}(z) \sim \left(\frac{2}{\pi z}\right)^{\frac{1}{2}} e^{i\varphi} \sum_{s=0}^{\infty} i^s \frac{a_s}{z^s}, \tag{1.03}$$

in which

$$(1.04) \qquad \varphi = z - \frac{1}{2}\nu\pi - \frac{1}{4}\pi, \qquad a_s = \frac{(4\nu^2-1^2)(4\nu^2-3^2)\dots\{4\nu^2-(2s-1)^2\}}{8^s\, s!}.$$

This expansion holds in Poincaré's sense [18] when $-\pi < \arg z < 2\pi$; in fact for arbitrary values of a positive number δ, it is uniformly valid in the sector $-\pi + \delta \le \arg z \le 2\pi - \delta$ in the accepted sense that if the series is truncated after m terms, then the constant implied in the error term $O(|z|^{-m})$ can be assigned independently of $\arg z$. Now it will be seen later (§7) that when 2ν is not an odd integer the accuracy yielded by the expansion (1.03), for a given value of $|z|$, actually deteriorates steadily and severely as $\arg z \to -\pi$ or $\arg z \to 2\pi$. To express this another way, the minimum value of the implied constant in the uniform error bound depends on δ and becomes increasingly large as $\delta \to 0$. As a consequence, the concepts of "validity" and "uniform validity" can be quite misleading in applications: an unsuspecting computer evaluating the series (1.03) by the usual computational procedure of truncation at the smallest term may obtain inaccurate results in the sectors $-\pi < \arg z < -\frac{1}{2}\pi$ and $\frac{3}{2}\pi < \arg z < 2\pi$, grossly so in the neighbourhoods of $-\pi$ and 2π.

This situation, although perhaps not widely appreciated, is really scarcely surprising, because (1.03) is known to break down completely on crossing the boundaries $\arg z = -\pi$ and 2π. It is more natural [8] to expect this failure to be gradual than abrupt as the boundaries are approached. The behaviour of an ordinary Taylor-series expansion of an analytic function is somewhat similar, inasmuch as the accuracy yielded by a fixed number of terms diminishes as the circle of convergence is approached. The analogy is not complete, however. A computer is warned of the inaccuracy of a truncated Taylor series near the boundary of its region of validity by a diminution in the rate of convergence. No similar warning is available for an asymptotic expansion, because its "rate of convergence", that is, rate of reduction of the magnitudes of successive early terms in the series, is independent of the proximity of the boundary.

Some way of excluding the direct use of an asymptotic expansion near the boundaries of its region of validity is therefore desirable, and it is in this sense that the Poincaré definition is insufficiently restrictive. In the next three sections we discuss this difficulty in general terms, then in the remaining part of the paper we return to the specific problem of Hankel and Bessel functions of large arguments, and derive some new results in connection with the expansion (1.03).

2. Complete asymptotic expansions. Practical dangers attending the use of asymptotic expansions have been stressed previously by Miller [10], [11]. In the expansions for the Weber functions given in

these references, Miller distinguishes between regions of validity in the sense of Poincaré and the more restrictive "complete sense of Watson". Essentially, the difference is that in the former sense all contributions of an exponentially small character are neglected (as they may be, according to the definition), whereas in the latter sense they are retained if they have numerical significance.

For example, if 2ν is not an odd integer the expansion (1.03) is completely valid only when $-\frac{1}{2}\pi \leq \arg z \leq \frac{3}{2}\pi$; this is demonstrated in §7 below. To achieve complete validity in the quadrant $\frac{3}{2}\pi \leq \arg z \leq 2\pi$ it is necessary to add the series

$$(1 + e^{-2\nu\pi i})\left(\frac{2}{\pi z}\right)^{\frac{1}{2}} e^{-i\varphi} \sum_{s=0}^{\infty} (-i)^s \frac{a_s}{z^s} \tag{2.01}$$

to the right of (1.03), whereas of course in the Poincaré sense (2.01) is negligible compared with the right of (1.03) when $\frac{3}{2}\pi \leq \arg z < 2\pi$. Similarly, to achieve complete validity in the quadrant $-\pi \leq \arg z \leq -\frac{1}{2}\pi$, (2.01) is subtracted from the right of (1.03).

By including exponentially small contributions of this type the numerical difficulties can be overcome satisfactorily in this example and in other cases. The process is difficult to justify mathematically however, without an investigation of the remainder term of the kind given in §§5–7 below. There is no readily applicable general definition of complete validity available, nor is it easy to frame one: "numerical significance" is too vague a criterion by itself. A drawback in practice of Watson's theory of the uniqueness of asymptotic expansions [16] is the need to assess properties of the remainder term which are not immediately available in many applications. Further, in cases where these properties are known it is quite possible that a realistic bound for the remainder term is also known, thereby obviating the need for the theory for numerical purposes. This is certainly true of the example given in Watson's paper [16], §11.

The difficulty of recognizing when to include the numerical contribution of an exponentially small term in an asymptotic expansion is illustrated by the following example, which arose some years ago in computations at the National Physical Laboratory, Teddington.

Let

$$I(n) = \int_0^{\pi} \frac{\cos nt}{t^2 + 1}\, dt . \tag{2.02}$$

By repeated integration by parts, we readily show that for large positive integer values of n, $I(n)$ has the Poincaré expansion

(2.03) $$I(n) \sim (-)^{n-1}\left(\frac{\lambda_1}{n^2} - \frac{\lambda_2}{n^4} + \frac{\lambda_3}{n^6} - \ldots\right),$$

in which the coefficients λ_s are given by

(2.04) $$\lambda_s = (\pi^2 + 1)^{-2s} p_{2s-1}(\pi),$$

the $p_s(t)$ being polynomials in t of degree s, defined recursively by $p_0(t) = 1$, and

(2.05) $$p_s(t) = 2st\, p_{s-1}(t) - (t^2+1)\, p'_{s-1}(t) \qquad (s = 1, 2, \ldots).$$

Explicit expressions for the first six polynomials are

(2.06) $$\begin{cases} p_0(t) = 1,\ p_1(t) = 2t,\ p_2(t) = 2(3t^2-1),\ p_3(t) = 24(t^3-t), \\ p_4(t) = 24(5t^4 - 10t^2 + 1),\ p_5(t) = 240(3t^5 - 10t^3 + 3t), \end{cases}$$

and on numerical evaluation, we obtain to five decimals

(2.07) $$\lambda_1 = 0.05318,\ \lambda_2 = 0.04791,\ \lambda_3 = 0.08985.$$

Thus for $n = 10$, the series (2.03) gives

(2.08) $$I(10) \sim -(0.00053\,18 - 0.00000\,48 + 0.00000\,01 - \ldots) = -0.00052\,71.$$

This answer is quite incorrect however, because direct numerical quadrature of the expression (2.02) yields, to seven decimals,

(2.09) $$I(10) = -0.00045\,58.$$

The inclusion of additional terms in the expansion would not help matters, and a partial explanation of the discrepancy is as follows. We may write

(2.10) $$I(n) = \int_0^\infty \frac{\cos nt}{t^2+1}\,dt - \int_\pi^\infty \frac{\cos nt}{t^2+1}\,dt.$$

The first of these integrals equals $\frac{1}{2}\pi e^{-n}$; the second may again be expanded by repeated partial integration. In this way, we find that

(2.11) $$I(n) \sim \frac{1}{2}\pi e^{-n} + (-)^{n-1}\left(\frac{\lambda_1}{n^2} - \frac{\lambda_2}{n^4} + \frac{\lambda_3}{n^6} - \cdots\right) ,$$

where the λ_s are the same as in (2.03). From this result we obtain the correct numerical value at $n = 10$, because

$$\frac{1}{2}\pi e^{-10} = 0.00007\,13 ,$$

which is exactly the discrepancy between the values (2.08) and (2.09).

An alternative way of deriving (2.11) is to apply the Residue theorem and Watson's lemma [18], page 236, to the contour integral

$$\int_C (t^2+1)^{-1} e^{int}\, dt,$$

where C is the perimeter of the rectangle having vertices $\pm\pi$ and $\pm\pi + i\infty$.

In the sense of Miller and Watson, (2.11) is apparently a complete asymptotic expansion for positive integer n, whereas (2.03) is incomplete. There is, however, no self-evident conclusive mathematical reason why this should be so, in fact (2.11) was obtained by less obvious procedures. It is even possible that (2.11) is itself incomplete, for without further investigation we do not know whether or not we have neglected other exponential terms, for example e^{-2n}, which make numerically significant contributions for smaller values of n.

3. The need for error bounds. The difficulty illustrated by the examples of the previous sections is linked to a fundamental weakness of the Poincaré definition: it provides no direct answer to the question "What is the precise relation between an asymptotic expansion and the function from which it is derived?" Thus strictly speaking there is no connection between pure asymptotics and applied mathematics, except in the limit $|z| = \infty$. To establish a connection, two courses are open. Either we can seek upper bounds for the differences between the partial sums of an asymptotic expansion and the function from which it was obtained, or we can endeavour to transform the expansion into a convergent form, as, for example, in [17] and [19]. In the present paper we confine ourselves to the former possibility.

Although the theory of pure asymptotics has been extensively developed and applied, the corresponding theory of error bounds has been comparatively neglected. The literature on this aspect consists mainly of scattered results applicable to special functions.

The few theorems of a general nature which have been discovered [3], [5], are concerned with asymptotic expansions of integral representations with real variables. (The example of §2, incidentally, is not covered by these theorems.) A possible reason for this neglect is the belief [1], §1.7, that when error bounds are needed they can be obtained merely by retracing the steps of the asymptotic proof. This is frequently a difficult and tedious undertaking, and the bounds it yields are often quite unrealistic. There is a need for readily applicable general theorems, and the writer's experience with expansions arising from differential equations indicates that in order to derive them it may often be necessary to develop substantially new proofs of the theorems of pure asymptotics before attempting to follow through explicit treatments of the error terms.

In this connection, attention may be drawn to the suggestion of Wyman [20] that the main direction in which the modern theory of asymptotics will move is towards the use of more general concepts in the theory of pure asymptotics. The importance of investigating such generalizations is indisputable, but perhaps it needs to be stressed that the bridging of a gap between pure and applied mathematics in this branch of analysis by the development of satisfactory theories of error bounds is also of importance. Moreover, such theories may sometimes provide an alternative way of overcoming one of the difficulties which has helped stimulate the recent further generalization [6] in the definition of an asymptotic expansion: the need to avoid narrow concepts concerning both the choice of asymptotic variable for a given expansion, and the nature of the uniformity of the expansion with respect to other variables.

This observation may be illustrated briefly by the following example. In [7], (6.31), Erdélyi and Wyman give a new generalized series expansion in terms of Airy functions for the Hankel function $H_\nu^{(1)}(x)$ when ν and x are real and positive, having a "scale" $\{\tau^{-1-(2m/5)}\}$ as $\tau \to \infty$, where

$$\tau = \left|\tfrac{1}{4}(\nu^2 - x^2)\right|^{\frac{1}{4}} + \left(\tfrac{1}{2}\nu\right)^{\frac{1}{3}} .$$

This means that for each fixed integer m, the $(m+1)$th partial sum of the series differs from $H_\nu^{(1)}(x)$ by $o\{\tau^{-1-(2m/5)}\}$ as $\tau \to \infty$. Thus these authors have succeeded in describing the behaviour of $H_\nu^{(1)}(x)$ when either x or ν is large by means of a single asymptotic expansion. Other investigators, using Poincaré expansions, have had to distinguish between the two cases. Recently however, the present writer [13] has derived sharp error bounds for the most powerful of the existing Poincaré-type expansions for $H_\nu^{(1)}(x)$ for large ν, namely the uniform expansion in terms of Airy functions. From these bounds it can be seen that although the expansion was derived on the assumption that ν is large, it also has an asymptotic property for large x. Indeed, without going into detailed proof, it can be stated that the uniform expansion in terms of Airy functions for large ν is also a generalized expansion in the sense of Erdélyi, this time with respect to the scale $\{(x+\nu)^{-1+\delta-m}\}$ as $x+\nu \to \infty$, for any positive number δ. This is, in fact, a considerably more powerful scale than that of the new expansion.

(Notwithstanding the generality and greater power of the Airy-function expansion, the Poincaré-type expansion of $H_\nu^{(1)}(x)$ for fixed ν and large x remains important, owing to its simplicity, and we make a further study of it in §§5-7.)

4. Nature of the error bounds. In seeking bounds for the error term of a typical expansion of the form (1.01), what kind of success can be hoped for? If f_m is non-zero, then on replacing x by the complex variable z, we have $\epsilon_m(z) \sim f_m z^{-m}$. Hence the most that can be established, in general, is that $|\epsilon_m(z)|$ is bounded by the modulus of the first (non-vanishing) neglected term of the series. This bound cannot apply when $|\arg\{f_{m+1}/(zf_m)\}| < \frac{1}{2}\pi$ however, for the modulus of the right side of the equation

$$\epsilon_m(z) = f_m z^{-m} + f_{m+1} z^{-m-1} + o(|z|^{-m-1})$$

would exceed that of its first term for all sufficiently large $|z|$. In particular, this happens when f_m and f_{m+1} are real and of the same sign, and z is real and positive.

A modification of this bound which would always be feasible is a multiple $\rho_m (>1)$ of the modulus of the first non-vanishing neglected term. This multiple itself could depend on z, and then ideally it would tend to unity as $|z| \to \infty$. The last condition is not essential from the standpoint of most applications however, and a bound of this kind is likely to be quite satisfactory with any value of ρ_m which is not too large. Perhaps this can be appreciated best by observing that for a specified precision in $f(z)$, the difference between having $\rho_m |f_m z^{-m}|$ and $|f_m z^{-m}|$ as bounds for $\epsilon_m(z)$ only affects the minimum allowable value of $|z|$ by the factor $(\rho_m)^{1/m}$. Certainly, for example, if $\rho_m < 10$ there are few situations in which such a reduction in the region of applicability is likely to be of importance. From this point of view, the expenditure of heavy analytical effort to achieve a slight reduction in the value of ρ_m is unjustified, except possibly in the case of the dominant term ($m = 1$) of the expansion.

A form of error bound which has emerged from recent investigations by the writer [12], [13] of the asymptotic solutions of certain second-order differential equations with respect to a parameter effectively consists of the variation, that is, the integral of the modulus of the derivative, of the first neglected term of the series taken over a suitable contour. More recent work, in preparation for publication, has shown that bounds of this type are also applicable, in certain cases, to asymptotic expansions of solutions for large values of the independent variable z. For the series (1.01) this would mean a bound for $|\epsilon_m(z)|$ of the form $m\int|f_m t^{-m-1}dt|$. The contour of integration would naturally be subject to certain restrictions, and from the observations made in §1 we might expect that as z approaches the boundaries of the regions of validity, the contour is constrained to pass increasingly close to the singularity of the integrand at the origin, causing the bound to increase in size.

In the remaining part of this paper, we show that this variational form of error bound is applicable to the expansions of cylinder functions of large argument, and that it does indeed have the feature just described.

5. Hankel functions of large argument. The following theorem is obtained from Theorem 7 of [12] by taking the parameter u occurring there to be unity, and making minor changes:

Let $f(z)$ *be regular in a simply-connected complex domain* D, *and a sequence of functions* $A_s(z)$ *be defined by* $A_0(z) = 1$ *and*

$$A_{s+1}(z) = -\frac{1}{2}A'_s(z) + \frac{1}{2}\int f(z)A_s(z)\,dz \qquad (s = 0, 1, \ldots) . \tag{5.01}$$

Then the differential equation

$$\frac{d^2w}{dz^2} = \{1 + f(z)\}w \tag{5.02}$$

has a solution $w_m(z)$, *depending on an arbitrary point* a *of* D *and an arbitrary positive integer* m, *such that*

$$w_m(z) = e^z\left[\sum_{s=0}^{m-1}{}' A_s(z) + \epsilon_m(z)\right] , \tag{5.03}$$

and

$$w'_m(z) = e^z\left[\sum_{s=0}^{m-1} \{A_s(z) + A'_s(z)\} + \eta_m(z)\right] , \tag{5.04}$$

where

(5.05) $|\epsilon_m(z)|,\ |\eta_m(z)| \le 2\exp\{2\mathcal{V}_{a,z}(A_1)\}\mathcal{V}_{a,z}(A_m) \quad (z \in \mathbf{H}(a))$.

In this result the symbol $\mathcal{V}_{a,z}(A_1)$ denotes the variation of the function A_1 over a path $\mathcal{P}$ connecting a and z, given by

(5.06) $$\mathcal{V}_{a,z}(A_1) = \int_a^z |A_1'(t)\,dt| \;;$$

similarly for $\mathcal{V}_{a,z}(A_m)$. The region $\mathbf{H}(a)$ is the subset of $\mathbf{D}$ comprising those points for which there exists a path $\mathcal{P}$ such that:

(i) $\mathcal{P}$ lies entirely in $\mathbf{D}$;

(ii) $\mathcal{P}$ consists of a finite number of Jordan arcs, each having a parametric equation of the form $t = t(\tau)$ with $t''(\tau)$ continuous and $t'(\tau)$ non-vanishing;

(iii) Re t is monotonic non-decreasing as t traverses $\mathcal{P}$ from a to z .

The point a, incidentally, may be the point at infinity on a straight line $\mathcal{L}$ lying in $\mathbf{D}$; in this event we suppose that $\mathcal{P}$ coincides with $\mathcal{L}$ for all sufficiently large $|t|$.

The original purpose of this theorem was to provide asymptotic developments of solutions of (5.02), complete with error bounds, when $f(z)$ depends on a large parameter u . Suppose, however, that the parameter is absent, and

(5.07) $$f(z) \sim kz^{-1-\sigma} \quad \text{as } |z| \to \infty ,$$

where k, σ are constants and $\sigma > 0$. Then for large $|z|$, (5.03) and (5.04) are generalized asymptotic developments, complete with error bounds. For if the limits of integration on the right of (5.01) are taken to be $-\infty$ and z, it readily follows by induction that $A_s(z) = O(|z|^{-s\sigma_1})$ $(s = 1, 2, \ldots)$, where $\sigma_1 = \min(\sigma, 1)$. Thence from (5.05), with $a = -\infty$, we derive $\epsilon_m(z),\ \eta_m(z) = O(|z|^{-m\sigma_1})$. Thus in the sense of Erdélyi [6], equations (5.03) and (5.04) are generalized asymptotic expansions with respect to the scale $\{|z|^{-m\sigma_1}\}$ as $|z| \to \infty$.

The expansion (5.03) is generally less convenient than the usual Thomé asymptotic expansions in descending powers of z [5], §3.2, because of the need to evaluate the functions $A_s(z)$. The case of Bessel's differential equation is special, however, in that the two forms of expansion become the same with a suitable choice of $f(z)$.

Set

$$f(z) = (\nu^2 - \tfrac{1}{4})/z^2 , \tag{5.08}$$

where ν is a constant. The solution of equation (5.02) is then given by $w = z^{\frac{1}{2}} \mathcal{C}_\nu(\pm iz)$, where $\mathcal{C}_\nu$ denotes the general cylinder function of order ν. Applying the theorem with $a = -\infty$, and replacing z by iz, we construct a solution

$$w_m = e^{iz} \left\{ \sum_{s=0}^{m-1} i^s \frac{a_s}{z^s} + \epsilon_m \right\} , \tag{5.09}$$

in which a_s is defined by (1.04) and

$$|\epsilon_m| \le 2 \exp\{|\nu^2 - \tfrac{1}{4}| \mathcal{V}_{i\infty, z}(t^{-1})\} \mathcal{V}_{i\infty, z}(a_m t^{-m}) . \tag{5.10}$$

The path of variation is subject to the condition that $\operatorname{Im} t$ is monotonic, and this restricts z to the region $-\pi < \arg z < 2\pi$.

Clearly

$$w_m = Az^{\frac{1}{2}} H_\nu^{(1)}(z) + Bz^{\frac{1}{2}} H_\nu^{(2)}(z) , \tag{5.11}$$

where A, B are independent of z. Letting $z \to i\infty$, we see that $\epsilon_m \to 0$ and $e^{-iz} w_m \to 1$. Using the known asymptotic forms of the Hankel functions [18], we deduce that $B = 0$ and $A = (\frac{1}{2}\pi)^{\frac{1}{2}} e^{i\pi(\frac{1}{2}\nu + \frac{1}{4})}$. Thus we derive the main result of this section:

$$H_\nu^{(1)}(z) = \left(\frac{2}{\pi z}\right)^{\frac{1}{2}} e^{i(z - \frac{1}{2}\nu\pi - \frac{1}{4}\pi)} \left\{ \sum_{s=0}^{m-1} i^s \frac{a_s}{z^s} + \epsilon_m \right\} , \tag{5.12}$$

when $-\pi < \arg z < 2\pi$, where ϵ_m is subject to (5.10). We now proceed to the evaluation of this bound.

6. <u>Evaluation of the variations</u>. The problem discussed in this section is the choice of the path $\mathcal{P}$, connecting $i\infty$ and z, to minimize the quantity

$$\mathcal{V}_{i\infty, z}(t^{-m}) = m \int_{\mathcal{P}} |t^{-m-1} dt| \quad (m \ge 1) . \tag{6.01}$$

We write $\theta = \arg z - \frac{1}{2}\pi$, and consider in turn the cases $|\theta| \le \frac{1}{2}\pi$, $\frac{1}{2}\pi < |\theta| \le \pi$, $\pi < |\theta| < \frac{3}{2}\pi$.

(i) $|\theta| \leq \frac{1}{2}\pi$. Consider the path which is indicated on Figure 1 when θ is positive and is its image in the imaginary axis when θ is negative. It comprises part of the imaginary axis, a

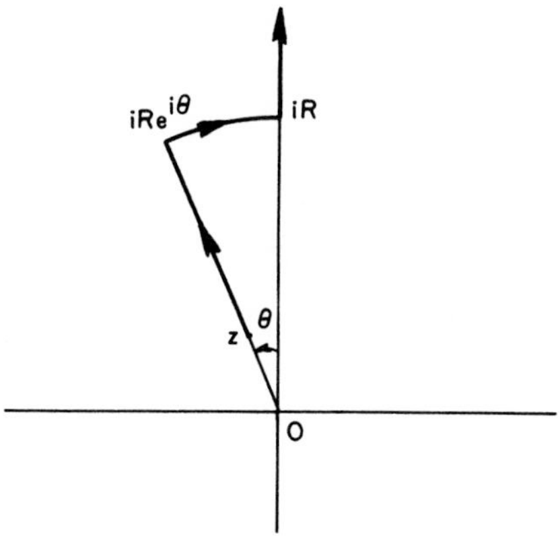

Figure 1. $0 \leq \theta \leq \frac{1}{2}\pi$.

circular arc of radius R centred at the origin, where $R\,(>|z|)$ is arbitrary, and the straight line with parametric equation

$$(6.02) \qquad t = z + \tau e^{i(\theta + \frac{1}{2}\pi)} \qquad (0 \leq \tau \leq R - |z|).$$

As $R \to \infty$ the contributions to the variation from the imaginary axis and the circular arc both vanish, and we obtain

$$(6.03) \quad \mathcal{V}_{i\infty, z}(t^{-m}) = \int_0^\infty \frac{m\,d\tau}{|z+\tau e^{i(\theta+\frac{1}{2}\pi)}|^{m+1}} = \int_0^\infty \frac{m\,d\tau}{(|z|+\tau)^{m+1}} = \frac{1}{|z|^m}.$$

Since this actually equals the modulus of the difference between the values of t^{-m} at the extremities of the path, no other path can yield a smaller variation.

(ii) $\frac{1}{2}\pi < |\theta| \leq \pi$. Consider the path indicated in Figure 2. Again, as the radius R of the circular arc tends to infinity the contributions from this arc and the imaginary axis both vanish, and we obtain

$$(6.04) \qquad \mathcal{V}_{i\infty, z}(t^{-m}) = \int_0^\infty \frac{m\,d\tau}{|z-\tau|^{m+1}} = \int_0^\infty \frac{m\,d\tau}{\{(\tau+|x|)^2+y^2\}^{\frac{1}{2}m+\frac{1}{2}}},$$

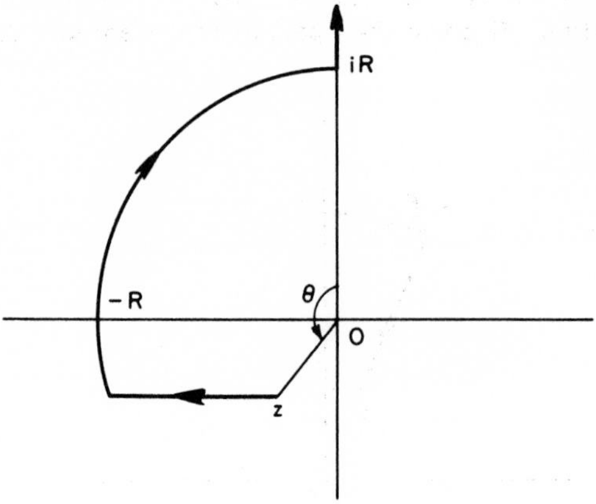

Figure 2. $\frac{1}{2}\pi < \theta \leq \pi$.

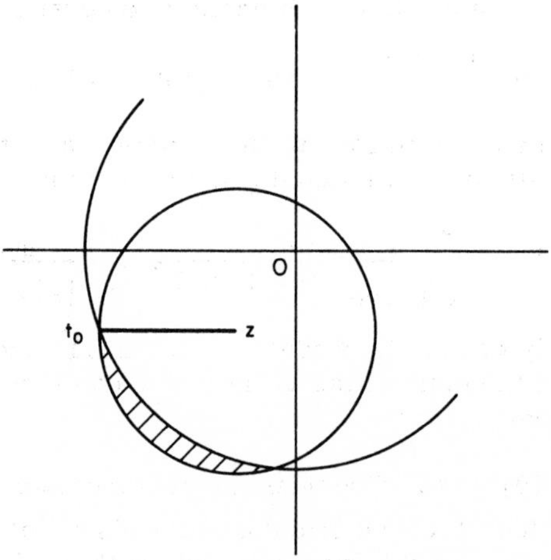

Figure 3. $\frac{1}{2}\pi < \theta \leq \pi$.

where x and y denote the real and imaginary parts of z, respectively.

That this path minimizes the variation can be seen as follows. Let us travel a prescribed distance τ along any admissible path from z, arriving at t, say. For the path of Figure 2 t is at $t_0 = z-\tau$, and for any other path t lies within or on the circle centred at z and passing through t_0; see Figure 3. Clearly $|t| > |t_0|$ only if t lies within the shaded lune bounded by this circle and the circular arc centred at the origin and passing through t_0. No path can be admitted to this lune however, because $\operatorname{Im} t < \operatorname{Im} z$ in its interior. Hence $|t| \leq |t_0|$, which leads to the stated result of this paragraph.

The integral (6.04) can be evaluated in terms of elementary functions for all integer values of m; for example

$$(6.05) \qquad \begin{cases} \mathcal{V}_{i\infty, z}(t^{-1}) = \dfrac{1}{|y|}\left(\dfrac{\pi}{2} - \tan^{-1}\left|\dfrac{x}{y}\right|\right) & (y \neq 0), \\ \mathcal{V}_{i\infty, z}(t^{-1}) = \dfrac{1}{|x|} & (y = 0). \end{cases}$$

To avoid unnecessary complication however, we bound it by the slightly weaker form

$$(6.06) \qquad \mathcal{V}_{i\infty, z}(t^{-m}) \leq \int_0^{\infty} \frac{m\,d\tau}{(\tau^2+x^2+y^2)^{\frac{1}{2}m+\frac{1}{2}}} = \frac{\chi(m)}{|z|^m},$$

in which

$$(6.07) \qquad \chi(m) = \sqrt{\pi}\ \Gamma(\tfrac{1}{2}m+1)/\Gamma(\tfrac{1}{2}m\ \ \tfrac{1}{2})$$

This bound is in fact attained when $x = 0$.

(iii) $\pi < |\theta| < \frac{3}{2}\pi$. The minimizing path is indicated on Figure 4. To prove this assertion, let any other path intersect the negative imaginary axis at the point $i\ell$. If $\ell = y$ the result follows immediately from (ii), hence we suppose that $0 > \ell > y$. On travelling a distance τ from $i\ell$ towards z we arrive at a point t somewhere within or on the smaller circle of Figure 5, whereas on travelling a distance τ from iy along the nominated path we arrive at $t_0 = iy+\tau$. Again we have $|t| \leq |t_0|$ except within an inadmissible lune.

On letting $R \to \infty$, we obtain

$$(6.08) \qquad \mathcal{V}_{i\infty, z}(t^{-m}) = \int_z^{iy-\infty} \left|\frac{m\,dt}{t^{m+1}}\right| = \int_0^{|x|} \frac{m\,d\tau}{|iy+\tau|^{m+1}} + \int_0^{\infty} \frac{m\,d\tau}{|iy-\tau|^{m+1}}.$$

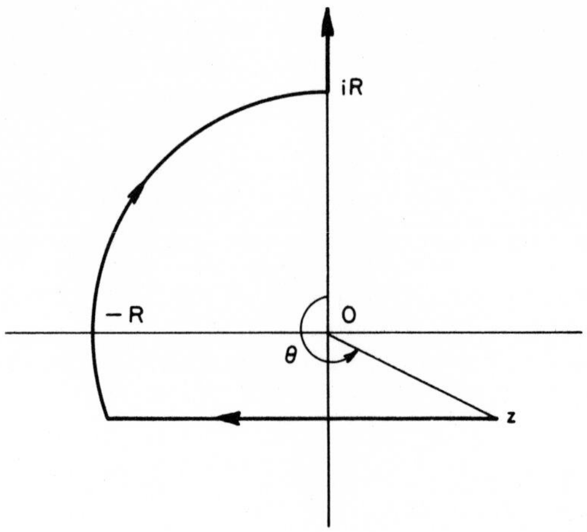

Figure 4. $\pi < \theta < \frac{3}{2}\pi$.

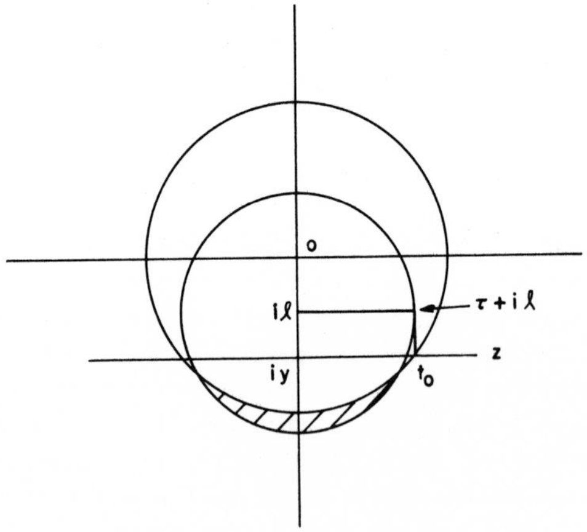

Figure 5. $\pi < \theta < \frac{3}{2}\pi$.

The last of these integrals equals $\chi(m)|y|^{-m}$ and the one before it is bounded by this quantity. Therefore

$$\mathcal{V}_{i\infty, z}(t^{-m}) < 2\chi(m)|\operatorname{Im} z|^{-m} . \tag{6.09}$$

We observe that as $\arg z$ approaches either of its extreme values $-\pi$ and 2π, $\mathcal{V}_{i\infty, z}(t^{-m})$ becomes increasingly large, as anticipated in §§1 and 4 above.

7. Collected results for cylinder functions. On combining the analysis of the last two sections and extending it by means of (5.04) to the derivative $H_\nu^{(1)\prime}(z)$, we have the following results, in which ν is an unrestricted real or complex number.

$$H_\nu^{(1)}(z) = \left(\frac{2}{\pi z}\right)^{\frac{1}{2}} e^{i\varphi}\left\{\sum_{s=0}^{m-1} i^s \frac{a_s}{z^s} + \epsilon_m\right\} , \tag{7.01}$$

$$H_\nu^{(1)\prime}(z) = \left(\frac{2}{\pi z}\right)^{\frac{1}{2}} ie^{i\varphi}\left\{\sum_{s=0}^{m-1} i^s \frac{b_s}{z^s} + i^m \frac{(b_m - a_m)}{z^m} + \eta_m + \frac{i}{2z}\epsilon_m\right\} , \tag{7.02}$$

where $\varphi = z - \frac{1}{2}\nu\pi - \frac{1}{4}\pi$,

$$a_s = \frac{(4\nu^2-1^2)(4\nu^2-3^2)\dots\{4\nu^2-(2s-1)^2\}}{8^s\, s!} , \quad b_s = \frac{4\nu^2+4s^2-1}{4\nu^2-(2s-1)^2} a_s , \tag{7.03}$$

$$|\epsilon_m|, \ |\eta_m| \le 2|a_m| \exp\{|\nu^2 - \tfrac{1}{4}|\mathcal{V}_{i\infty, z}(t^{-1})\}\mathcal{V}_{i\infty, z}(t^{-m}) , \tag{7.04}$$

and

$$\mathcal{V}_{i\infty, z}(t^{-m}) \le \begin{cases} |z|^{-m} & (0 \le \arg z \le \pi) , \\ \chi(m)|z|^{-m} & (-\frac{1}{2}\pi \le \arg z < 0 \text{ or } \pi < \arg z \le \frac{3}{2}\pi) , \\ 2\chi(m)|\operatorname{Im} z|^{-m} & (-\pi < \arg z < -\frac{1}{2}\pi \text{ or } \frac{3}{2}\pi < \arg z < 2\pi). \end{cases} \tag{7.05}$$

In (7.01) and (7.02) the branch of $z^{\frac{1}{2}}$ is $\exp(\frac{1}{2}\ln|z| + \frac{1}{2}i \arg z)$, and in (7.05) $\chi(m)$ is defined by (6.07) . The values of the first ten $\chi(m)$ to two decimal places are as follows:

m	$\chi(m)$	m	$\chi(m)$
1	1.57	6	3.20
2	2.00	7	3.44
3	2.36	8	3.66
4	2.67	9	3.87
5	2.95	10	4.06

For large m, $\chi(m) \sim \sqrt{\frac{1}{2}m\pi}$.

The corresponding results for $H_\nu^{(2)}(z)$ and its derivative are obtained by changing the sign of i throughout, and replacing the z-regions in (7.05) by their respective conjugates.

In applying these results, the bounds for the quantity $\mathcal{V}_{i\infty, z}(t^{-1})$ appearing in (7.04) are obtained by setting m = 1 and $\chi(1) = \frac{1}{2}\pi$ in (7.05). It should be observed that for all values of z in the region $-\frac{1}{2}\pi \le \arg z \le \frac{3}{2}\pi$ for which the expansions (7.01) and (7.02) are computationally useful, the factor $\exp\{|\nu^2 - \frac{1}{4}|\mathcal{V}_{i\infty, z}(t^{-1})\}$ is approximately unity, because a necessary condition that $|a_m z^{-m}|$ be small compared with the leading term 1 of each series is that $|z| >> |\nu^2 - \frac{1}{4}|$.

For other ranges of arg z use may be made of the connection formula [18], §3.62,

(7.06)

$$H_\nu^{(1)}(ze^{n\pi i}) = \sin(1-n)\nu\pi \operatorname{cosec} \nu\pi H_\nu^{(1)}(z) + \sin n\nu\pi \operatorname{cosec} \nu\pi H_\nu^{(1)}(ze^{\pi i}) ,$$

in which n is a positive or negative integer. In the application of this formula, arg z can always be taken in the range $(-\frac{1}{2}\pi, \frac{1}{2}\pi)$, which means that the use of (7.01) and (7.02) can be confined to the sector $-\frac{1}{2}\pi \le \arg z \le \frac{3}{2}\pi$. Thus the direct use of (7.01) and (7.02) in the sectors $-\pi < \arg z < -\frac{1}{2}\pi$ and $\frac{3}{2}\pi < \arg z < 2\pi$, which is fraught with the danger of a large error term, can be avoided altogether. In effect, the more accurate connection-formula procedure improves the accuracy of (7.01) and (7.02) in these two sectors by adding in appropriate contributions of an exponentially small nature, and accordingly provides a rigorous justification, in the present example, of Miller's use of complete asymptotic expansions (§2).

Corresponding results for the functions $J_\nu(z)$ and $Y_\nu(z)$ are immediately deducible from those for the Hankel functions by means of the relations

$$(7.07)\quad J_\nu(z) = \frac{1}{2}\{H_\nu^{(1)}(z) + H_\nu^{(2)}(z)\},\ Y_\nu(z) = \frac{1}{2}i\{H_\nu^{(2)}(z) - H_\nu^{(1)}(z)\}.$$

We find that

$$J_\nu(z) = \left(\frac{2}{\pi z}\right)^{\frac{1}{2}} \left\{\cos\varphi \sum_{s=0}^{m-1} (-)^s \frac{a_{2s}}{z^{2s}} - \sin\varphi \sum_{s=0}^{m-1} (-)^s \frac{a_{2s+1}}{z^{2s+1}} + \alpha_{2m}\right\}$$

$$(7.08)\qquad = \left(\frac{2}{\pi z}\right)^{\frac{1}{2}} \left\{\cos\varphi \sum_{s=0}^{m} (-)^s \frac{a_{2s}}{z^{2s}} - \sin\varphi \sum_{s=0}^{m-1} (-)^s \frac{a_{2s+1}}{z^{2s+1}} + \alpha_{2m+1}\right\},$$

and

$$Y_\nu(z) = \left(\frac{2}{\pi z}\right)^{\frac{1}{2}} \left\{\sin\varphi \sum_{s=0}^{m-1} (-)^s \frac{a_{2s}}{z^{2s}} + \cos\varphi \sum_{s=0}^{m-1} (-)^s \frac{a_{2s+1}}{z^{2s+1}} + \beta_{2m}\right\}$$

$$(7.09)\qquad = \left(\frac{2}{\pi z}\right)^{\frac{1}{2}} \left\{\sin\varphi \sum_{s=0}^{m} (-)^s \frac{a_{2s}}{z^{2s}} + \cos\varphi \sum_{s=0}^{m-1} (-)^s \frac{a_{2s+1}}{z^{2s+1}} + \beta_{2m+1}\right\},$$

where

(7.10)

$$|\alpha_m|,\ |\beta_m| \le (|e^{\nu\pi i/2}| + |e^{-\nu\pi i/2}|)\exp\left(\frac{|\nu^2 - \frac{1}{4}|}{z}\right)\frac{|a_m|}{z^m} \qquad (\arg z = 0),$$

(7.11)

$$|\alpha_m|,\ |\beta_m| \le \{|e^{\pm i\varphi}| + \chi(m)|e^{\mp i\varphi}|\}\exp\left(\frac{\pi|\nu^2 - \frac{1}{4}|}{2|z|}\right)\frac{|a_m|}{|z|^m} \quad (0 < |\arg z| \le \tfrac{1}{2}\pi),$$

(7.12)

$$|\alpha_m|,\ |\beta_m| \le \{|e^{\pm i\varphi}| + 2\chi(m)|e^{\mp i\varphi}|\}\exp\left(\frac{\pi|\nu^2 - \frac{1}{4}|}{|\mathrm{Im}\, z|}\right)\frac{|a_m|}{|\mathrm{Im}\, z|^m}$$

$$(\tfrac{1}{2}\pi < |\arg z| < \pi).$$

The upper or lower signs are taken in (7.11) and (7.12), according as $\arg z$ is positive or negative. Again, we see that to achieve maximum accuracy the use of (7.08) and (7.09) should be confined to the half-plane $|\arg z| \le \frac{1}{2}\pi$ and connection formulae used elsewhere.

Next, we consider the modified Bessel functions:

(7.13)

$$K_\nu(z) = \frac{1}{2}\pi e^{\frac{1}{2}(\nu+1)\pi i} H_\nu^{(1)}(e^{\frac{1}{2}\pi i} z), \quad I_\nu(z) = \frac{1}{2} e^{-\frac{1}{2}\nu\pi i} \{H_\nu^{(1)}(e^{\frac{1}{2}\pi i} z) + H_\nu^{(2)}(e^{\frac{1}{2}\pi i} z)\}.$$

For the former, we derive immediately from (7.01)

$$K_\nu(z) = \left(\frac{\pi}{2z}\right)^{\frac{1}{2}} e^{-z} \left\{\sum_{s=0}^{m-1} \frac{a_s}{z^s} + \gamma_m\right\}, \tag{7.14}$$

where

$$|\gamma_m| \le \begin{cases} 2\exp\left(\dfrac{|\nu^2 - \frac{1}{4}|}{|z|}\right)\dfrac{|a_m|}{|z|^m} & (|\arg z| \le \frac{1}{2}\pi), \\[2ex] 2\chi(m)\exp\left(\dfrac{\pi|\nu^2 - \frac{1}{4}|}{2|z|}\right)\dfrac{|a_m|}{|z|^m} & (\frac{1}{2}\pi < |\arg z| \le \pi, \\[2ex] 4\chi(m)\exp\left(\dfrac{\pi|\nu^2 - \frac{1}{4}|}{|\mathrm{Re}\, z|}\right)\dfrac{|a_m|}{|\mathrm{Re}\, z|^m} & (\pi < |\arg z| < \frac{3}{2}\pi). \end{cases} \tag{7.15}$$

For the latter, we find that

(7.16)

$$I_\nu(z) = \frac{e^z}{(2\pi z)^{\frac{1}{2}}}\left\{\sum_{s=0}^{m-1}(-)^s \frac{a_s}{z^s} + \delta_m\right\} - ie^{-\nu\pi i}\frac{e^{-z}}{(2\pi z)^{\frac{1}{2}}}\left\{\sum_{s=0}^{m-1}\frac{a_s}{z^s} + \gamma_m\right\}$$

$$(-\tfrac{3}{2}\pi < \arg z < \tfrac{1}{2}\pi).$$

Here γ_m is the same as in (7.14) and is therefore bounded by (7.15); δ_m also is subject to (7.15) except that the applicable regions are changed to

$$-\frac{3}{2}\pi \le \arg z \le -\frac{1}{2}\pi, \quad -\frac{1}{2}\pi < \arg z \le 0, \quad 0 < \arg z < \frac{1}{2}\pi,$$

respectively.

Again, the use of (7.14) and (7.16) should be confined to the regions $|\arg z| \le \pi$ and $-\pi \le \arg z \le 0$, respectively, and connection formulae used elsewhere. In particular, by using the relation

$I_\nu(z) = e^{\nu\pi i} I_\nu(e^{-\pi i}z)$ we deduce from (7.16) its conjugate form applicable to the region $0 \leq \arg z \leq \pi$.

Finally, we observe that by setting $\nu = \frac{1}{3}$ and $\frac{2}{3}$ we may deduce error bounds for the asymptotic expansions of the Airy functions and their derivatives, but we shall not record these results here.

The above bounds are by no means the first which have been given for the remainder terms in the Hankel expansions. Watson [18], pages 205-220, describes in detail researches of Hankel, Stieltjes and himself for real ν and positive z, and of Weber and Schläfli for complex ν and z. Subsequently Schläfli's results have been extended by Meijer [9]. Quite recently, Döring [4] has critically examined the bounds of Schläfli and Meijer in the case of real ν, and effected simplifications to make them more readily computable. Except for Weber each author derives his results from integral representations of the Hankel functions. Weber uses the defining differential equation in a way which bears some resemblance to the theorem of §5 above, but is more complicated.

It is not claimed that the present bounds are superior to previous results in every respect. Indeed, for certain combinations of ν and z, particularly real ν, some of the earlier results are simpler and sharper, although it must be added that in regions in which the expansions are meaningful the sharpening seldom exceeds a factor of 2 (compare the remarks made in the second paragraph of §4). We do claim, however, that for the general combination of complex values of ν and z, the present results are considerably simpler than the aggregate of earlier results, and furthermore that they are completely realistic for all combinations of the variables. Of the earlier results, the most complete are those of Meijer. They are more complicated than (7.01) to (7.16), involving the solution of a transcendental equation in some regions. Moreover, they break down for complex values of ν arbitrarily close to, though not lying on, the lines $\mathrm{Re}\,\nu = \pm\frac{1}{2}, \pm\frac{3}{2}, \ldots$.

8. Summary. In the first part of this paper we discussed, in general terms, practical difficulties in the use of asymptotic expansions, particularly in the vicinity of the boundaries of their regions of validity in the complex plane. We pointed out that the use of "complete asymptotic expansions" in the sense of Watson and Miller, though often expedient in practice, is difficult to place on a firm mathematical foundation. We indicated, however, that the practical difficulties could be overcome by the development of satisfactory theories of error bounds. We also suggested that such theories may throw light on the theoretical nature of an asymptotic expansion involving two or more variables, and in this respect provide an alternative or supplementary mathematical tool to generalizations of Poincaré's definition.

In the second part of the paper new error bounds were derived for the well-known Hankel asymptotic expansions for cylinder functions of large complex argument and given real or complex order. These bounds were obtained by application of the asymptotic theory of ordinary differential equations. A characteristic feature of their evaluation was the minimization of the variation of the first neglected term of the series over a prescribed type of contour in the complex plane. The bounds appear to be the first ones for the Hankel expansions which are completely satisfactory for all combinations of the variables. They are well adapted to the control of accuracy in the construction of general-purpose automatic computing routines for the cylinder functions.

REFERENCES

1. N. G. de Bruijn, Asymptotic methods in analysis, (Amsterdam, North-Holland; Interscience, New York; 1958).

2. J. G. van der Corput, Asymptotic developments I. Fundamental theorems of asymptotics, J. d'Analyse Math., 4 (1956), 341-418.

3. J. G. van der Corput and J. Franklin, Approximation of integrals by integration by parts, Koninkl. Nederlandse Akad. Wetensch. Proc., A, 54 (1951), 213-219.

4. B. Döring, Über Fehlerschranken zu den Hankelschen asymptotischen Entwicklungen der Besselfunktionen für komplexes Argument und reellen Index, Z. angew. Math. Mech., 42 (1962), 62-76.

5. A. Erdélyi, Asymptotic expansions, (Dover, New York, 1956).

6. __________, General asymptotic expansions of Laplace integrals, Arch. Rational Mech. Anal., 7 (1961), 1 - 20.

7. A. Erdélyi and M. Wyman, The asymptotic evaluation of certain integrals, Arch. Rational Mech. Anal., 14 (1963), 217-260.

8. G. E. Forsythe, Singularity and near singularity in numerical analysis, Amer. Math. Mon., 65 (1958), 229-240.

9. C. S. Meijer, Asymptotische Entwicklungen von Besselschen, Hankelschen und verwandten Funktionen. I-IV. Koninkl. Nederlandse Akad. Wetensch. Proc., 35 (1932), 656-667, 852-866, 948-958, 1079-1090.

10. J. C. P. Miller, Tables of Weber parabolic cylinder functions, (London, H. M. S. O., 1955).

11. National Bureau of Standards, Handbook of mathematical functions, Appl. Math. Ser. 55 (Washington, G. P. O., 1964). Chapter 19.

12. F. W. J. Olver, Error bounds for the Liouville-Green (or WKB) approximation, Proc. Cambridge Philos. Soc., 57 (1961), 790-810.

13. __________, Error bounds for asymptotic expansions in turning-point problems, J. Soc. Indust. Appl. Math., 12(1964), 200-214.

14. H. Poincaré, Sur les intégrales irrégulières des équations linéaires, Acta Math., 8 (1886), 295-344.

15. H. Schmidt, Beiträge zu einer Theorie der allgemeinen asymptotischen Darstellungen, Math. Ann., 113 (1937), 629-656.

16. G. N. Watson, A theory of asymptotic series, Phil. Trans. Roy. Soc. London A, 211 (1911), 279-313.

17. __________, The transformation of an asymptotic series into a convergent series of inverse factorials, Rend. Circolo Mat. Palermo 34 (1912), 1-48.

18. __________, Theory of Bessel functions, (Cambridge U. P. Second edition, 1944).

19. A. van Wijngaarden, A transformation of formal series. I, Koninkl. Nederlandse Akad. Wetensch. Proc., A, 56 (1953), 522-543.

20. M. Wyman, The asymptotic behaviour of the Hermite polynomials, Canad. J. Math., 15 (1963), 332-349.

The author acknowledges helpful criticisms of this paper by Mr. G. F. Miller and Dr. J. C. P. Miller.

ROBERT A. CLARK

Asymptotic Solutions of Elastic Shell Problems

1. Introduction. The word shell is used to describe a three dimensional structure which has one dimension (the thickness) that is small compared to all other characteristic dimensions including the radii of surface curvature. Our purpose here is to describe some problems within the mathematical theory of shells composed of elastic material. More specifically, we shall discuss problems to which methods of asymptotic integration of ordinary differential equations may be applied, especially some of those methods extensively developed by Professor R. E. Langer.

Many problems of the type mentioned occur in the theory of small rotationally symmetric deformations of shells associated with smooth surfaces of revolution and we shall limit our attention primarily to problems within this theory. However, a few remarks about general shell theory may be in order. The ratio of the thickness of a shell to some representative shell length determines a small parameter and the presence of this parameter enables one to use various perturbation or asymptotic methods to great advantage in obtaining approximate solutions of complex problems. In fact, shell theory itself represents an asymptotic first approximation to the three dimensional theory of elastic materials. However, the nature of the relationship between three dimensional elasticity and shell theory has yet to be established in a completely rigorous fashion. Much important work has been concerned with this relationship and many interesting problems exist. Two recent contributions are by A. L. Goldenveizer [15] and E. Reissner [29].

Within shell theory itself there are many applications of asymptotic methods and the extensive monograph [14] by Goldenviezer is almost exclusively devoted to such techniques. The reasoning is usually heuristic as a sufficiently general rigorous theory of asymptotic solutions of partial differential equations does not yet exist, although there are efforts in this direction [36].

Within the theory of symmetric deformations of shells of revolution, which involves only ordinary differential equations, it is possible to be more precise. One finds that the historical development of shell theory largely parallels the development of the mathematical theory of asymptotic solutions. A breakthrough in shell theory occurred in 1912 when H. Reissner [30] succeeded in reducing the equations for a spherical shell to a symmetric pair of coupled second order differential equations. Acquainted with the work of his colleague, Blumenthal [2], Reissner also gave formal asymptotic solutions of the now classical type. Blumenthal [3], in turn, established the asymptotic nature of such solutions in a rigorous fashion.

In 1913, Meissner [21] generalized H. Reissner's reduction to arbitrary shells of revolution. Classical asymptotic solutions of the resulting equations have since been applied to a large variety of shell problems and may be found in standard textbooks on shell theory.

Apparently, no one applied uniform asymptotic solutions of the turning point type to shell problems until the 1940's. This was partly due, probably, to the lack of adequate tables for the Bessel functions involved in the representations. However, three independent applications of such solutions to toroidal shells were published from 1949 to 1951 [4, 37, 38]. Since 1950, there have been a great many applications of turning point methods to shell problems, some of which will be described below.

2. <u>Symmetric deformations of shells of revolution.</u> We shall sketch a brief derivation of the basic equations which borrows from the work of E. Reissner [26] and V. V. Novozhilov [25] and which attempts to show clearly the relationship between different formulations which exist in the literature. We shall limit ourselves to the linear or small deformation theory of isotropic shells of uniform thickness subject to static, rotationally symmetric loads.

The underlying shell theory hypotheses (in addition to the relative thinness of a shell) are (1) that normals to the shell's middle surface deform into normals to the deformed middle surface without extension (this implies that the transverse shear and normal strains are negligible), (2) that the transverse normal stress is negligible, and (3) that the components of displacement u and w and the rotation β are sufficiently small to neglect second order terms while the middle surface strains, ϵ_s and ϵ_θ, are negligible compared to unity.

Cylindrical coordinates of a point on the middle surface of the undeformed shell are denoted by (r, θ, z). Figure 1 shows a portion of a meridian of the middle surface. When it is revolved about the z-axis, the meridian generates the middle surface of the shell. The shell is always assumed either to be closed (e.g., a complete sphere) or to have at most two edges formed by intersections with cones

φ = constant, where φ is the angle of inclination of the normal to a meridian with respect to the z-axis. With s denoting the arc length of a meridian in the direction of increasing φ, the following geometric relations hold:

$$(1) \qquad r = R_\theta \sin\varphi\,, \quad r' = \frac{dr}{ds} = \cos\varphi\,, \quad \frac{d^2r}{ds^2} = -\frac{r}{R_s R_\theta}\,, \quad \frac{d\varphi}{ds} = \frac{1}{R_s}\,,$$

where R_θ, R_s are the principal radii of curvature of the middle surface in the circumferential and meridional directions, respectively.

The quantities u, w and β denote the changes in r, z, and φ due to deformation of the shell, while $\epsilon_s, \epsilon_\theta$ are the strains of the middle surface due to stretching and κ_s, κ_θ are the changes in the principal curvatures of the middle surface due to bending. For small deformations, the following relations hold (where primes indicate differentiation with respect to the arc length s):

$$(2) \qquad \epsilon_s = u' \cos\varphi - w' \sin\varphi\,, \quad \epsilon_\theta = u/r\,,$$

$$(3) \qquad \kappa_s = \beta'\,, \qquad \kappa_\theta = r' \beta/r$$

$$(4) \qquad \beta = -u' \sin\varphi - w' \cos\varphi\,.$$

Solving (2) and (4) for u' and w' yields

$$(5) \qquad u' = -\beta \sin\varphi + \epsilon_s \cos\varphi\,, \; w' = -\beta\cos\varphi - \epsilon_s \sin\varphi\,.$$

By eliminating u and w from the above equations and making use of equations (1), one may obtain the following compatibility equations:

$$(C_1) \qquad (r\epsilon_\theta)' - r'\epsilon_s + \frac{r}{R_\theta}\beta = 0\,,$$

$$(C_2) \qquad (r\beta)' - r(\kappa_s + \kappa_\theta) = 0\,,$$

$$(C_3) \qquad (r\kappa_\theta)' - r'\kappa_s + \frac{r\beta}{R_s R_\theta} = 0\,.$$

The last two equations are merely identities that result from equations (3).

Stress resultants N_s, N_θ, Q and stress couples M_s, M_θ correspond to the average and first moment across the shell thickness of three-dimensional components of stress. The equilibrium equations satisfied by these stress quantities may be written as

$$(E_1) \qquad (rN_s)' - r'N_\theta + \frac{r}{R_s} Q + rp_s = 0 ,$$

$$(E_2) \qquad (rQ)' - \frac{r}{R_s} N_s - \frac{r}{R_\theta} N_\theta + rp_n = 0 ,$$

$$(E_3) \qquad (rM_s)' - r'M_\theta - rQ = 0 ,$$

where p_s and p_n are the components of surface load intensity in the tangential and normal directions.

Defining (in accordance with Fig. 1)

$$(6) \qquad \begin{aligned} H &= N_s \cos\varphi + Q \sin\varphi , \\ V &= N_s \sin\varphi - Q \cos\varphi , \end{aligned}$$

it follows that equations (E_1) and (E_2) may be combined to yield

$$(7) \quad = \quad (E_1) \cos\varphi + (E_2) \sin\varphi : \qquad (rH)' - N_\theta + r\,p_H = 0 ,$$

$$(8) \quad = \quad (E_1) \sin\varphi - (E_2) \cos\varphi : \qquad (rV)' + rp_V = 0 ,$$

where p_H and p_V are components of load intensity defined by equations analogous to (6). The "vertical" resultant V is determined by direct integration of (8). If we define $\psi = rH$, then from (6), (7) and (1) we may write

$$(9) \qquad N_s = \frac{r'}{r} \psi + \frac{rV}{R_\theta} ,$$

$$(10) \qquad N_\theta = \psi' + rp_H$$

$$(11) \qquad R_\theta Q = \psi - r' R_\theta V .$$

Thus, with V known, N_s, N_θ, and Q are given in terms of the single unknown function ψ. Alternatively, N_s and N_θ may be expressed in terms of the combination $R_\theta Q$ by substituting for ψ from equation (11).

For an isotropic shell, the stress and strain quantities are assumed to be related by the following generalized Hooke's law:

$$\text{(12)} \qquad \begin{aligned} C\epsilon_s &= N_s - \nu N_\theta, & (1-\nu^2)\, D\kappa_s &= M_s - \nu M_\theta, \\ C\epsilon_\theta &= N_\theta - \nu N_s, & (1-\nu^2)\, D\kappa_\theta &= M_\theta - \nu M_s, \end{aligned}$$

where the constant coefficients are defined by

$$C = Eh, \quad D = \bar{h}^2 C, \quad \bar{h} = h/[12(1-\nu^2)] .$$

Here, h is the shell thickness, while E and ν are the elastic constants known as Young's modulus and Poisson's ratio.

3. Reduction of equations to a fourth-order system. By substituting from the stress-strain relations, the compatibility equations may be written in terms of the stress quantities. The resulting equations may, in turn, be combined with the equilibrium equations to obtain a simple set of four first-order differential equations. The resulting equations contain the quantities N and M defined by

$$\text{(13)} \qquad N = N_s + N_\theta, \quad M = M_s + M_\theta .$$

Using $R_\theta Q$ instead ψ in equations (9) and (10), the final equations may be written in the form:

$$\text{(I)} \; = (9) + (10): \qquad N = \frac{1}{r}\frac{d}{ds}(rR_\theta Q) + N_M,$$

$$\text{(II)} \; = \frac{\bar{h}C}{r}(C_2): \qquad \frac{M}{(1+\nu)\bar{h}} = \frac{\bar{h}C}{r}\frac{d}{ds}(r\beta),$$

$$\text{(III)} \; = \frac{C}{r}(C_1) + \frac{1+\nu}{r}(E_1): \quad \frac{dN}{ds} = \frac{-1}{\bar{h}R_\theta}\Big[(\bar{h}C\beta) + \underline{(1+\nu)\frac{\bar{h}}{R_s}(R_\theta Q)}\Big] - (1+\nu)p_s,$$

$$\text{(IV)} \; = (1-\nu)\frac{\bar{h}C}{r}(C_3) + \frac{(E_3)}{\bar{h}r}: \quad \frac{d}{ds}\Big[\frac{M}{(1+\nu)\bar{h}}\Big] = \frac{1}{\bar{h}R_\theta}\Big[(R_\theta Q) - \underline{(1-\nu)\frac{\bar{h}}{R_s}(\bar{h}C\beta)}\Big],$$

On the left we have written the combinations of the previous equations which result in the given equations. The quantity N_M in (I) is given by

(14) $$N_M = R_\theta p_n + \left(1 - \frac{R_\theta}{R_s}\right) \frac{R_\theta V}{r} .$$

It is the value of N given by the so-called membrane theory, when M_s, M_θ, and Q are negligible. The reason for writing (II) and (IV) in the above form will be apparent later.

In the solution of particular problems it becomes clear that the combinations $R\theta Q$ and $\bar{h}C\beta$ are of the same order of magnitude in general. Consequently, the underlined terms in (III) and (IV) are of relative order $\bar{h}/R_s$, which must be small compared to unity for a true shell. Furthermore, one can show explicitly that the coefficient of the underlined term in (III) is modified if transverse shear strains are not neglected, so that the relative error of shell theory itself is of the order $\bar{h}/R$. It is therefore consistent with our basic hypotheses to drop both of the underlined terms in the above equations.

If N and M are eliminated from equations (I) to (IV), one obtains the pair of equations for β and $R_\theta Q$ originally derived by Meissner [21], who retained the underlined terms. Dropping the underlined terms and eliminating β and $R_\theta Q$, one obtains a pair of equations for N and M which corresponds to Novozhilov's formulation [25].

Substituting for $R_\theta Q$ from equation (11) (and dropping the underlined terms), we may also write the basic system of equations in the form:

(I)' $$N = \frac{1}{r}\frac{d}{ds}(r\psi) + \frac{rV}{R_\theta} + rp_H ,$$

(II)' $$\frac{M}{(1+\nu)\bar{h}} = \frac{\bar{h}C}{r}\frac{d}{ds}(r\beta) ,$$

(III)' $$\frac{dN}{ds} = -\frac{C\beta}{R_\theta} - (1+\nu)\, p_s ,$$

(IV)' $$\frac{d}{ds}\left[\frac{M}{(1+\nu)\bar{h}}\right] = \frac{1}{\bar{h}r}\left[\psi \sin\varphi - (rV)\cos\varphi\right] .$$

If one eliminates N and M from this system, the pair of equations obtained for β and ψ corresponds to Reissner's formulation [26] except that he retains terms which correspond to those underlined in equations (III) and (IV).

The first and second pairs of equations in the above systems may be combined into complex-valued equations by defining the complex-valued quantities

$$\widetilde{N} = N + \frac{iM}{(1+\nu)\bar{h}}, \quad \widetilde{\beta} = \beta - i\frac{R_\theta Q}{\bar{h}C}, \quad \widetilde{\psi} = \psi + i\bar{h}C\beta. \tag{15}$$

The two alternate systems may now be written as

$$\widetilde{N} = i\frac{\bar{h}C}{r}\frac{d}{ds}(r\widetilde{\beta}) + N_M = \frac{1}{r}\frac{d}{ds}(r\widetilde{\psi}) + \frac{rV}{R_\theta} + rp_H, \tag{16}$$

$$\frac{d\widetilde{N}}{ds} = -\frac{C\widetilde{\beta}}{R_\theta} - (1+\nu)p_s = \frac{i\widetilde{\psi}}{\bar{h}R_\theta} - i\frac{r'V}{\bar{h}} - (1+\nu)p_s. \tag{17}$$

Eliminating $\widetilde{\beta}$ yields Novozhilov's single complex-valued equation

$$i\frac{\bar{h}}{r}\frac{d}{ds}[rR_\theta\frac{d\widetilde{N}}{ds}] + \widetilde{N} = N_M - i(1+\nu)\frac{\bar{h}}{r}\frac{d}{ds}(rR_\theta p_s), \tag{N}$$

where the last term is usually negligible except possibly for special loadings. Eliminating $\widetilde{N}$ yields the two alternate equations

$$i\bar{h}R_\theta\frac{d}{ds}[\frac{1}{r}\frac{d}{ds}(r\widetilde{\beta})] + \widetilde{\beta} = \beta_M = -\frac{R_\theta}{C}\frac{dN_M}{ds} - (1+\nu)p_s, \tag{M}$$

$$i\bar{h}R_\theta\frac{d}{ds}[\frac{1}{r}\frac{d}{ds}(r\widetilde{\psi})] + \widetilde{\psi} = r'R_\theta V - i\bar{h}R_\theta[\frac{d}{ds}(\frac{rV}{R_\theta} + rp_H) + (1+\nu)p_s]. \tag{R}$$

Equation (M) corresponds to Meissner's formulation and equation (R) to Reissner's formulation. The last term on the right hand side of equation (R) is usually negligible.

Equations (N), (M) and (R) as written above, all take the form of a singular perturbation equation with $\bar{h}$ playing the formal role of a small parameter. In each case the formal limit as $\bar{h} \to 0$ yields the membrane theory value of the quantities involved. In the interior of a shell, away from a bending boundary layer near an edge, these limiting values may furnish satisfactory approximate solutions of the differential equations. However, such formal solutions are not always valid as is the case in the toroidal shell problems discussed in Section 5.

For completeness we list below formulas from which all other quantities may be obtained (we recall the primes denote differentiation with respect to the meridional arc length s):

$$rV = -\int r p_V \, ds\,, \quad N_M = R_\theta p_n + \left(1 - \frac{R_\theta}{R_s}\right)\frac{R_\theta V}{r}\,,$$

$$N_s = \frac{r'}{r}\psi + \frac{rV}{R_\theta} = \frac{r'}{r}(R_\theta Q) + \frac{R_\theta V}{r} = \bar{h} R_\theta \frac{r'}{r}\,\mathrm{Im}\{\widetilde{N}'\} + \frac{R_\theta V}{r}\,,$$

$$N_\theta = \psi' + r p_H = (R_\theta Q)' + R_\theta p_n - \frac{R_\theta}{R_s}\frac{R_\theta V}{r} = \mathrm{Re}\,\{\widetilde{N}\} - N_s\,,$$

$$M_s = D(\beta' + \nu\frac{r'}{r}\beta) = \frac{M}{1+\nu} - (1-\nu)\,D\frac{r'}{r}\beta$$

$$(18) \qquad = \bar{h}\;\mathrm{Im}\,\{\widetilde{N}\} + (1-\nu)\,\bar{h}^{2} R_\theta \frac{r'}{r}[\,\mathrm{Re}\,\{\widetilde{N}\} + (1+\nu)p_s]\,,$$

$$M_\theta = D(\nu\beta' + \frac{r'}{r}\beta) = \frac{\nu M}{1+\nu} + (1-\nu)\,D\frac{r'}{r}\beta = M - M_s\,,$$

$$Q = M'/(1+\nu) = \bar{h}\;\mathrm{Im}\;\{\widetilde{N}'\}\,,$$

$$C\beta = -R_\theta[\,\mathrm{Re}\,\{\widetilde{N}'\} + (1+\nu)\,p_s]\,, \quad Cu = r\,(N_\theta - \nu N_s)\,,$$

$$Cw = -\int [C\beta\cos\varphi + (N_s - \nu N_\theta)\,\sin\varphi]\,ds\,.$$

4. Asymptotic solutions of an exponential or classical type.

Classical methods of asymptotic integration were first applied to shell problems in 1912 by H. Reissner [30] and O. Blumenthal [3]. A recent and more detailed account of such methods has been given by F. B. Hildebrand [17], who discusses both the homogeneous and the nonhomogeneous equations of the Meissner form. Here, we shall discuss briefly the homogeneous equations which must be solved to obtain solutions of a boundary layer type for shells subject to edge loads.

First, it is convenient to make standard transformations which reduce the equations to the form (the homogeneous equation for $\widetilde{\psi}$ has the same form as that for $\widetilde{\beta}$):

$$(19) \qquad \frac{d^2}{ds^2}(r^{1/2}\widetilde{\beta}) - \left[\frac{i}{\bar{h}R_\theta}\left(1 - \underline{\frac{i\bar{h}}{2R_s}}\right) + \frac{3}{4}\left(\frac{r'}{r}\right)^2\right](r^{1/2}\widetilde{\beta}) = 0\,,$$

(20) $$\frac{d^2}{ds^2}[(rR_\theta)^{1/2}\tilde{N}] - [\frac{i}{\bar{h}R_\theta} + \Omega_N][(rR_\theta)^{1/2}\tilde{N}] = 0,$$

where $\Omega_N = (rR_\theta)^{-1/2}[(rR_\theta)^{1/2}]''$ may be reduced to

(21) $$\Omega_N = -\frac{1}{r^2}\frac{R_\theta}{R_s}(1 - \frac{3}{4}\frac{R_\theta}{R_s}) - \frac{1}{4}\frac{1}{R_s^2} + \frac{1}{2}\frac{r'}{r}\frac{R_\theta}{R_s}\frac{R_s'}{R_s}.$$

It is consistent with our earlier approximations to drop the underlined term in equation (19).

Next, let ℓ denote a representative distance along a meridian of the shell's middle surface and write

(22) $$s = \ell\xi + s_o, \qquad \mu = \ell^2/(\bar{h}R_o)$$

where ξ is then a dimensionless parameter and where s_o and R_o denote reference values of s and R_θ at some point on a meridian. With $W = r^{1/2}\tilde{\beta}$ or $(rR_\theta)^{1/2}\tilde{N}$ and with $\Omega = \Omega_M = (3/4)(r'/r)^2$ or Ω_N as given by (21), equations (19) and (20) both take the form:

(23) $$\frac{d^2W}{d\xi^2} - [i\mu\frac{R_o}{R_\theta} + \ell^2\Omega] \; W = 0 .$$

If on some interval, $\xi_1 \leq \xi \leq \xi_2$, R_o/R_θ and $\ell^2\Omega$ are both bounded and R_o/R_θ is also bounded from zero, then it is well known that for sufficiently large values of the parameter μ asymptotic solutions of the following form exist:

(24) $$W(\xi) = (R_\theta/R_o)^{1/4} e^{\pm(i\mu)^{1/2}\omega(\xi)}[1+O(\mu^{-1/2})],$$

where

(25) $$\omega(\xi) = \int_0^\xi (R_o/R_\theta)^{1/2} d\xi .$$

Equation (24) lists the first term of an asymptotic series for which higher terms may be calculated. However, it appears that even the second term, of relative order $\mu^{-1/2}$, would be modified somewhat if the effect of transverse shear strains were included in shell theory. Thus, adding on higher order terms does not necessarily yield a more accurate solution of shell problems as compared to a possible solution of the equations of three dimensional elasticity theory. This is a question which, in the author's opinion, has yet to be answered in a completely satisfactory and rigorous way except for the special case of a cylindrical shell.

In the case of a cylindrical shell, $\Omega = 0$ and $R_\theta = R_o$, so that $\omega(\xi) = \xi$. The first term of (24) is then an exact solution of equation (23). In a sense, the asymptotic solutions (24) become less accurate the more radically the portion of a shell concerned departs from cylindrical shape. From the behavior of solutions (24) we may deduce that the effect of a bending couple or a transverse shear stress on an edge of a shell (the conical surface, φ = constant) decays exponentially as the distance from the edge increases. The stresses produced by such edge loads are then of importance only in an edge zone or boundary layer with a width of the order $\xi = O(\mu^{-1/2})$ or $s = O[(R_o h)^{1/2}]$, where R_o is the value of R_θ at the edge.

5. Turning point problems - toroidal shells. If R_θ becomes infinite for a value of ξ in the range of interest, the coefficient of μ in equation (23) vanishes. Such a point is called a turning point and, since $1/R_\theta = (\sin\varphi)/r$, such points occur whenever the normal to the middle surface is parallel to the axis of revolution at a point not on the axis. A typical example is a toroidal shell. Classical asymptotic methods fail for the homogeneous equation and the membrane solution is generally not valid as a particular solution of the nonhomogeneous equation.

Substituting the following expressions into Reissner's equation, one obtains the explicit differential equation listed below:

$$r = a + b\sin\varphi, \quad R_o = a, \quad R_s = b = \ell, \quad s = b\varphi,$$

(26)

$$\lambda = b/a, \quad \mu = b^2/a\bar{h}, \quad \tilde{\psi} = (1+\lambda\sin\varphi)^{-1/2} W,$$

$$\frac{d^2W}{d\varphi^2} - \left[\frac{i\mu\sin\varphi}{1+\lambda\sin\varphi} + \frac{3}{4}\left(\frac{\lambda\cos\varphi}{1+\lambda\sin\varphi}\right)^2\right] W$$

(27)

$$= -\frac{i\mu a V_o\cos\varphi}{(1+\lambda\sin\varphi)^{1/2}}$$

For simplicity, we have assumed that the components of surface load intensity vanish, in which case the load function, $rV = aV_0$, becomes at most a constant.

It is apparent that the differential equation has a first order turning point at $\varphi = 0$. For problems such as that illustrated in Figure 2a, only solutions of the homogeneous equation are required. Professor Langer [18] indicated more than thirty years ago how asymptotic solutions of such equations may be represented in terms of Bessel functions of order 1/3, but it was not until 1950 that his work was applied directly to shell problems [4]. Quite satisfactory numerical results may be obtained using only the leading term of the possible asymptotic expansions. Similar approximate solutions of toroidal shell problems were developed independently in Germany during World War II [37] and in Russia in 1951 [38].

Probably of greater physical interest is the problem posed by the non-homogeneous differential equation. A typical case is illustrated in Figure 2b. Assuming that the horizontal shear H and the rotation β are both zero at the edges, the problem is to solve equation (27) subject to the homogeneous boundary conditions, $W(\pm\pi/2) = 0$.

Proceeding formally, the result of dividing (27) by μ and letting $\mu \to \infty$ yields the membrane solution,

$$W = aV_0 \cot\varphi\,(1+\lambda \sin\varphi)^{1/2} . \tag{28}$$

While this satisfies the boundary conditions, it is not finite at $\varphi = 0$. In other words, as $\mu \to \infty$ the solution of the boundary value problem does not approach a continuous limit function. Instead there is an internal bending layer in the neighborhood of $\varphi = 0$. According to Goldenveizer [14], such behavior may be expected in the neighborhood of an asymptotic line on the middle surface of an arbitrary shell.

Introducing the transformations

$$\begin{aligned} &x(\varphi) = \mu^{1/3}(3\omega/2)^{2/3}, \quad \omega(\varphi) = \int_0^{\varphi}\left(\frac{\sin\varphi}{1+\lambda\sin\varphi}\right)^{1/2} d\varphi, \\ &W(\varphi) = P(\varphi)\,u(x), \quad P(\varphi) = (1+\lambda\sin\varphi)^{1/4}[x/(\mu^{1/3}\sin\varphi)]^{1/4}, \end{aligned} \tag{29}$$

equation (27) becomes

$$u''(x) - ix\,u(x) + \mu^{-2/3} f(x)\,u(x) = -i\mu^{1/3} g(x) , \tag{30}$$

where primes now denote differentiation with respect to the written argument of a function and where

$$f(x(\varphi)) = [\lambda \cos\varphi/(1+\lambda \sin\varphi)]^2 P^4(\varphi) + P''(\varphi) P^3(\varphi) , \tag{31}$$

$$g(x(\varphi)) = aV_o \cos\varphi(1 + \sin\varphi)^{-1/2} P^3(\varphi) .$$

All functions have continuous derivatives of all orders and, in particular, $f(x(\varphi))$ and $g(x(\varphi))$ are bounded on $-\pi/2 \leq \varphi \leq \pi/2$ independent of μ.

By neglecting the term in $\mu^{-2/3}$ on the left side of (30), one may obtain an integral representation of an appropriate solution in terms of the Green's function associated with the remaining differential operator and the boundary conditions: $u(x) \to 0$ as $x \to \pm\infty$. Integrating by parts, a representation to within terms of relative order $\mu^{-2/3}$ may be obtained which does not involve integrals over the function g. This was shown in [5] and the results were applied to toroidal shell problems in [6]. The same type of solution was developed independently in [35]. However, the approach is not easily extended to include terms of order $\mu^{-2/3}$ and higher.

Although the higher order terms may not be appropriate for shell problems, as they are probably of the order of the error of the shell theory itself, the mathematical problem is of interest. By extending the work of Professor Langer [20] on homogeneous equations, complete asymptotic expansions of solutions of the nonhomogeneous equation are obtained in [7], including the possibility of a term of order $\mu^{1/2}$ in the coefficient of the original equation for W.

The asymptotic representations discussed above all depend on a function T which satisfies the conditions:

$$T''(x) - i x T(x) = 1, \quad T(x) \sim i/x \text{ as } |x| \to \infty . \tag{32}$$

The function T has the Fourier integral representation,

$$T(x) = - \int_0^\infty \exp[-ixt - (t^3/3)]\, dt .$$

Brief tables and further properties of the real and imaginary parts of $T(x)$ and its derivative are given in [4] and in [16]. In terms of T, an asymptotic solution of the boundary value problem associated with equation (27) is given by

$$(33) \quad W(\varphi) = -i\mu^{1/3} aV_o \Big\{ P(\varphi)\ T(x) + i\frac{1+\lambda \sin\varphi}{\mu^{1/3}\sin\varphi}\left[\frac{\cos\varphi}{(1+\lambda\sin\varphi)^{1/2}} - \frac{1}{P^3(\varphi)}\right] + O(\frac{1}{\mu^{2/3}})\Big\}.$$

Since $P(\varphi) = 1 + O(\varphi)$, the term with $1/\sin\varphi$ remains bounded at $\varphi = 0$. From the asymptotic properties of $T(x)$ for large $|x|$, it follows that $W(\varphi)$ vanishes at $\varphi = \pm\pi/2$ to within terms of the order of those omitted.

The same mathematical problem occurs in the bending of curved tubes and other applications of the above type of asymptotic solution may be found in [8, 9, 11, 16, 22, 31].

6. A second order turning point problem. If toroidal shells of arbitrary cross section are considered, it is possible to have a turning point of higher than first order. No literature on such shells is known to the author. However, a non-linear membrane problem for a toroidal shell of circular cross section results in an equation with a second order turning point. Again, the problem involves a nonhomogeneous differential equation and an internal "boundary layer".

The problem is to consider a complete toroidal shell subject only to a uniform internal pressure p. With $p_V = -p\sin\varphi$, $p_H = p\cos\varphi$, the load function rV becomes

$$rV = (1/2)\,p(r^2 - a^2) + aV_o$$

where $-V_o$ represents the value of the shear resultant Q at $\varphi = 0$. According to linear membrane theory, the shear vanishes so that $V_o = 0$. With $Q \equiv 0$, the linear membrane theory values of the direct stress resultants, N_s and N_θ are found from equations (18) to be

$$(34) \quad \begin{aligned} N_{sLM} &= R_\theta V/r = (1/2)\,bp\,[1 + (a/r)]\,, \\ N_{\theta LM} &= R_\theta p_n - (R_\theta/R_s)(R_\theta V)/r = (1/2)\,bp\,. \end{aligned}$$

However, the membrane theory value of β given by

$$C\beta_{LM} = -R_\theta dN/ds = (abp/2r)\cot\varphi\,,$$

becomes infinite at $\varphi = 0$.

According to linear bending theory, V_o does not vanish and a solution analogous to (33) must be obtained. Finally, the unknown value of the constant V_o is determined by the symmetry condition that the axial component of displacement be the same at $\varphi = \pm \pi/2$.

However, for sufficiently thin shells one expects that there should be little bending action. The inadequacy of the linear membrane theory is due to the fact that the shear resultant is referred to the undeformed shape of the shell. Using the subscript L to denote the linear theory values, Q_L and N_{sL}, of the stress resultants in directions normal and tangential to the undeformed meridian curve of the middle surface, while Q is the shear resultant normal to the deformed meridian curve, it follows that

$$Q = Q_L \cos \beta + N_{sL} \sin \beta \approx Q_L + \beta N_{sL} ,$$

where β is the angle of rotation of the normal to a meridian due to deformation. For a nonlinear membrane theory, it is the actual shear Q, rather than Q_L, which vanishes.

As shown by Reissner [28], it is possible to develop equations which contain both linear bending theory and nonlinear membrane theory as limiting cases, and we shall now give a brief development of these equations for a general shell. Since we do not expect the circular cross section of the torus to be distorted appreciably, β will be small and second order terms in β may be neglected. It will then be sufficient to modify the equations of the linear theory only to the extent of writing $Q_L + \beta N_{sL}$ in place of Q in the basic equation (IV). Furthermore, it will be appropriate to use the linear membrane value N_{sLM} in the nonlinear term βN_{sL}. Resolving Q_L into radial and axial components, the modified version of equation (IV), or actually (IV)', now becomes

$$\frac{d}{ds}\left(\frac{M}{1+\nu}\right) = \frac{1}{r}(\psi \sin \varphi - rV \cos \varphi) + N_{sLM}\beta .$$

Following Reissner, we write ψ and V as sums of the linear membrane value and a supplementary term; namely,

$$\psi = \psi_{LM} + \psi_S , \quad V = V_{LM} + V_S , \quad \text{where } \psi_{LM} = rV_{LM} \cot \varphi .$$

For the toroidal shell under uniform pressure p,

$$rV_{LM} = (1/2)\, p\,(r^2 - a^2), \quad rV_S = aV_o , \quad \psi_{LM} = (1/2)\, bp(r+a) \cos \varphi .$$

Noting that in general

$$\frac{1}{r}\frac{d}{ds}(r\psi_{LM}) + \frac{rV_{LM}}{R_\theta} + rp_H = N_{sLM} + N_{\theta LM} = N_{LM},$$

the basic set of first order differential equations now reduces to the following:

$$N = \frac{1}{r}\frac{d}{ds}(r\psi_S) + N_{LM} + \frac{rV_S}{R_\theta}, \quad \frac{dN}{ds} = -\frac{C\beta}{R_\theta} - (1+\nu)p_s,$$

$$\frac{M}{1+\nu} = \frac{D}{r}\frac{d}{ds}(r\beta), \quad \frac{d}{ds}\left(\frac{M}{1+\nu}\right) = \frac{1}{r}(\psi_S \sin\varphi - rV_S\cos\varphi) + N_{sLM}\beta.$$

Eliminating N and M, one obtains Reissner's equations. Taking $p_S = 0$, they are

$$\frac{d}{ds}\left[\frac{1}{r}\frac{d}{ds}(r\psi_S)\right] = -\frac{1}{r}C\beta\sin\varphi - \frac{d}{ds}\left(N_{LM} + \frac{rV_S}{R_\theta}\right), \tag{35}$$

$$D\frac{d}{ds}\left[\frac{1}{r}\frac{d}{ds}(r\beta)\right] = \frac{1}{r}(\psi_S\sin\varphi - rV_S\cos\varphi) + N_{sLM}\beta. \tag{36}$$

Except for the term with V_S in equation (35), which is ordinarily insignificant and is neglected below, the above equations correspond to Reissner's equations (VII) and (VIII), page 181 of [28], for a shell of constant thickness (again, Reissner has additional terms which correspond to retaining the underlined terms in (III) and (IV) of Section 3).

Equations for a nonlinear membrane theory may be obtained from the above by setting the bending stiffness $D = 0$. Substituting the resulting value for β into equation (35) yields the following single equation for ψ_S:

$$\frac{d}{ds}\left[\frac{1}{r}\frac{d}{ds}(r\psi_S)\right] - \frac{C}{N_{sLM}}\left(\frac{\sin\varphi}{r}\right)^2\psi_S = -\frac{C}{N_{sLM}}\,\frac{rV_S\sin\varphi\cos\varphi}{r^2} - \frac{dN_{LM}}{ds}. \tag{37}$$

Equation (37) takes the following form for a toroidal shell of circular cross section:

$$(38)\quad \frac{d}{d\varphi}\left[\frac{1}{r}\frac{d}{d\varphi}(r\psi_S)\right] - \frac{\mu^2}{\rho}\frac{\sin^2\varphi\ \psi_S}{(r/a)(1+(1/2)\lambda\sin\varphi)}$$

$$= -\frac{\mu^2}{\rho}\frac{aV_o\sin\varphi\cos\varphi}{(r/a)(1+(1/2)\lambda\sin\varphi)} + \frac{\lambda}{2}\frac{b^2 p\cos\varphi}{(r/a)^2},$$

where

$$r = a(1+\lambda\sin\varphi),\quad \lambda = \frac{b}{a},\quad \mu = \frac{b^2}{a\bar{h}},\quad \rho = \frac{b^3 p}{D} = \frac{b^3 p}{\bar{h}^2 C}.$$

Reissner shows that nonlinear membrane theory, or equation (38), is valid provided $1 << \mu << \rho^{3/2}$. Equation (38) is to be solved subject to the boundary conditions, $\psi_S(\pm\pi/2) = 0$, which follow from the symmetry of the problem with respect to the plane $z = 0$. The unknown constant V_o is again determined by the condition that the axial component of displacement vanish at $\varphi = \pm\pi/2$.

J. L. Sanders and A. A. Liepins [32] have formulated the above problem somewhat differently but they also obtain a nonhomogeneous differential equation with a second order turning point completely analogous to equation (38). Under the assumption that $\mu^2 >> \rho$, they have constructed an asymptotic solution of the problem in a manner similar to that discussed in Section 5. Their solution is represented in terms of two functions T_1 and T_2 which satisfy the following conditions:

$$T_1''(x) - x^2 T_1(x) = -1,\quad T_1(x) \sim x^{-2}\quad \text{as } |x| \to \infty,$$

$$T_2''(x) - x^2 T_2(x) = -x,\quad T_2(x) \sim x^{-1}\quad \text{as } |x| \to \infty.$$

The problem of obtaining an asymptotic solution of the pair of equations which correspond to (35) and (36) when $\mu = O(\rho^{3/2})$ with $\rho >> 1$ is still open. For this range of the parameters linear bending action and nonlinear membrane action are of equal importance. A problem with a second order turning point and a singular term is considered in [27].

7. Asymptotic solutions for differential equations with a singular point. Another type of asymptotic solution occurs in connection with shells of revolution which have an apex on the axis of revolution. An example is an ellipsoidal shell. Ordinarily, membrane theory furnishes

an adequate particular integral so that one is concerned with obtaining asymptotic solutions of a homogeneous equation.

If the arc length s is measured from the apex of such a shell and if the middle surface of the shell is sufficiently smooth at the apex (in particular, a tangent plane exists), then the radial coordinate r has an expansion in powers of s of the form

$$r(s) = s - [s^3/(6R_o^2)] + \dots ,$$

where $R_o = R_s(0) = R_\theta(0)$ is the common value of the radii of curvature at the apex. It is now apparent that the second term of the coefficient in the general equations (19) and (20) of Section 4 has a pole of second order at $s = 0$, or at the apex. In a paper [19] published in 1935, Professor Langer developed asymptotic representations of solutions of such equations in terms of Bessel functions.

As an example, consider an ellipsoidal shell of revolution. The elliptical meridian of the middle surface of the shell is most conveniently represented by the parametric equations

$$r = a \sin \xi , \quad z = \cos \xi .$$

Other quantities may be expressed in terms of ξ as follows:

$$ds = \alpha \, d\xi , \quad \alpha(\xi) = (a^2 \cos^2 \xi + b^2 \sin^2 \xi)^{1/2}$$

$$R_\theta = \frac{a}{b}\alpha , \quad R_s = \frac{\alpha^3}{ab} , \quad \sin \varphi = \frac{b}{\alpha} \sin \xi , \quad \cos \varphi = \frac{a}{\alpha} \cos \xi .$$

Novozhilov's equation now takes the form

$$\text{(39)} \qquad \frac{d^2 \tilde{N}}{d\xi^2} + \cot \xi \frac{d\tilde{N}}{d\xi} - i\lambda^2 \frac{\alpha(\xi)}{a} \tilde{N} = 0 ,$$

where

$$\lambda^2 = \frac{b}{h} = \frac{a^2}{R_o h} , \quad \frac{\alpha(\xi)}{a} = [1 + \frac{b^2 - a^2}{a^2} \sin^2 \xi]^{1/2}$$

and R_o is again the common value of R_s and R_θ at $\xi = 0$.

Following Professor Langer's methods, we may construct a related differential equation

$$\text{(40)} \qquad \frac{d^2 Y}{d\xi^2} + \cot \xi \frac{dY}{d\xi} + [- i\lambda^2 \frac{\alpha(\xi)}{a} + \Omega(\xi)] \, Y = 0$$

which agrees with equation (39) except for the presence the term Ω. Defining

$$\eta(\xi) = \int_0^\xi [\alpha(\xi)/a]^{1/2} d\xi ,$$

one finds that for (primes denote $d/d\xi$)

(41) $$\Omega(\xi) = \frac{\alpha/a}{4\eta^2} - \frac{1}{4}\cot^2\xi - \frac{1}{2} + \frac{1}{4}\frac{\alpha''}{\alpha} - \frac{5}{16}\left(\frac{\alpha'}{\alpha}\right)^2$$

$$= \frac{\alpha/a}{4\eta^2} - \frac{1}{4}\cot^2\xi - \frac{1}{2} + \frac{b^2 - a^2}{4\alpha^2}\cos 2\xi - \frac{9}{64}\frac{(b^2-a^2)^2}{\alpha^4}\sin^2 2\xi$$

appropriate solutions of (40) are given exactly by

(42)
$$Y_1(\xi) = \left(\frac{\alpha}{a}\right)^{-1/4}\left(\frac{\eta}{\sin\xi}\right)^{1/2} J_o(i^{3/2}\lambda\eta) ,$$

$$Y_2(\xi) = \left(\frac{\alpha}{a}\right)^{-1/4}\left(\frac{\eta}{\sin\xi}\right)^{1/2} K_o(i^{1/2}\lambda\eta) .$$

Here, J_o and K_o are the standard Bessel function and modified Bessel function of order zero. The real and imaginary parts

$$J_o(i^{3/2}x) = \mathrm{ber}(x) + i\,\mathrm{bei}(x) , \quad K_o(i^{1/2}x) = \mathrm{ker}(x) + i\,\mathrm{kei}(x)$$

are the extensively tabulated Kelvin functions.

For $\lambda >> 1$, Professor Langer has shown that Y_1 and Y_2 furnish asymptotic solutions of equation (39) to within terms of relative order $1/\lambda$ uniformly on an interval $0 \le \xi \le \xi_1 < \pi$ provided the function $\Omega(\xi) = O(1)$ on the interval. For the case of an ellipsoidal shell, the expression for $\Omega(\xi)$, given by equation (41), remains bounded for $0 \le \xi \le \xi_1 < \pi$ but its value also depends on the ratio b/a. In particular, one may show that

$$\Omega(0) = (1/3)(b/a)^2 - (2/3) .$$

There are two cases to consider. First, if $b >> a$, then $\Omega(\xi)$ is largest in the neighborhood of $\xi = 0$. Also, the least radius of curvature of a meridian occurs at $\xi = 0$ and is given by $R_o = a^2/b$. Since one must have $R_o/\bar{h} = a^2/b\bar{h} >> 1$ for shell theory to be valid, it follows that $\lambda^2 = b/\bar{h} >> (b/a)^2$, so that the asymptotic solutions

(42) are still valid even when $(b/a)^2$ or $\Omega(0) >> 1$.

In the second case, when $b << a$, the least radius of curvature occurs at the ends of an equatorial diameter and is given by

$R_{min.} = R_s(\pi/2) = b^2/a$. At $\xi = \pi/2$, $\alpha = b$ and $\Omega(\pi/2) = O(a/b)^2$.

Thus, for the term $\lambda^2(\alpha/a)$ to be large compared to Ω in the neighborhood of $\xi = \pi/2$, one must have $\lambda^2(b/a) = R_{min.}/\bar{h} >> (a/b)^2$, and the validity of the asymptotic solutions is guaranteed only if this relationship holds. However, thin shell theory is still valid when $R_{min}/\bar{h} = 0(a/b)^2$ provided $(a/b)^2 >> 1$. Similarly, it was established in [10] that the membrane solution of a complete ellipsoidal shell subject only to uniform internal pressure, which corresponds to a solution of equation (39) with a nonhomogeneous term, is generally valid only if $R_{min.}/\bar{h} >> (a/b)^2$ when $(a/b)^2 >> 1$.

The case of a spherical shell is obtained from the above by taking $b = a$. Then ξ may be identified with the angle of inclination of the normal φ. Also, $\alpha = a$ is constant, so that $\eta = \xi = \varphi$, and

$$Y_1(\varphi) = (\varphi/\sin\varphi)^{1/2)} J_o(i^{3/2}\lambda\varphi), \quad Y_2(\varphi) = (\varphi/\sin\varphi)^{1/2} K_o(i^{1/2}\lambda\varphi)$$

where now $\lambda^2 = a/\bar{h}$ and a is the radius of the spherical middle surface. If attention is restricted to shallow spherical shells for which $0 \le \varphi \le \varphi_1 = 0(\lambda^{-1/2})$, then to within terms of relative order $1/\lambda$ the factor $(\varphi/\sin\varphi)^{1/2}$ may be approximated by unity and the standard solution for shallow spherical shells is obtained.

There have been many applications of the asymptotic solutions of the above type to shell problems. In 1954, Naghdi and DeSilva [24] first applied such methods to ellipsoidal shells, although their formulation differs somewhat from that given above. They have also mentioned or applied asymptotic solutions of the same general type in a series of papers [13, 23]. In [12] the coefficient of the large parameter has a simple pole. Baker and Cline [1] have used such solutions to determine influence coefficients for a whole family of dome-shaped shells.

Recently, Steele and Hartung [34] have used asymptotic methods to solve problems for dome-spaped orthotropic shells of revolution. Their solutions involve Bessel functions of non-integral order. Also, since membrane solutions for an orthotropic shell may not be valid in a neighborhood of the apex, they have developed asymptotic solutions of the nonhomogeneous equation in terms of Lommel functions (which satisfy a nonhomogeneous Bessel equation). The solutions are analogous to those discussed earlier for the turning point problems.

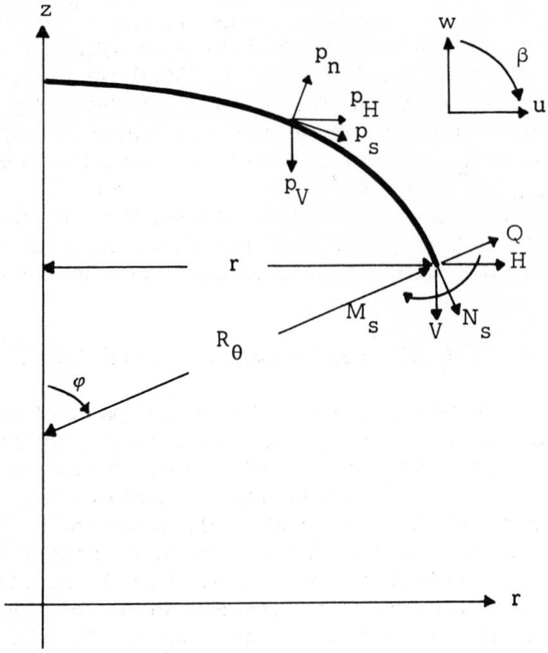

Figure 1. Axial section of shell's middle surface indicating stress resultants acting in the rz-plane.

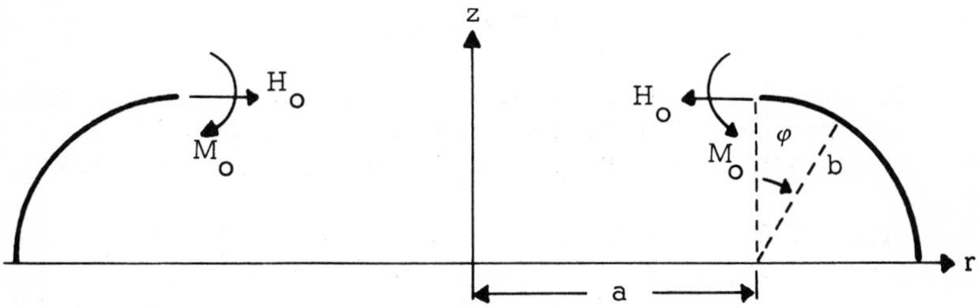

Figure 2a

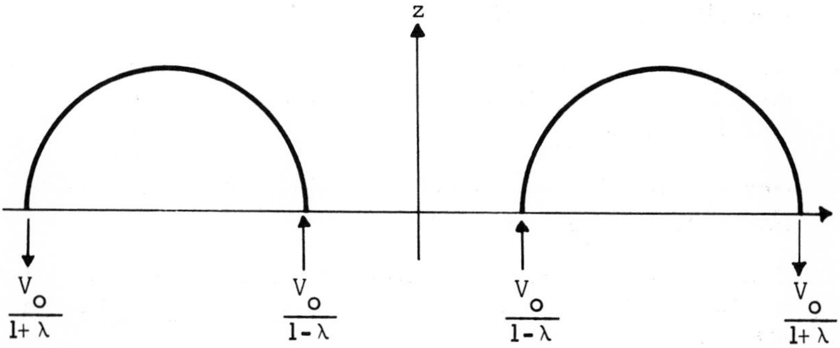

Figure 2b. Axial cross section of a toroidal shell

8. Bibliography. The list of references given below is by no means complete but is hopefully representative of papers which apply or develop asymptotic solutions related to those discussed in the paper.

REFERENCES

1. Baker, B. R., and Cline, G. B., "Influence coefficients for thin smooth shells of revolution subjected to symmetric loads," Trans. ASME, Serie E (J. Appl. Mech.) **29** (1962) 335-339.

2. Blumenthal, O.,"Uber asymptotische Integration Linear Differentialgliechungen, mit Anwendungen auf eine asymptotische Theorie der Kugelfunktionen," Archiv d. Math. u. Physik (3), **19** (1912), 136, 174.

3. Blumenthal, O., "Uber asymptotische Integration von Differentialgleichungen mit Anwendung auf die Berechnung von Spannungen in Kugelschalen," Proc. of the Fifth Internat. Cong. of Math. II (1912), pp. 319-327; Zeit. f. Math. u. Phys. **62** (1914), 343-358.

4. Clark, R. A., "On the theory of thin elastic toroidal shells," J. of Math. and Phys. **29** (1950), 146-178.

5. Clark, R. A., "Asymptotic integration of a nonhomogeneous differential equation," O.O.R Tech. Report, Contract DA-33-019-ORD-1193, (1954), 14 pp.

6. Clark, R. A., "Asymptotic solutions of toroidal shell problems," Quart. Appl. Math., **16** (1958), 47-60.

7. Clark, R. A., "Asymptotic solutions of a nonhomogeneous differential equation with a turning point," Archive Rational Mech. Anal. **12** (1963), 34-51.

8. Clark, R. A., Gilroy, T. I., and Reissner, E., "Stresses and deformations of toroidal shells of elliptical cross section," J. Appl. Mech., **19** (1952), 37-48.

9. Clark, R. A., and Reissner, E., "Bending of Curved Tubes," Advances in Applied Mechanics, II, Academic Press, New York, 1951.

10. Clark, R. A., and Reissner, E., "On stresses and deformations of ellipsoidal shells subject to internal pressure," J. Mech. Phys. Solids, (1957), 63-70.

11. Crandall, S. H., and Dahl, N. C., "The influence of pressure on the bending of curved tubes," Proc. 9th Internatl. Cong. Appl. Mech., 1956.

12. DeSilva, C. N., "Thermal stresses in the bending of ogival shells," J. of the Aerospace Sciences, **29** (1962), 207-212.

13. DeSilva, C. N. and Naghdi, P. M., "Asymptotic solutions of a class of elastic shells of revolution with variable thickness," Q. Appl. Math. **15** (1957), 169-182.

14. Gol'denveizer, A. L., Theory of Elastic Thin Shells, (transl. from 1953 Russian ed.), Pergamon, New York, 1961.

15. Gol'denveizer, A. L., "Derivation of an approximate theory of shells by means of asymptotic integration of the equations of the theory of elasticity," Appl. Math. Mech. (Prikl. Mat. Mekh transl. ASME) **27** (1963), 903-924.

16. Hetényi, M. and Timms, R. J., "Analysis of axially loaded annular shells with applications to welded bellows," Trans. ASME **82** D (1960), 741-755.

17. Hildebrand, F. B., "On asymptotic integration in shell theory," Proc. Symposia in Appl. Math. III, 1950, pp. 53-66.

18. Langer, R. E., "On the asymptotic solutions of ordinary differential equations," Trans. Amer. Math. Soc. **33** (1931), 23-64.

19. Langer, R. E., "On the asymptotic solutions of ordinary differential equations with reference to the Stokes' phenomenon about a singular point," Trans. Amer. Math. Soc. **37** (1935), 397-416.

20. Langer, R. E., "Asymptotic solutions of ordinary linear differential equations of second order," Trans. Amer. Math. Soc., **67** (1949), 461-490.

21. Meissner, E., "Das Elastizitatsproblem fur dunne Schalen von Ringflachen-Kugel - und Kegel-form," Phys. Zeitschrift. **14** (1913), 343-349.

22. Mescall, J., "On a particular integral for toroidal shell segments," Trans. ASME, Serie E (J. Appl. Mech.) **30** (1963), 136.

23. Naghdi, P. M., "The effect of transverse shear deformation on the bending of elastic shells of revolution," Quart. Appl. Math. **15** (1957), 41-52.

24. Naghdi, P. M. and DeSilva, C. N., "Deformations of elastic elliposidal shells of revolution," Proc. 2nd. U. S. Nat. Cong. Appl. Mech. Ann Arbor, 1954, A. S. M. E. (1955), pp. 333-343.

25. Novozhilov, V. V., The Theory of Thin Shells, (transl. from 1951 Russian ed.), Noordhoff, Groningen, 1959.

26. Reissner, E., "On the theory of thin elastic shells," H.Reissner Anniversary Volume, Edwards, Ann Arbor, 1949, pp. 231-247.

27. Reissner, E., "On pure bending of pressurized toroidal membranes," J. Math. and Phys. **42** (1963), 38-46.

28. Reissner, E., "On stresses and deformations in toroidal shells of circular cross section which are acted upon by uniform normal pressure," Quart. Appl. Math. **21** (1963), 177-187.

29. Reissner, E., "On the derivation of the theory of thin elastic shells," J. of Math. and Phys. **42** (1963), 263-277.

30. Reissner, H., "Spannungen in Kugelschalen (Kuppeln)," Muller-Breslau Festschrift, Leipzig, 1912, pp. 181-193.

31. Rodabaugh, E. C., and George, H. H., "Effect of internal pressure on flexibility and stress intensification factors of curved pipes or welding bellows," Trans. ASME **79** (1957), 939-948.

32. Sanders, J. L., Jr., and Liepins, A. A., "Toroidal membrane under internal pressure," AIAA Journal **1** (1963), 2105-2110.

33. Steele, C. R., "Nonsymmetric deformation of dome-shaped shells of revolution," Trans. ASME, Series E (J. Appl. Mech.) **29** (1962), 353-361.

34. Steele, C. R. and Hartung, R. F., "Symmetric loading of orthotropic shells of revolution," Lockheed Missiles and Space Co. Technical Report, March, 1964.

35. Tumarkin, S. A., "Asymptotic solution of a linear nonhomogeneous second order differential equation with a transition point and its application to the computations of toroidal shells and propeller blades," Appl. Math. Mech. (Prikl. Mat. Mech. transl. ASME), **23** (1959), 1549-1565.

36. Vishik, M. I. and Lyusternik, L. A., "Regular degeneration and boundary layer for linear differential equations with a small parameter," Amer. Math. Soc. Translations (2), **20** (1962),

37. Wei, Chang, "Der Spannungszustand in Kreisringschale und ahnlichen Schalen mit Scheitelkreisringen unter drehsymmetrischer Belastung," Science Reports, National Tsing Hua Univ. Series A, **5** (1949), 289-349.

38. Zenova, E. F. and Novoshilov, V. V., "Symmetric deformation of a toroidal shell", (in Russian), Prikl. Mat. Mekh. **15** (1951), 521-530.

ARTHUR ERDÉLYI

The Integral Equations of Asymptotic Theory

1. Introduction. The investigation of the asymptotic behavior of solutions of ordinary differential equations often consists of two distinct phases. In the first phase one attempts to construct formal solutions, approximate solutions, or a "related equation" (which is sufficiently close to the given equation and possesses solutions whose properties are known); in the second phase one attempts to show that the formal solution is an asymptotic expansion of or the approximate solution is an approximation to a solution of the given equation, or else one compares solutions of the related equation with corresponding solutions of the given equation.

The first phase has generally been regarded as the more challenging one [1]; it requires considerable insight into the problem on hand, and it demands technical skill, ingenuity, inventiveness. Much of Professor Langer's work belongs to this phase: since it has been discussed in earlier lectures, the first phase will not concern us here.

By comparison, the second phase is almost dull following, as it does, well-established lines and using well-understood techniques. Nevertheless, in many cases it cannot be circumvented since there are no general theorems available that would yield the desired results. Indeed, in many cases only this second phase of the investigation will reveal the conditions that must be imposed on the coefficients of the given differential equation to insure the validity of the approximations and this phase will reveal the precise relationship between corresponding solutions of the given differential equation and the related equation.

Ever since Liouville's classical investigations [2], the principal tools employed in the second phase of asymptotic investigations were integral and integro-differential equations. In the simplest case one has a linear Volterra integral equation,

$$y(x) = \overline{y}(x) + \int_c^x K(x,t)\,y(t)\,dt \tag{1.1}$$

where y is the "unknown" solution of the given differential equation, $\bar{y}$ is a partial sum of the formal solution, the tentative approximation, or a solution of the related equation, and the kernel of the integral equation, $K(s,t)$, is also known. In more complicated cases systems of integral equations, Fredholm or singular Fredholm equations, integro-differential equations, and non-linear functional equations arise in place of (1.1).

Considering for a moment the simplest case, (1.1), we recall that in the general theory of Volterra integral equations the functions entering into such an equation are subjected to certain continuity, boundedness, or integrability conditions, and that uniform appraisals of y or $y - \bar{y}$ are available only if the variables are restricted to compact intervals. These conditions fail in many significant applications to asymptotic theory, so that one faces singular Volterra integral equations. The domain of x may be unbounded, singularities of the given equation may lie at c or on the boundary of the domain or may be introduced by the comparison technique; and in many cases the kernel will fail to be integrable, and the integral will exist only in consequence of the compensating behaviour of y which in its turn depends on the behaviour of $\bar{y}$.

The singular character of the integral equations arising in asymptotic theory was recognized fifty years ago by Horn [3 and numerous other papers], but no systematic investigation of such equations appears to have been undertaken until fairly recently. Instead, either suitable restrictions were introduced to insure that the classical theory of Volterra integral equations applies, or else the work proceeded from first principles as it were, construction of the solution by successive approximations and ad hoc appraisal of the integrals arising in this construction. The first of these expedients is satisfactory only in a restricted number of simple cases and the second, while perfectly straightforward, is somewhat laborious, since the estimates of the integrals depend on a detailed appraisal of the constituent parts of $\bar{y}$ and of the kernel near the singularity or near the boundary of the domain. Such an appraisal is made more difficult by the circumstance that in many cases the successive terms of $\bar{y}$ and K are determined recurrently and do not admit of a convenient general representation.

In recent years a number of investigations were carried out aiming at a sharpening of available results and at producing general results that can be applied in a number of cases and reduce the ad hoc investigations to a minimum. It is perhaps not inappropriate to discuss these investigations at this symposium, since some of the early "sharpening" is due to Professor Langer [4 and other papers], while some "general" results first appeared in a report [5] written by the present author when he, at the invitation of Professor Langer, spent a summer at the Madison U. S. Army Mathematics Research

Center. Since the appearance of that report further developments occurred. For instance, the author and his colleagues extended the results to systems of integral equations [6] and to non-linear equations [7-10], Dr. Olver [11, 12] has sharpened the estimates in special cases considerably and provided useful numerical bounds, while Pike [13] re-examined the second phase with a view to applications to physical problems.

The present lecture is devoted largely to a description of some results on integral equations which have been found useful in asymptotic theory, and to a brief indication of the application of these results. We shall assume x to be a real variable. There are corresponding results for Volterra integral equations involving analytic functions of a complex variable but they will not be discussed here.

2. Let x vary over an interval I (which may be bounded or unbounded, open, half-open or closed), let c be a point or an end-point of I (in the latter case c need not belong to I), denote by R the set of those points (x, t) for which x is in I and t is between c and x, and denote by R_x a section of R, i.e., the set of those (x, t) with x fixed. A property, such as uniform convergence or integrability will be said to hold locally if it holds on each interval bounded by c and a point of I, that is, if it holds on each section of R. The terms "measurable on I" and "a.e. in I" (a.e. = almost everywhere) will refer to one-dimensional (linear) measure, and "measurable on R" and "a.e. in R", to two-dimensional (plane) measure.

Instead of a single integral equation (1.1) we may consider a system of integral equations which we again write in the form

$$(2.1) \qquad y(x) = \bar{y}(x) + \int_c^x K(x,t)\,y(t)\,dt \ .$$

In the most general context, let us consider a Banach space V together with the Banach space $E(V)$ of the endomorphisms of V, denoting by $\|y\|$ and $\|K\|$ the norms of $y \in V$ and $K \in E(V)$. y and $\bar{y}$ in (2.1) are functions on I with values $y(x)$ and $\bar{y}(x)$ in V, and K is a function on R with values $K(x, y)$ in $E(V)$. For such vector-valued functions measurability will mean strong measurability, and the integrals will accordingly be Bochner integrals [14 sections 3.5, 3.7]. For numerical functions we have simply Lebesgue measurability and Lebesgue integrals.

In applications to ordinary differential equations, V is a finite-dimensional, say n-dimensional, vector space, and $E(V)$ the corresponding space of square matrices (or linear transformations). In many cases, convenient norms for $y = (y_1, \dots, y_n)$ and

$K = [k_{ij} : 1 \leq i, j \leq n]$ will be

$$\|y\| = \max\{|y_i| : 1 \leq i \leq n\}$$

$$\|K\| = \max\{\sum_{j=1}^{n} |k_{ij}| : 1 \leq i, j \leq n\},$$

but any other norms (including some that depend on the asymptotic parameter) may be used. Strong measurability in this case amounts to Lebesgue measurability of each component (element), and the Bochner integral of a finite-dimensional vector or matrix is the vector or matrix formed by the Lebesgue integrals of the components (elements).

In this setting we consider the integral equation (2.1) in which $\overline{y}$ and K are given functions on, respectively, I and R, and y is the unknown function. At this stage it is worth while to consider how this integral equation arises from the comparison of the related differential equations,

$$y'(x) = [A(x) + F(x)]\, y(x) \tag{2.2}$$

$$\overline{y}'(x) = A(x)\overline{y}(x) \ . \tag{2.3}$$

Here we shall consider y and $\overline{y}$ finite-dimensional column vectors and, accordingly, A and F as square matrices. It is assumed that the properties of the solutions of (2.3) are known, and it is desired to compare solutions of (2.2) with "corresponding" solutions of (2.3).

Let $Y(x)$ be a non-singular square matrix solution of (2.3), so that $Y' = AY$. [The columns of Y are any linearly independent system of vector solutions of (2.3)]. If c is a point of I, a simple computation gives

$$y(x) = Y(x)Y^{-1}(c)y(c) + \int_c^x Y(x)Y^{-1}(t)F(t)y(t)\,dt \ .$$

This is the integral equation (2.1) with

$$K(x,t) = Y(x)Y^{-1}(t)F(t) \tag{2.4}$$

and

$$\overline{y}(x) = Y(x)Y^{-1}(c)y(c) \tag{2.5}$$

that solution of (2.3) satisfying the initial condition $\bar{y}(c) = y(c)$.

If c is not in I (but an end-point of I), one again has the integral equation (2.1). The explicit formula (2.5) for $\bar{y}$ may fail: $\bar{y}$ is then that solution of (2.3) behaving, in some appropriate sense, similarly to y as $x \to c$.

It is seen from (2.4) that in the comparison technique, the elements of $K(x,t)$ are sums of products of functions of x with functions of t. Using estimates for certain solutions of (2.3) and for the reciprocals of certain other solutions, one is lead to estimates of the following form:

$$\|K(x,t)\| \, \eta(t) \le \eta(x) g(t) \tag{2.6}$$

on R. An examination of the "second phase" of many investigations of the asymptotic behaviour of solutions of differential equations shows that in each case estimates of the form (2.6) were responsible for the success of the ad hoc methods. We shall indeed see that the validity of (2.6) will ensure the existence of a unique solution of (2.1) for a large class of functions.

We make the following assumptions:

(i) K is measurable on R;

(ii) there exists a measurable and a.e. finite function η and a locally integrable function g on I so that (2.6) holds a.e. on R;

(iii) $\bar{y}$ is measurable on I and

$$\|\bar{y}(x)\| \le \eta(x) \tag{2.7}$$

a.e. on I.

Using the notations

$$g_1(x) = \left| \int_c^x g(t)\,dt \right| \tag{2.8}$$

$$e_n(z) = e^z - \sum_{k=0}^{n-1} \frac{z^k}{k!} \le \frac{1}{n!} z^n e^z \qquad n = 1, 2, \xi, \dots, z \ge 0 \tag{2.9}$$

we can then show [6] that, under these assumptions, the integral equation (2.1) possesses a unique solution y that is $0(\eta)$ locally a.e. on I;

$$(2.10) \qquad \|y(x)\| \leq \eta(x) e^{g_1(x)}$$

a.e. on I;

$$(2.11) \qquad y(x) = \sum_{n=0}^{\infty} y_n(x) \;,$$

where

$$(2.12) \quad y_0(x) = \bar{y}(x), \qquad y_n(x) = \int_c^x K(x,t) y_{n-1}(t)\,dt \qquad n = 1, 2, \ldots;$$

and

$$(2.13) \qquad \|y(x) - \sum_{k=0}^{n-1} y_k(x)\| \leq \eta(x) e_n(g_1(x)) \;.$$

This result is proved by showing by induction that

$$\|y_n(x)\| \leq \eta(x) \frac{[g_1(x)]^n}{n!} \;.$$

In the proof of the latter relation from (2.12), one uses (2.6) in combination with $g(t) = |g_1'(t)|$.

In some applications of (2.1) to differential equations of the second (or higher) order it is of interest to have appraisals for the derivative (or derivatives) of y. In these applications $K(t,t) = 0$, see (2.14), and the inclusion of the seemingly irrelevant function h in the assumptions below serves to minimize the differentiability conditions on the coefficients of the differential equation.

We make, in addition to (i), (ii), (iii) above, the following assumptions:

(iv) there is a measurable function L on R so that

$$(2.14) \qquad h(x) K(x,t) = \int_t^x L(s,t)\,ds;$$

(v) there is a measurable function ζ on I so that ζg_1 is locally integrable, and

$$\|L(x,t)\|\eta(t) \leq \zeta(x)g(t) \tag{2.15}$$

a.e. on R;

(vi) $h\bar{y}$ possesses a measurable derivative, and

$$\left\|\frac{d}{dx}[h(x)\bar{y}(x)]\right\| \leq \zeta(x) \tag{2.16}$$

a.e. on I.

Under conditions (i) - (vi) one can show that, for a.e. x, hy and hy_k for k = 1, 2, 3, ... are differentiable,

$$\left\|\frac{d}{dx}[h(x)y(x)]\right\| \leq \zeta(x)e^{g_1(x)} , \tag{2.17}$$

and

$$\left\|\frac{d}{dx}\{h(x)[y(x) - \sum_{k=0}^{n-1} y_k(x)]\}\right\| \leq \zeta(x)e_n(g_1(x)) \tag{2.18}$$

$$n = 1, 2, 3, \ldots .$$

The proof of this result in the scalar case is given in [4]: this proof can easily be extended to the vector integral equation (2.1).

3. We can now briefly indicate the application of the basic results to the asymptotic theory of differential equations. We choose a simple (scalar) differential equation

$$y'' + \lambda^2 y = f(x, \lambda)y \tag{3.1}$$

where λ is a parameter, and f is a locally integrable function of x.

Two distinct cases of interest arise in connection with (3.1). One case is that of a differential equation with a large parameter. Here λ is large, $|\lambda| \to \infty$, while f is in some sense small in comparison with λ^2 - it will be seen later that $f(x, \lambda) = o(\lambda)$ as $\lambda \to \infty$ will ensure the asymptotic validity of our results. The other case concerns the asymptotic behavior of solutions of a differential equation in the neighborhood of an essential singularity. Here λ is fixed, c is a point at infinity, and f is small, at least integrable, at infinity.

In either of these two cases the appropriate comparison equation is

(3.2) $$\bar{y}'' + \lambda^2 \bar{y} = 0 \ ,$$

and the connection between corresponding solutions of (3.1) and (3.2) is expressed by the scalar integral equation

(3.3) $$y(x) = \bar{y}(x) + \lambda^{-1} \int_c^x \sin[\lambda(x-t)] f(t,\lambda) y(t)\, dt$$

which is of the form (2.1). We assume that for each λ, f is a locally integrable function.

A comparison of (2.1) and (3.3) shows that

(3.4) $$K(x,t) = \lambda^{-1} f(t,\lambda) \sin \lambda(x-t)$$

in the present case. We shall assume for the time being that c is finite and t is between c and x. We then have

(3.5) $$|\sin \lambda(x-t)|\, e^{|\mathrm{Im}\, \lambda(t-c)|} \le e^{|\mathrm{Im}\, \lambda(x-c)|} \ .$$

This inequality holds for all complex values of λ. It is easy to see that for imaginary λ a sharper inequality, with a factor $\frac{1}{2}$ inserted on the right-hand side, holds. Generally speaking, the inequality could be sharpened by inserting on the right-hand side a factor that depends on $\arg \lambda$ and does not exceed unity; but we shall not make use of this factor here. We also have

$$\frac{\partial K}{\partial x}(x,t) = f(t,\lambda) \cos \lambda(x-t)$$

and

$$|\cos \lambda(x-t)|\, e^{|\mathrm{Im}\, \lambda(t-c)|} \le e^{|\mathrm{Im}\, \lambda(x-c)|} \ .$$

thus, for our kernel we have the estimates (2.6) and (2.15) with

(3.6) $$h(x) = 1$$

$$|\lambda|^{-1} \zeta(x) = \eta(x) = e^{|\mathrm{Im}\, \lambda(x-c)|}$$

$$g(x) = |\lambda^{-1} f(x,\lambda)|, \quad g_1(x,c) = \left|\lambda^{-1} \int_c^x |f(t,\lambda)|\, dt\right| \ .$$

We can now use the results of section 2 to give estimates for a pair of linearly independent solutions of (3.1) on any closed subinterval $[a, b]$ of I.

Let $m = \pm 1$. Then $\bar{y}(x) = e^{im\lambda(x-c)}$ is a solution of (3.2). According to our results, there is a unique solution, y_m, of (3.1) satisfying the initial conditions

$$(3.7) \qquad y_m(c) = 1, \quad y'_m(c) = im\lambda ,$$

and for this solution (2.13) and (2.18) with $n = 1$ yield the appraisals

$$(3.8) \quad |y_m(x) - e^{im\lambda(x-c)}| \le e^{-\mathrm{Im}\, m\lambda(x-c)} e_1(g_1(x, c))$$

$$|y'_m(x) - im\lambda\, e^{im\lambda(x-c)}| \le |\lambda| e^{-\mathrm{Im}\, m\lambda(x-c)} e_1(g_1(x, c))$$

$$\text{for } m = \pm 1, \qquad \mathrm{Im}\, m\lambda(x-c) \le 0 .$$

If λ is real, (3.8) is valid on the entire interval I. If λ is not real, we may take $\mathrm{Im}\,\lambda > 0$. In this case we must have $x \le c$ for $m = 1$, and $x \ge c$ for $m = -1$. Let $[a, b]$ be any closed interval in I. Then we take $c = b$ for $m = 1$, $c = a$ for $m = -1$ and obtain estimates for a pair of linearly independent solutions of (3.1) on the interval $[a, b]$. We may take $[a, b] = I$ if I is a bounded closed interval. If I is open at its left end-point, we may still take $c = a$ for $m = -1$ provided that f is integrable at a so that $g_1(x, a)$ makes sense; and similarly for b.

In order to extend these results to infinite intervals, we use solutions

$$y^*_m(x) = y_m(x) e^{im\lambda c}$$

satisfying the initial conditions

$$(3.9) \qquad y^*_m(c) = e^{im\lambda c}, \quad y^{*\prime}_m(c) = im\lambda e^{im\lambda c}$$

For these solutions the appraisals (3.8), with $\mathrm{Im}\,\lambda \ge 0$, yield

$$(3.10) \quad |y^*_m(x) - e^{im\lambda x}| \le e^{-\mathrm{Im}\, m\lambda x} e_1(g_1(x, c))$$

$$|y^{*\prime}_m(x) - im\lambda e^{im\lambda x}| \le |\lambda| e^{-\mathrm{Im}\, m\lambda x} e_1(g_1(x, c)|$$

$$x < c \text{ if } m = 1, \quad x > c \text{ if } m - 1.$$

Here we may choose $c = +\infty$ for $m = 1$, or $c = -\infty$ for $m = -1$, provided that f is integrable at $\pm\infty$ so that $g_1(x, \infty)$ or $g_1(x, -\infty)$ exist. However, in this case the boundary conditions (3.9) must be replaced by

$$(3.11) \qquad e^{-im\lambda x} y_m^*(x) \to 1 \quad \text{as } mx \to \infty .$$

The results briefly presented above are special cases of those developed in [5]. (3.10) for real or imaginary λ has also been proved by Olver [11]. Indeed, in the case of λ imaginary, Olver has an improved form of (3.10) in which g_1 is replaced by $\frac{1}{2}g_1$ (this can be justified by the remark following (3.5)): he also gives alternative bounds and comparisons with some older results.

The developments briefly outlined above are typical for the application of the results of section 2 to differential equations in the absence of turning points or singularities. In this case the appropriate comparison equation is one with constant coefficients, and simple estimates for trigonometric or exponential functions will lead to inequalities of the form (2.6) and (2.15). In the presence of turning points or singularities the solutions of the comparison equation will no longer be elementary functions. Nevertheless, in many cases it is possible to find comparison equations with solutions whose properties are sufficiently well known: Airy functions, Bessel functions, and parabolic cylinder functions occur in this context. Known bounds on the solutions of the comparison equation will then lead to inequalities of the form (2.6) and (2.15) and thus to the application of the results of section 2. For a second order differential equation with a single simple transition point this was carried out briefly in [15] and [5], and in more detail and with considerably more precision (including the numerical determination of the constants appearing in the bounds) by Olver [12].

So far we have made no contact with asymptotic theory: indeed, the basic appraisals (3.8) and (3.10) are valid for general values of λ and x. We shall obtain asymptotic results under circumstances that make g_1 approach zero. This will happen either if $|\lambda| \to \infty$ and $g_1(x, \lambda) = o(\lambda)$ locally as $|\lambda| \to \infty$ (differential equation with a large parameter) or if λ is fixed, $x \to c$, and c is either $\pm\infty$ or a singularity of f (significant if c is an irregular singularity of (3.1)). In either of these two cases we shall have

$$(3.12) \qquad y_m^*(x) \sim e^{im\lambda x}$$

under the conditions elucidated above, and according to (3.10) this asymptotic representation may be differentiated.

The right-hand side of (3.12) is but the first term of an asymptotic expansion, and our results on integral equations can be used to establish asymptotic expansions to any number of terms for solutions of (3.1). This can be achieved in several distinct ways.

To begin with, under circumstances which make $g_1 \to 0$, (2.13) shows that the convergent expansion $y = \Sigma y_k$ is also an asymptotic expansion (a "general asymptotic expansion" in the sense of [5] section 4), with respect to the asymptotic sequence, or scale, $\{\eta g_1^n\}$. Moreover, (2.13) gives a quantitative bound for the remainder of this asymptotic expansion, and (2.18) gives a similar bound for the differentiated series. This result is of a sweeping generality: it applies both to differential equations with a large parameter and to differential equations with an essential singularity, and it requires no elaborate assumptions regarding the detailed structure of f.

From the practical point of view, the asymptotic expansion $y \sim \Sigma y_k$ has certain disadvantages. The successive terms, y_k, are not easy to calculate, and they are usually complicated functions of λ and x that do not lend themselves easily to numerical computation. Simpler expansions can be obtained. The process for obtaining these is somewhat different in the two cases $\lambda \to \infty$ and $x \to c$, and we shall restrict ourselves here to differential equations with a large parameter, i.e., $\lambda \to \infty$.

In older investigations (see, e.g., [16] Chapter 4) it is usual to assume that $f(x, \lambda)$ possesses an asymptotic expansion "of Poincaré type",

$$f(x, \lambda) \sim \sum_{k=0}^{\infty} f_k(x) \lambda^{-k} ,$$

whereupon it is shown that (3.1) possesses a formal solution

$$e^{im\lambda x} \sum_{k=0}^{\infty} \alpha_k(x) \lambda^{-k}$$

whose coefficients can be determined by substitution into (3.1) and a comparison of coefficients of like powers of λ. The proof of the asymptotic character of this formal solution is given by first constructing the differential equation satisfied by

$$\bar{y}(x) = e^{im\lambda x} \sum_{k=0}^{n-1} \alpha_k(x)\lambda^{-k} ,$$

using this differential equation as the comparison equation, and then estimating $y(x) - \bar{y}(x)$ by means of the results of section 2.

An alternative, newer, approach that appears to place fewer restrictions on f employs "general asymptotic expansions". Here f is assumed to possess an asymptotic expansion of the form

$$f(x,\lambda) \sim \sum_{k=0}^{\infty} f_k(x,\lambda)\lambda^{-k}$$

(not excluding the possibility $f_o = f$, $f_1 = f_2 = \ldots 0$), and for y too an expansion of the form

$$y(x) \sim e^{im\lambda x} \sum_{k=0}^{\infty} \alpha_k(x,\lambda)\lambda^{-k}$$

is obtained. There is now no unique way for the determination of the α_k. Once a rule for the recurrent calculation of the α_k has been given, an integral equation of the form (2.1) may be derived for the remainder, whereupon (2.10) and (2.17) lead to a numerical estimate for the remainder and its derivative. In [5] and in an unpublished enlarged revision of that report the entire work is based on the integral equation (3.3), while Olver [11] bases the determination of the α_k on the differential equation (3.1), and uses the integral equation for estimating the remainder. Olver's work, which is restricted to the case of real and imaginary λ and assumes $f = f_o$, has the valuable feature of relating the error,

$$y(x) - e^{im\lambda x} \sum_{k=0}^{n-1} \alpha_k(x,\lambda)\lambda^{-k}$$

to

$$\int_c^x |\alpha_n'(t,\lambda)|\,dt .$$

The corresponding expansions for the case of a single simple transition point have been indicated briefly in [5]. A more detailed and more precise investigation is due to Olver [17].

4. The basic results on linear Volterra integral equations can be extended to non-linear integral equations of the form

$$(4.1) \qquad y(x) = \overline{y}(x) + \int_c^x f(x, t, y(t))\, dt$$

in which f is a vector-valued function of its variables.

Let V, I, R, x, t, c, $y(x)$, $\overline{y}(x)$ have the same meaning as in section 2, let $A(x,t)$ be a positive (numerical) function defined in R, and let S denote the collection of those triplets (x, t, y) for which (x, t) is in R, y is in V, and $\|y\| < A(x, t)$. We make the following assumptions in which k is a measurable function on R, η is a measurable and a.e. finite function, and g is a locally integrable function, on I:

(i) $f(x, t, o) = 0$ for (x, t) in R and

$$\|f(x, t, y) - f(x, t, z)\| \leq k(x, t) \|y - z\|$$

for (x, t, y) and (x, t, z) in S;

(ii) $f(x, t, y(t))$ is measurable on R provided that y is measurable on I, and $(x, t, y(t))$ is in S for each (x, t) in R;

(iii) we have, a.e. in R,

$$k(x, t)\eta(t) \leq \eta(x)g(t), \qquad \eta(t)e^{g_1(t)} < A(x, t),$$

where g_1 is given by (2.8);

(iv) $\overline{y}$ is measurable on I and

$$\|\overline{y}(x)\| \leq \eta(x)$$

a.e. on I.

The first part of assumption (i) is not an essential restriction since the replacement of $f(x, t, y)$ by $f(x, t, y) - f(x, t, 0)$ merely changes $\overline{y}$. The second part of assumption (i) is a Lipschitz condition which implies continuity of f as a function of y. Assumption (ii) is neded to make the integral in (4.1) meaningful, and assumptions (iii) and (iv) are analogous to the assumptions in the linear case, with an inequality added to ensure that the solution of (4.1) remains in S.

Under these assumptions, the solution of (4.1) can be constructed by successive approximations, with

(4.2) $y_{-1}(x) = 0, \quad y_o(x) = \bar{y}(x),$

$$y_n(x) = \bar{y}(x) + \int_c^x f(x, t, y_{n-1}(t))\, dt \qquad n = 1, 2, \dots .$$

One can prove by induction that y_n is a measurable function on I,

(4.3) $\|y_n(x) - y_{n-1}(x)\| \le \eta(x) g_1^n(x)/n!$

a.e. on I. Since

$$y_n(x) = \sum_{k=0}^{n} [y_k(x) - y_{k-1}(x)] ,$$

it follows that $(x, t, y_n(t))$ is in S. Moreover, the infinite series in

(4.4) $y(x) = \sum_{k=0}^{\infty} [y_k(x) - y_{k-1}(x)]$

converges absolutely a.e. in I and defines a measurable function y on I, and this function can be shown to satisfy (3.1) and certain inequalities.

In this manner one can prove [7] that under the above assumptions the integral equation (4.1) possesses a unique solution y that is $0(\eta)$ locally a.e. on I and for which $(x, t, y(t))$ is in S for each (x, t) in R; this solution is given by (4.4) and satisfies (2.6) a.e. on I; and

(4.5) $\|y(x) - y_n(x)\| \le \eta(x) e_{n+1}(g_1(x))$

a.e. on I.

Instead of imposing bounds with regard to x and integrability conditions with regard to t, we could impose integrability conditions for p-th and q-th powers respectively, where $p^{-1} + q^{-1} = 1$. We shall not describe this variation of the above result but will outline some results that are similar in character to, if different in detail from, the above results. The work to be outlined is due to Willett [9] and has been found useful in singular perturbation problems concerning non-linear ordinary differential equations.

Let V, I, R, x, t, c, y(x), $\bar{y}(x)$ have the same meaning as in section 2, let $\delta(t)$ be a non-negative measurable function on I for which $[\delta(t)]^p$ is integrable on I, and let W be the collection of those vector-valued measurable functions y on I for which

$$\|y(t) - \bar{y}(t)\| \le \delta(t) \qquad \text{a. e. on } I .$$

Integrals in which the limits of integration are not indicated will be understood to be extended over the entire interval I.

Willett considers the integral equation (4.1) under the following assumptions:

(i) $\bar{y}$ is measurable on I and $\int \|\bar{y}(x)\|^p dx$ exists;

(ii) for each y in W (and in particular, for $y = \bar{y}$), $f(x, t, y(t))$ is measurable on R;

(iii) there exist measurable and non-negative numerical functions α on I and k on R for which

$$\int [\alpha(x)]^p dx \qquad \text{and} \qquad \int (\int [k(x, t)]^q dt)^{p/q} dx$$

exist,

$$\|f(x, t, \bar{y}(t)\| \le k(x, t)\alpha(t) \qquad \text{a. e. on } R$$

and for each y and z in W,

$$\|f(x, t, y(t)) - f(x, t, z(t)\| \le k(x, t)\, \|y(t) - z(t)\| ;$$

(iv)

$$(4.6) \quad \theta(x) = \delta(x) - (\int_c^x [\alpha(t)]^p dt)^{1/p} (\int [k(x, t)]^q dt)^{1/q}$$

$$\times \sum_{n=0}^{\infty} (n!)^{-1/p} (\int_c^x (\int [k(s, t)]^q dt)^{p/q} ds)^{n/p}$$

$$\ge 0 \qquad \text{a. e. on } I .$$

Under these assumptions, the existence of a unique solution in W of the integral equation (4.1) can be established by the process of successive approximations indicated in (4.2). Actually, Willett proves that instead of taking $y_0 = \bar{y}$, one may start with any y_0 in W for which

$$\|y_o(x) - \bar{y}(x)\| \le \theta(x) \qquad \text{a.e. on } I .$$

(θ is defined in (4.6)).

5. So far the discussion was restricted to functional equations of the Volterra type. These possess unique solutions without any restriction as to the size of the kernel. Indeed, in the linear case we had only qualitative restrictions (local integrability of g in (2.6)), and the quantitative restrictions introduced in connection with (4.1) were necessitated by the limited domain of definition of f and in no sense demand that this function be small. Indeed, if $f(x, t, y)$ is defined for all y, then $A(x, t)$ or $\delta(t)$, as the case may be, may be taken as $+\infty$, and the quantitative restrictions $\eta \exp g_1 < A$ and (4.6) respectively are nugatory.

If the integral equation is written in the form $y = T(y)$, where T is a non-linear operator on a suitably defined metric space, then it turns out that in the case of Volterra operators T, iterates of sufficiently high order are contraction mappings; and this property of Volterra operators is used for the construction of the solution by successive approximations.

In the applications to ordinary differential equations, Volterra functional equations arise naturally in the case of initial value problems; and if the differential equation is linear, then every solution can be expressed as a linear combination of solutions determined by initial conditions. However, in connection with boundary value problems involving non-linear differential equations, and also in the direct approach to linear boundary value problems, one encounters functional equations of the Fredholm type

$$(5.1) \qquad y(x) = \bar{y}(x) + \int_a^b h(x, t, y(t))\, dt .$$

For these, some quantitative conditions are needed to insure the existence of a unique solution for a suitable class of given $\bar{y}$, and the construction of solutions by successive approximations is feasible only if h is sufficiently small.

In some, but not in all, cases h may be made small by choosing the large paramater λ occurring in the differential equation sufficiently large. In other cases only a part of h will become small for large λ. In these cases the following artifice has proved useful.

Writing the integral equation in the form $y = T(y)$, where T is the operator defined by the right hand side of (5.1), we attempt to break up T as $T = T_1 + T_2$ in such a manner that $1 - T_1$ possesses an inverse, while T_2 is small. Then $y = T(y)$ is re-written in the form $y = (1 - T_1)^{-1}(T_2(y)) = T_3(y)$, say. For sufficiently small T_2,

T_3 will be a contraction mapping. The existence of a unique solution to $y = T(y)$ can be proved by means of the contraction mapping principle (applied to T_3), and the solution may be constructed by successive approximations applied to T_3. In particular, the existence of $(1 - T_1)^{-1}$ will be assured if T_1 can be chosen as a Volterra operator.

This process has been carried out in a particular case, and applied to a singular perturbation problem, in [18] and [19]. It has been formulated in a more general context by Willett [9].

Willett writes (5.1) in the form

$$y(x) = \bar{y}(x) + \int_c^x f(x, t, y(t))\,dt + \int_a^b g(x, t, y(t))\,dt\,, \tag{5.2}$$

where g is "small". Under the conditions imposed on f in section 4, the integral equation

$$y(x) = u(x) + \int_c^x f(x, t, y(t))\,dt$$

will have a unique solution for all u satisfying the conditions imposed on $\bar{y}$ in section 4. With this as a background, Willett shows that under mild restrictions on g, $\bar{y}$ and z, the integral equation for y,

$$y(x) = \bar{y}(x) + \int_a^b g(x, t, z(t))\,dt + \int_c^x f(x, t, y(t))\,dt \tag{5.3}$$

possesses a unique solution y, and thus defines a transformation T_3 such that $y = T_3 z$. If, in addition, g is small, T_3 is a contraction mapping and has a unique fixed point which is the solution of (5.2). For the detailed assumptions on g, and the proof, reference may be made to [9].

REFERENCES

1. R. E. Langer, Asymptotic theories for linear ordinary differential equations depending upon a parameter. J. Soc. Indust. Appl. Math. 7(1959) 298-305.

2. J. Liouville, Second mémoire sur le développement des fonctions on parties de fonctions en séries dont divers termes sont assujettis à satisfaire a une même équation différentielle du second ordre contenant un paramètre variable. J. Math. Pure et Appl. 2 (1837) 16-35.

3. J. Horn, Integration linearer Differentialgleichungen durch Laplacesche Integrale und Fakultätenreihen. Jahresb. Deutsch. Math.-Ver. 24 (1915) 309-329 and 25 (1961) 74-83.

4. R. E. Langer, The asymptotic solutions of ordinary linear differential equations of the second order, with special reference to a turning point. Trans. Amer. Math. Soc. 67 (1949) 461-490.

5. A. Erdélyi, Singular Volterra integral equations and their use in asymptotic expansions. MRC Technical Summary Report No. 194 (1960).

6. A. Erdélyi, An example in singular perturbations. Monatsh. f. Math. 66 (1962) 123-128.

7. A. Erdélyi, A result on non-linear Volterra integral equations. Studies in mathematical analysis and related topics; Essays in Honor of George Pólya, 1962, p. 104-109.

8. D. W. Willett, Solutions of nonlinear integral equations and their application to singular perturbation problems. Ph. D. thesis, California Institute of Technology. 1963.

9. D. W. Willett, Nonlinear vector integral equations as contraction mappings. Arch. Rat. Mech. Anal. 15(1964) 79-86.

10. J. Macki, Singular perturbations of a boundary value problem for a system of nonlinear differential equations. Ph. D. Thesis, California Institute of Technology, 1964.

11. F. W. J. Olver, Error bounds for the Liouville-Green (or WKB) approximations. Proc. Cambridge Phil. Soc. 57(1961) 790-810.

12. F. W. J. Olver, Error bounds in first approximations in turning point problems. J. Soc. Indust. Appl. Math. 11 (1963) 748-772.

13. E. R. Pike, On the related-equation method of asymptotic approximation (W. K. B. or A-A method), with some quantum-mechanical illustrations. R. R. E. Memorandum No. 1923, Royal Radar Establishment, Malvern, Worcs., 1962.

14. E. Hille and R. S. Phillips, Functional analysis and semi-groups. Amer. Math. Soc. Coll. Publ. v. 31, 1957.

15. A. Erdélyi, Differential equations with transition points. I. The first approximation. Tech. Rep. 6, Contract Nonr-220(11). Department of Mathematics, California Institute of Technology, 1955.

16. A Erdélyi, Asymptotic expansions. Dover Publications, 1956.

17. F. W. J. Olver, Error bounds for asymptotic expansions in turning point problems. J. Soc. Indust. Appl. Math. 12(1964) 200-214.

18. A. Erdélyi, Singular perturbations. Bull. Amer. Math. Soc. 68(1962) 420-424.

19 A. Erdélyi, On a nonlinear boundary value problem involving a small parameter. J. Austral. Math. Soc. 2(1962) 425-439.

This work was sponsored in part by the National Science Foundation under grant no. GP-213.

NICHOLAS D. KAZARINOFF

Application of Langer's Theory of Turning Points to Diffraction Problems

1. Introduction. The asymptotic theory of ordinary differential equations with turning points, initiated by Professor Langer and developed by him, his students and others, is perhaps more closely connected to problems in diffraction theory than to physical problems of any other type. Professor Langer discovered that Airy functions of a certain argument uniformly approximate, as $|\lambda| \to \infty$, solutions of a second order differential equation

$$\frac{d^2u}{dz^2} + \left[\lambda^2 zq(z) + p(z, \lambda)\right] u = 0 \qquad (q \neq 0)$$

over a full neighborhood of the turning point at the origin. This result was presented to the American Mathematical Society in the spring of 1930 [19]. Almost one hundred years earlier the function

$$\int_0^\infty \cos\left[\frac{2\pi}{\lambda}(x^3 - zx)\right] dx$$

arose naturally in Sir George B. Airy's famous investigation of light in the neighborhood of a caustic [1]. It is now called an Airy Function. Thus did a theory of the rainbow provide the footings for the mathematical theory of differential equations with turning points.

In 1918, G. N. Watson unified and improved a number of previous researches upon the phenomenon of diffraction of radio waves by the earth [27]. Watson did not employ Airy's functions although he, as Langer was to be in 1930, was interested in the problem of asymptotic evaluation of cylinder functions $C_\nu(z)$ for large $|\nu|$. Subsequently, research upon this diffraction problem continued, Dutch mathematicians such as B. van der Pol and H. Bremmer playing a leading role. They eventually applied their results to Airy's original problem [2].

With the rise of quantum mechanics, the need for methods of asymptotics became acute. It was the desire to show agreement at high energies between the results of quantum theory and those of classical mechanics and optics that brought forth the W-K-B method, stimulated the work of H. Jeffreys and finally led to Professor Langer's uniform approximation of solutions to turning point problems. In his thesis Jeffreys used Airy functions to obtain connection formulas for solutions of simple-turning-point problems, but he failed to realize their full potential [13].

With the advent of radar, a fertile field for application of Professor Langer's theory developed. He was one of the first to realize this [21]. In the past decade especially, numerous problems in diffraction theory have been solved with the aid of Langer's method. Currently it is being used in high energy physics again in discussions on Regge poles, and it is even being used in analyzing the pressure waves generated by a nuclear explosion in the earth's atmosphere. (The gravity wave mode exists in this problem as it does in the solar corona problem to which Professor Lin referred in his lecture.)

It is my goal to describe briefly some of the problems in diffraction theory that have been solved with the aid of Professor Langer's method and to present their salient mathematical features to you.

2. Diffraction by a sphere. I shall begin with a modified version of the problem considered by Watson, diffraction by a sphere. One may seek to determine the function

$$u = \left.\frac{\partial\psi}{\partial r}\right|_{r=a} ,$$

where ψ is the solution of

$$(\nabla^2 + k^2)\psi = 0 \qquad (r>a)$$

$$\psi(a,\theta) = 0$$

that satisfies the Sommerfeld radiation condition

$$\lim_{r\to\infty} r\left(\frac{\partial\psi}{\partial r} - ik\psi\right) = 0$$

uniformly in $\vec{r}/r$ or, equivalently, that is square integrable over the region exterior to the sphere of radius a if $\mathrm{Im}(k^2) < 0$.

If we separate the scalar wave equation and solve the eigenvalue problems that result, we find that

$$u = \sum_0^\infty (n+\tfrac{1}{2})\,P_n(\cos\theta)\,e^{-n\pi i/2}\Big/\zeta_n^{(1)}(ka) ,$$

where

$$\zeta_n^{(1)}(z) = z h_n^{(1)}(z) ,$$

$h_n^{(1)}$ being a spherical Hankel function. This series may be thought of as a residue series and may be written as a contour integral

$$u = \alpha_1 \int_{C_0} \nu e^{-\pi i/2} \frac{P_{\nu-\frac{1}{2}}(-\cos\theta)}{\cos \pi\nu \zeta_{\nu-\frac{1}{2}}^{(1)}(ka)} d\nu , \tag{1}$$

where C_0 is an oriented contour encircling the positive axis of reals clockwise.

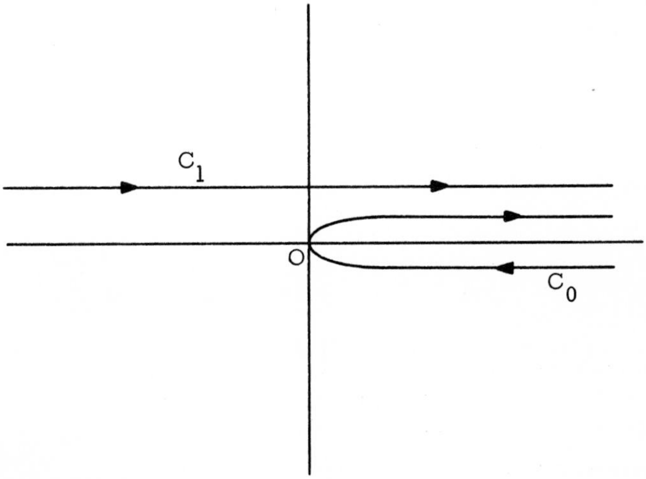

Figure 1

The integrand is an odd function of ν . Therefore we may replace the path C_0 by a path C_1 lying just above the real axis. The zeros of $\zeta_{\nu-\frac{1}{2}}^{(1)}(ka)$ are in the first quadrant and lie in the union of a large disc and a small sector containing the positive axis of the imaginaries.

Now for $\pi/6 < \theta < 5\pi/6$,

$$\sec\pi\nu P_{\nu-\frac{1}{2}}(-\cos\theta) = e^{\pi i/2}\sum_{0}^{\infty}(-1)^n\left[P^{(+)}_{\nu-\frac{1}{2}}(\theta+2\pi n) - P^{(+)}_{\nu-\frac{1}{2}}\left[2(n+1)\pi-\theta\right]\right],$$

where

$$P^{(+)}_{\nu-\frac{1}{2}}(\theta) = \frac{1}{(2i\sin\theta)^{1/2}}\frac{\Gamma(\nu+\frac{1}{2})}{\Gamma(\nu+1)}e^{i\nu\theta}\,{}_2F_1\left(1/2, 1/2; \nu+1; \frac{e^{i\theta}}{2i\sin\theta}\right).$$

Let

$$\phi = \theta - \frac{\pi}{2} \quad \text{and} \quad \phi' = \frac{3\pi}{2} - \theta ,$$

and write

$$I(\phi) = \int_{C_1}\frac{\nu\Gamma(\nu+\frac{1}{2})\,e^{i\nu\phi}\,{}_2F_1\left(1/2, 1/2; \nu+1; \frac{e^{i\phi}}{2\cos\phi}\right)}{\Gamma(\nu+1)\,\zeta^{(1)}_{\nu-\frac{1}{2}}(ka)}\,d\nu . \tag{2}$$

Then

$$u = \frac{\alpha_2}{(\sin\theta)^{1/2}}\sum_{0}^{\infty}(-1)^n\left[I(\phi+2\pi n) - iI(\phi'+2\pi n)\right]. \tag{3}$$

It was Watson's idea to replace the path C_0 by the path C_1 and to evaluate the new integral as the sum of the residues contributed by the zeros of $\zeta^{(1)}_{\nu-\frac{1}{2}}(ka)$. The procedure is called the Watson transformation. The decomposition (3) was introduced by W. Franz [6]. Each of the terms of a residue series for one of the integrals in (3) is called a creeping wave. The creeping waves are grouped in modes, one mode for each zero of $\zeta^{(1)}_{\nu-\frac{1}{2}}(ka)$. Their phases are determined by the numbers $\phi + 2n\pi$ and $\phi' + 2n\pi$. (See Figure 2).

A zero $\nu_m = \nu_m(ka)$ of $\zeta^{(1)}_{\nu-\frac{1}{2}}(ka)$ is of the form

$$ka + \text{const. } e^{i\pi/3}(ka)^{1/3} + \dots ,$$

where the constant is related to the zeros of $Ai(x)$. This means that $i\nu_m\phi$ has a negative real part so that each creeping wave decays as it moves along the surface of the sphere. (For a complete discussion of the diffraction of electro-magnetic waves by a sphere see [10].)

There are three mathematical questions that I feel are of interest in connection with this analysis. The first is whether or not the contour C_1 may be closed in the upper half-plane and the residue series, thereby, summed. The second is the location of the zeros of $\zeta^{(1)}_{\nu-\frac{1}{2}}(ka)$

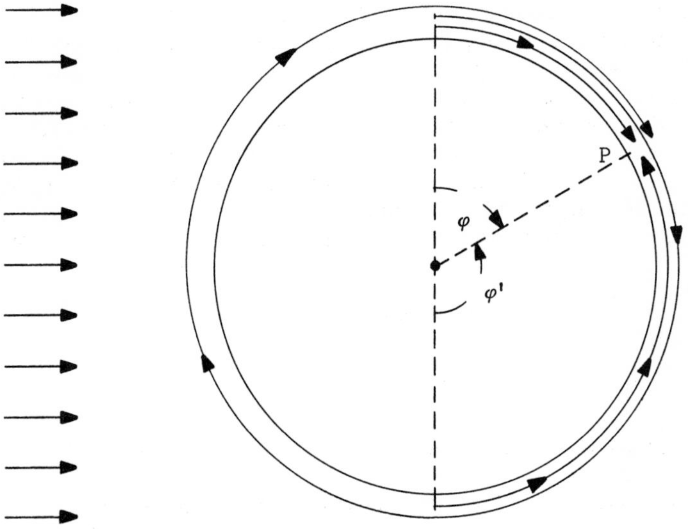

Figure 2

and computation of the residues. The third is to extend the analysis to other shapes.

The delicate question involved in choosing the contour is to estimate the integrand properly, for $|\nu|$ large, in a small sector containing the poles. Curiously, neither Watson nor a large number of subsequent investigators made a proper estimate of the integrand and proved that the contour could be closed. R. F. Goodrich and I finally supplied a proof [8, Section 3]. The key to the proof is very simple. One simply writes the Hankel function as a linear combination of Bessel functions, which are their own asymptotic expansions in ν.

The location of the zeros $\nu_n(ka)$ of $\zeta^{(1)}_{\nu-\frac{1}{2}}(ka)$ may be achieved by study of the equation

$$u'' + \lambda^2(e^{2x} - 1)u = 0 ,$$

which has solutions $C_\lambda(\lambda e^x)$. This equation has a simple turning point at $x = 0$, and it is the first one to which Professor Langer applied his theory [19].

3. Other shapes. Can the analysis be extended to other bodies? The answer is a somewhat unsatisfactory one at present. It has been

extended to so-called separable bodies: the parabolic cylinder and paraboloid of revolution, the elliptic cylinder, prolate and oblate spheroids, for example, [25, 8, 9, 11, 12, 15, 16, 18, 22]. V.A. Fock and J.B. Keller have derived, on the basis of physical assumptions, an extension of the theory of geometric optics that describes the solutions of the scalar and vector diffraction problems for arbitrary convex bodies in terms of creeping waves and a geometric optics contribution [5, 7, 17]. V.S. Buslaev has recently claimed to have found a mathematical derivation of Fock's theory [3].

For a separable body, the solution to the scalar diffraction problem

$$\begin{cases} (\nabla^2 + k^2)u = \delta(x - x_0) \\ u\big|_B = 0 \text{ or } \dfrac{\partial u}{\partial n}\Big|_B = 0 \\ u \text{ satisfies the Sommerfeld radiation condition} \end{cases}$$

may be expressed by an integral of the same general type as (2):

$$\frac{1}{2\pi i}\int_C G(r, r', \nu)\,\widetilde{G}(\theta, \theta', \nu)\,d\nu ,$$

where G and $\widetilde{G}$ are the radial and angular Green's functions for the operators into which $(\nabla^2 + k^2)$ separates (assuming axial symmetry) and where C is a contour separating their poles [15]. The question of convergence of the radial residue series presents no new difficulties in these cases, but the location of the poles does. Almost the full range of the turning point theory for second order ordinary differential equations is required. Some of the equations which arise are listed below.

The elliptic cylinder:

$$\frac{d^2y}{d\xi^2} + (\gamma^2 \sinh^2 \xi + \nu)y = 0, \quad \frac{d^2y}{d\eta^2} + (\gamma^2 \sin^2 \eta - \nu)y = 0 .$$

Here γ is a large parameter, which corresponds to the ka in Section 2. If the cylinder is fat, then an Airy function approximation may be used in studying solutions of the first equation [16, 22]. For η small or for a thin enough cylinder, the second order turning points at $\eta = 0$ and $\zeta = 0$ must be taken into account [9]. The asymptotic theory used is one of R. W. McKelvey's [23]. If the cylinder is fat, then the solution behaves as the creeping wave theory predicts it should. If the cylinder is thin enough, then the creeping waves degenerate into traveling waves that radiate appreciably only at the leading and trailing edges of the cylinder [9, Section 8].

The prolate spheroid:

$$\frac{d^2w}{d\xi^2}+\left[\gamma^2+\frac{\nu}{\xi^2-1}+\frac{1}{(\xi^2-1)^2}\right]w=0,\quad \frac{d^2w}{d\eta^2}+\left[\gamma^2-\frac{\nu}{1-\eta^2}+\frac{1}{(1-\eta^2)^2}\right]w=0\,.$$

If the spheroid is fat, the simple turning point theory again suffices for a study of the radial equation (the ξ-equation) [15, 18]. In addition, another theory of Langer's [20] is used to study the angular equation for η near to the pole at ± 1. For a thin spheroid, the pole at $\xi = 1$ must be considered. The zeros $\nu_m(\xi)$ are $O(\gamma)$ if ξ is close enough to 1. In this case a different theory of McKelvey's [24] is used [8].

The oblate spheroid:

$$\frac{d^2w}{d\xi^2}-\left[\frac{\gamma^2\xi^2}{\xi^2+1}-\frac{\nu}{\xi^2+1}+\frac{1}{(\xi^2+1)^2}\right]w=0\,,$$

$$\frac{d^2w}{d\eta^2}+\left[\frac{\gamma^2\eta^2}{1-\eta^2}-\frac{\nu}{1-\eta^2}+\frac{1}{(1-\eta^2)^2}\right]w=0\,.$$

If the oblate spheroid is thick, the simple turning point theory is used to study the radial equation. The angular equation must be studied near both $\eta = 0$, and $\eta = \pm 1$ [14, 23]. In the case of a thin oblate spheroid, the second order turning point of the radial equation must be taken into account [11].

4. Resonance. Let a be the semi-major axis of an elliptic cylinder, and suppose that $2\pi a/\lambda$ is large, λ being the wave length of plane waves traveling in the direction of the major axis of the elliptic cylinder. Then as b, the semi-minor axis, decreases from a value much larger than λ to a value much less than λ, a resonance phenomenon occurs. Small changes in b, if b is a small multiple of λ, cause relatively large changes in the scattered field. The mathematical difficulty in explaining this resonance phenomenon may be described as follows.

In elliptical-cylindrical coordinates (ξ, η, z), $\xi = 0$ corresponds to a strip (eccentricity is sech ξ). For large γ, solutions of the radial equation $d^2y/d\xi^2 + (\gamma^2 \sinh^2 \xi + \nu)y = 0$ are describable in terms of parabolic cylinder functions

$$D_{\frac{1}{2}(-1 \pm i\nu/\gamma)}\left[e^{-m\pi i}\left(-4i\gamma[\cosh\xi - 1]\right)^{1/2}\right] .$$

If $|\gamma(\cosh\xi - 1)|$ is small, and ν/γ is not large, the power series for these functions may be used in their evaluation, the first zeros ν_m can be shown to be of order γ, and the first ν_m can be asymptotically evaluated. However, as ξ increases, for γ large and fixed, it becomes increasingly awkward to use the power series-- a rather good qualitative approximation is needed to provide the functional behavior of the zeros ν_m. For ξ large enough an Airy function approximation to the parabolic cylinder functions may be used, the first zeros ν_m can easily be shown to be of order γ^2, and they can be asymptotically evaluated. The difficulty is to approximate $D_\mu(z)$ for values μ and z of moderate size. The problem is similar to that of studying an entire function f over the whole z-plane. For $|z|$ small or large, the task is not difficult: the power series is available for small $|z|$ and asymptotic estimates are available for large $|z|$. For intermediate values of z, special methods depending upon the nature of f must be used, and a satisfactory general qualitative description of f may be rather difficult to achieve.

The asymptotic theory required to solve the resonance problem in the case of an elliptic cylinder is, therefore, the following one: to obtain an approximation, uniform in ϵ and γ $(0 \le \epsilon \le 1,\ \gamma \ge N)$, for solutions of

$$\frac{d^2y}{d\xi^2} + \gamma^2(\sinh^2\xi - \epsilon^2)y = 0$$

for $0 \le \xi \le 1$. This problem appears to be beyond the range of known techniques. Nevertheless, it is representative of a class of important problems arising in scattering theory and elsewhere. It deserves serious attention.

5. Pressure waves and Regge poles. I now wish to discuss briefly two other types of problem. David van Hulsteyn, a graduate student at The University of Michigan, has recently given a description of the pressure wave that an observer located on the ground will detect at a distance of a few thousand kilometers from a low altitude nuclear explosion [26]. He assumes the atmosphere to be isothermal and he shows that this assumption is sufficiently accurate for predicting the initial low frequency pulse. He does not use a point source; but, using Huygen's principle, he is able to represent the explosion by a flow of energy across a sphere whose radius is large enough that, exterior to the sphere, the hydrodynamic equations may be linearized.

By analysis of microbarograph recordings of Soviet and U. S. nuclear detonations, it has been shown that the atmospheric disturbance felt far away consists of a pulse of relatively long period, followed, after a few cycles, by oscillations of higher frequency. van Hulsteyn shows that the low frequency oscillation is produced by the gravity wave and that it has an amplitude that varies proportionally to the energy of the explosion and a period that is almost independent of the energy.

His analysis is based upon a time independent pressure equation, derived by means of the Laplace transform, due to V. Weston:

$$(\nabla \cdot \vec{L})\rho_0^{-1/2} p + \frac{1}{h(r)} \frac{q(r)}{r^2} (\rho_0^{-1/2} p) = 0 ,$$

where

$$\vec{L} = \left(\frac{1}{h} \frac{\partial}{\partial r}, \frac{1}{r} \frac{\partial}{\partial \theta}, \frac{1}{r \sin\theta} \frac{\partial}{\partial \psi} \right) ,$$

p is the pressure, ρ_0 is the density of the atmosphere, and q and h are known functions of r. Here (r, θ, ψ) are spherical coördinates with origin at the center of the earth and (r_0, θ_0, ψ_0) are spherical coördinates with origin at the center of the sphere S_0 that models the explosion.

Let $G(\vec{r}, \vec{r}_0, \omega)$ be the Green's function such that

$$(\nabla \cdot \vec{L}) G + \frac{1}{h} \frac{q}{r^2} G = \delta(r - r_0) .$$

Then

$$\rho_0^{-1/2} p(\vec{r}, \omega) = \int_{S_0} [G\vec{L}(\rho_0^{-1/2} p) - (\rho_0^{-1/2} p)\vec{L} G] \cdot \vec{n}\, d\sigma ,$$

$$G(\vec{r}, \vec{r}_0, \omega) = \frac{1}{2\pi i} \int_C (2\lambda + 1) g(r, r_0) \tilde{g}(\theta, \theta_0) d\lambda ,$$

where $g, \tilde{g}$ are the Green's functions for the operators into which $\nabla \cdot \vec{L} + \frac{1}{h} \frac{q}{r^2}$ separates. Evaluating the integral for G by the residue series contributed by the poles of g, van Hulsteyn obtains his results.

The first pole yields the gravity wave mode; the rest yield the high frequency oscillations. Interestingly, the first pole lies in a different half-plane from the remaining ones. (The eigenvalue problem is to find the zeros of

$$\left[\frac{d}{d\xi} H_\nu^{(1)}(\xi) + \beta H_\nu^{(1)}(\xi)\right]_{r=a} = 0 \qquad \text{where } \xi = \xi(r) \text{ and } \beta = \beta(r).)$$

The gravity wave mode does not have an analogue in the theory of diffraction of electromagnetic waves by the earth. However, the remaining modes do correspond to the creeping wave modes found in diffraction by a sphere.

Lastly, I wish to make a brief mention of Regge poles. Physicists have recently tried to carry out Waston's transformation in the case of potential scattering. This problem presents new mathematical difficulties. If the Schrödinger equation is separated (a spherically symmetric potential is assumed), the following radial equation results:

$$\frac{d^2u}{dr^2} + \left[E + \frac{V(r)}{r} + \frac{\nu - \frac{1}{4}}{r^2}\right] u = 0 .$$

(The Yukawa potential $V(r) = e^{-r}$ gives an interesting example.) Regge poles, which might more properly be called Watson poles, are the poles of the radial part of the Green's function for the Schrodinger equation.

In order to find the radial Green's function for the problem, the behavior of the e^{ikr} solution of the radial equation must be determined for $r = 0$. This connection problem appears to be extremely difficult. A way around this difficulty, which to me at least is not unrealistic, is to consider "hard core" potentials, that is, to study the radial equation with a boundary condition at $r = a > 0$. One could carry out Watson's analysis in this case without too much difficulty, I believe. A recent attempt to do this [4] was not successful because the geometric optics term was not subtracted from the integral representation of the solution before the Watson transformation was applied. A divergent integral resulted. Perhaps, at this time, physicists could profit by becoming acquainted with the scattering theory developed for the understanding of electromagnetic problems.

REFERENCES

1. G. B. Airy, On the intensity of light in the neighborhood of a caustic, Trans. Camb. Phil. Soc, VI (1838), 379-402.

2. H. Bremmer and B. van der Pol, The diffraction of electromagnetic waves from an electrical point source round a finitely conducting sphere, with application to radiotelegraphy and the theory of the rainbow, Phil. Mag. Ser. 7, 24(1937), 141-176 and 825-863.

3. V. S. Buslaev, On formulas of short wave asymptotics in the problem of diffraction by convex bodies, Vestnik Leningrad Univ. No. 17 (1962), 1-21.

4. J. W. Durso and P. Signell, Regge poles and potentials with cores, J. Mathematical Phys. 5(1964), 350-354.

5. V. A. Fock, Diffraction of radio waves around the earth's surface, J. Physics 9 (1945), 255-266.

6. W. Franz, Ueber die Greenschen Funktionen des Zylinders und der Kugel, Z. Naturforsch. 9a(1954), 705-716.

7. R. F. Goodrich, Fock theory - an appraisal and exposition, IRE Trans. on Ant. and Prop. AP-7 (1959), S28-S36.

8. R. F. Goodrich and N. D. Kazarinoff, Scalar diffraction by prolate spheroids whose eccentricities are almost one, Proc. Camb. Phil. Soc. 59(1963), 167-183.

9. R. F. Goodrich and N. D. Kazarinoff, Scalar diffraction by elliptic cylinders whose eccentricities are almost one, Michigan Math. J. 10(1963), 105-127.

10. R. F. Goodrich and T. B. A. Senior, Scattering by a sphere, Proc. Inst. Elec. Eng. (London) Part C, to appear in 1964.

11. R. F. Goodrich, N. D. Kazarinoff and V. H. Weston, Scalar diffraction by a thin oblate spheroid, Int. series of monographs on electromagnetic waves, vol. 6. Electromagnetic theory and antennas, Part 1, pp. 27-38, Pergamon Press, London, 1963.

12. E. B. Hansen, Scalar diffraction by an infinite strip and a circular disc, J. Math. and Phys. 41 (1962), 229-245.

13. H. Jeffreys, On certain approximate solutions of linear differential equations of the second order, Proc. London Math. Soc. (2) 23 (1925), 428-436.

14. N. D. Kazarinoff, Asymptotic solutions with respect to a parameter of ordinary differential equations having a regular singular point, Michigan Math. J. 4(1957), 207-220.

15. N. D. Kazarinoff and R. K. Ritt, On the theory of scalar diffraction and its application to the prolate spheroid, Ann. of Phys. 6 (1959), 277-299.

16. N. D. Kazarinoff and R. K. Ritt, Scalar diffraction by an elliptic cylinder, IRE Trans. on Ant. and Prop. AP-7 (1959), S21-S27.

17. J. B. Keller and B. R. Levy, Diffraction by a smooth object, Comm. Pure and Appl. Math. 12(1959), 159-209.

18. J. B. Keller and B. R. Levy, Diffraction by a spheroid, Canad. J. Phys. 38 (1960), 128-144.

19. R. E. Langer, On the asymptotic solutions of ordinary differential equations with an application to the Bessel functions of large order, Trans. Amer. Math. Soc. 33 (1931), 23-64.

20. R. E. Langer, On the asymptotic solutions of ordinary differential equations with reference to the Stokes' phenomenon about a singular point, Trans. Amer. Math. Soc. 37 (1935), 397-416.

21. R. E. Langer, Asymptotic solution of a differential equation in the theory of microwave propagation, Comm. Pure and Appl. Math. 3(1950), 427-438.

22. B. R. Levy, Diffraction by an elliptic cylinder, J. Math. Mech. 9(1960), 147-165.

23. R. W. McKelvey, The solutions of second order linear ordinary differential equations about a turning point of order two, Trans. Amer. Math. Soc. 79(1955), 103-123.

24. R. W. McKelvey, Solution about a singular point of a linear differential equation involving a large parameter, Trans. Amer. Math. Soc. 91(1959), 410-424.

25. S. O. Rice, Diffraction of plane radio waves by a parabolic cylinder, Bell System Tech. J. 33 (1954), 417-504.

26. D. B. van Hulsteyn, The atmospheric pressure wave generated by a nuclear explosion, Univ. of Mich., Radiation Lab. Dept. of Elec. Eng., Tech. Rept. 5033-1-T, 1964.

27. G. N. Watson, The diffraction of electric waves by the earth, Proc. Royal Soc. London, Ser. A, 95 (1918), 83-89.

INDEX

Pekenis
J. App. Phys.
v. 17, 1946
pp. 1108-1124